Democracy in Western Germany

£ 3.50

Democracy in Western Germany

Parties and Politics in the Federal Republic

Gordon Smith
Reader in Government
London School of Economics
and Political Science

HEINEMANN · LONDON

Heinemann Educational Books Ltd
22 Bedford Square, London WC1B 3HH

LONDON   EDINBURGH   MELBOURNE   AUCKLAND
HONG KONG   SINGAPORE   KUALA LUMPUR   NEW DELHI
IBADAN   NAIROBI   JOHANNESBURG
EXETER (NH)   KINGSTON   PORT OF SPAIN

British Library Cataloguing in Publication Data
Smith, Gordon, *b.1927*
    Democracy in Western Germany.
    1. Germany, West – Politics and government
    I. Title
    320.9′43′087   JN3971.A2

    ISBN 0-435-83789-3
    ISBN 0-435-83790-7 Pbk

Printed in Great Britain by
Biddles Ltd, Guildford, Surrey

Contents

Preface

My aim in writing *Democracy in Western Germany* has been to show how liberal democracy in the Federal Republic has emerged s a stable system of power. The approach I have adopted concentrates on the party system – its development and the terms on which it now operates. The metamorphosis which has taken place in Germany since 1945 can only properly be appreciated by taking into account the vicissitudes of democratic politics over the past century and setting the contemporary Federal Republic against the backcloth of historical perspective.

This account is pitched well short of proposing a single theory which would explain the German transformation convincingly – that remains a daunting venture. But it does explore some of the special nuances in the West German version of liberal democracy and shows the contraints which still affect the working of the political system.

I should particularly like to thank both Hans-Werner Lohneis of Ealing College of Higher Education and Dorothea Smith for all their helpful advice and comment. An award from the British Academy Wolfson Foundation enabled me to make a preliminary study on which the present book is based.

G.S.
July 1979

List of Tables

List of Figures

Glossary of Party Abbreviations

ADF	Aktion Demokratischer Fortschritt
AVP	Aktionsgemeinschaft Vierte Partei
BHE	Block der Heimatvertriebenen und Entrechteten
BP	Bayern Partei
BVP	Bayerische Volkspartei
CDU	Christlich Demokratische Union
CSU	Christlich-Soziale Union
DDP	Deutsche Demokratische Partei
DFU	Deutsche Friedens Union
DKP	Deutsche Kommunistische Partei
DNVP	Deutschnationale Volkspartei
DP	Deutsche Partei
DReP	Deutsche Rechts-Partei
DRP	Deutsche Reichs-Partei
DStP	Deutsche Staatspartei
DVP	Deutsche Volkspartei
FDP	Freie Demokratische Partei Deutschlands
GB	Gesamtdeutscher Block
GDP	Gesamtdeutsche Partei
GIM	Gruppe Internationale Marxisten
GVP	Gesamtdeutsche Volkspartei
KBW	Kommunistischer Bund Westdeutschland
KPD	Kommunistische Partei Deutschlands
NPD	Nationaldemokratische Partei Deutschlands
NSDAP	Nationalsozialistische Deutsche Arbeiterpartei
SED	Sozialistische Einheitspartei Deutschlands
SPD	Sozialdemokratische Partei Deutschlands
SRP	Sozialistische Reichspartei

SSW	Südschleswigscher Wählerverband
USPD	Unabhängige Sozialdemokratische Partei Deutschlands
WAV	Wirtschaftliche Aufbau Vereinigung
WP	Wirtschaftspartei
Z	Zentrumspartei

1 Historical Perspectives

The Democratic Problem

Thomas Mann once wrote: 'I confess to being deeply convinced that Germans will never have a liking for political democracy – for the simple reason that they do not like politics, and further that the much-maligned *Obrigkeitsstaat* is and will remain the most fitting and congenial one for the German people – basically it is the form of state they most admire' (*Betrachtungen eines Unpolitischen*). Mann's judgement has to be related to the time when it was made – during the First World War and before the collapse of the imperial order – but it stands as a general commentary on the uneasy German relationship with 'politics' – equated by Mann with parliamentary government and party democracy. If we consider the subsequent fate of the Weimar Republic and the mass enthusiasm for National Socialism, then Mann's view is amply confirmed: Germans showed an inability to handle political conflict and apparently preferred the security offered by the authoritarian state.

The importance of historical factors

But why did Germans 'not like' politics? Answers to this question are necessarily varied, for they would involve a consideration of Germany's whole historical development. Some of the underlying causes may well lie in the more distant past – in the political impact of the Reformation and in the numbing effects of the Thirty Years' War. Those experiences and the political fragmentation of Germany deeply affected social attitudes and induced a passivity in the population at large. But the effects remained dormant until a general challenge was mounted against the traditional basis of

1

authority in the European states. It was only when radical thought and the ideas of popular democracy stimulated by the French Revolution blazed through Europe that certain German peculiarities were revealed.

Logically, the patchwork of the numerous German states should have been swept aside early in the nineteenth century. Increasingly they became an anachronism in modern Europe, backwaters of absolutist power or at best supporting an enlightened despotism. Yet although these states tottered during the Napoleonic Wars, afterwards they emerged sufficiently intact for their rulers to be propped in place again. The reinstatement of the old regimes postponed for more than a generation any advance towards constitutional and democratic government.

Authoritarian government happened to survive in Germany, but it was more than just chance. The spirit of the French Revolution brought about a direct confrontation between the ideas of modern democracy and what came to be represented as specifically German values; the revolutionary ideals were treated as intrusive forces, not universal truths. One reaction can be seen in the later course taken by German nationalism: the drive to national unity proved to be an alternative to, rather an expression of, a democratic impulse. Instead of the national idea becoming firmly harnessed to popular democracy, it was the unreformed Prussian state which in the end identified itself with the German cause.

In the negative German reaction to the French Revolution we can see how little political democracy attracted the mass of the people. But we also have to take into account the resilience of the *Obrigkeitsstaat* itself which was able to resist claims for democratic participation; in particular there was the entrenched power of the state elites and the ruling classes. Why was it that those sections of German society which might have been expected to challenge the existing order failed to do so? We have to bear in mind that Germany did not become substantially industrialised until late in the nineteenth century: the lack of a large industrial proletariat placed the onus for seeking radical change on two main groups, the intellectuals and the middle classes. Yet both largely capitulated in the face of – or even embraced – the power of the authoritarian state.

The place of the intellectual elite
Intellectual accommodation to the prevailing structure of power took three major forms. One reaction was apparently 'non-

political', a withdrawal from political engagement, which in its literary form is associated with the German Romantic movement. A central trait of Romanticism was a rejection of rationalism in favour of mystical values. In its German version Romanticism was a reaction against the Enlightenment and therefore just as much against the spirit of rationality behind the French Revolution. The leanings of the Romantics can best be appreciated in the expression they gave to the national idea. For them its essence lay in a natural historical growth, not a rational construction. The bonds of the nation were to be found in the past, not just through a shared history but in distant origins; to that end the Romantics idealised the Middle Ages and invoked the tales of German mythology. Following Herder, who had used the notion of the *Volksgeist* as an expression of the unity of a people brought about by the agencies of history, language, and culture, the Romantics elevated the concept of *Volk* to an almost mystical level. For them the communality of the *Volk* led to an uncritical admiration of all that which could be regarded as *völkisch* in character. German Romanticism was not overtly political, but there was nevertheless a latent political message contained in the sanctity accorded to traditional ways: the claims of established authority were to be respected in preference to those of formal and rational democratic equality.

A second intellectual support of the ruling order was provided by the development in Germany of a particular philosophy of the state, which is especially associated with the work of Friedrich Hegel. Basic to this body of thought which predominated in the nineteenth century was the insistence on the separation of the state from society, a divorce which had profound political implications. According to the doctrine, 'society' represented a wholly 'subjective' order, for it was composed of jostling interests, the partial and fragmenting forces of society. By contrast, the 'state' was imbued with the qualities of unity, order and permanence, characteristics which gave it an impartial and 'objective' appearance. If the terms of this formulation were accepted, then it followed that the separation of society and the state should be maintained at all costs: constitutional reforms and democratic inroads which led to the popular control over government would lead to a weakening of the state – and would actually result in a loss of freedom. The impartiality of the state and its objective dispensations meant that the state was the guarantor of freedom, even, in Hegel's view, its 'realisation'. Ordered liberty was to be found within the state, not in opposition to it or its legitimate representatives.

According to this philosophical view, the state was not simply distinct from society but was also a self-sufficient organic and moral entity which could both justify and serve its own purposes. That higher morality has parallels with the 'mystical identity' which the Romantics imputed to the *Volk* and shared their resistance to any rational or 'utilitarian' assessment. In the later extension and vulgarisation of Hegel's philosophy the way was opened to an unashamed veneration of state power. Thus Heinrich von Treitschke in his *History of Germany in the Nineteenth Century* (the first volume of which appeared in 1879) succeeded in grafting a form of political Darwinism on to Hegel's ideas in order to chart and glorify the triumphant course of the Prussian state. According to Treitschke, Europe 'lived in an age of war', and the duty of the state, the German Reich as it had then become, was to increase its power, for only the strong states deserved to survive. In effect, the military might of Prussia represented the highest values of the state: admiration of its power stood in complete antithesis to democratic beliefs. German philosophy helped to underpin the power structure of the authoritarian state by showing that it was the most legitimate form of government.

A third characteristic of the intellectuals' position related to the political function of the academic class in the universities. German universities developed as institutions of the state, a form of subordination which may in part account for the direction which academic involvement in political life tended to take: the under-writing of the state's claims to authority and a rejection of demo-cratic encroachment. The phenomenon of the *Gelehrtenpolitik* gave the academics a special function. Felix Gilbert in his essay on 'Political Power and Academic Responsibility' portrayed the contribution of the 'political academics' such as Treitschke in these terms: 'They clothed the empire, its genesis and its institutions in an idealistic garb. In German intellectual history the development from idealism to realism was constructed as a logically necessary process.' The academic scholar '. . . served the ruling elite as an expert, and he postulated loyalty to the existing system by explain-ing and proclaiming the excellence of the political order in which the nation lived. . . . The professor was the defender of the ruling group.'[1] The consensus amongst the German elites was not complete but it was sufficiently powerful to hinder the rise of a home-grown democratic tradition.

The middle class and politics

For the other important grouping which could have challenged the authoritarian system, the middle class, the practical benefits of stability were probably decisive. The citizens were content with the service of efficient administrators, they could rely on the personal security provided to them by the German *Rechtsstaat*, and they were able to enjoy the material progress of the second half of the nineteenth century. These factors all worked against a determined demand for constitutional and political reform. Only once, in the revolutionary year of 1848, did the middle-class activists come near to bringing down the old regimes. The eventual failure of the 1848 Revolution may be ascribed to the weakness of the middle-class leadership or even to the 'treachery' of the middle classes who failed to fulfil their historic task. But the more convincing explanation is that, for this section of German society at least, there were no overriding discontents, no great economic or social crisis which made the existing political system unworkable.

The failure of the Revolution in 1848 nonetheless had an incalculable effect on later political development. For the middle classes and for German liberalism there was little alternative but to accept the continued leadership of the established elites – and at a time when Germany was rapidly entering the industrial era. At that juncture of development the lack of a self-confident, independent middle class ensured that the Reich took a political path different from those of the other countries of Western Europe. Many German liberals were never reconciled to the power system of the 'Prusso-German' state which emerged, but others acquiesced or even made a willing capitulation. A leading liberal historian, Hermann Baumgarten, much later wrote a 'self-criticism' of the radical action of 1848: 'We thought that by our agitation we could transform Germany. . . . The victory of our principles would have brought misery upon us, whereas the defeat of our principles has brought us boundless salvation.'[2]

The liberal and middle-class 'salvation' took the form of the Prussian 'conquest' of Germany. The inability of the radicals to realise either of their chief aims in 1848 – constitutional reform and national unity – meant that leadership was retained by the traditional elites. The Prussians' success in unifying Germany ensured that their hegemony was maintained and their values prevailed over the democratic ones. The Prussian state was prosaic, even drab, but laced with the national sentiment which swept Germany, the new Reich of 1871 won a strong loyalty from Germans of all classes: the modern *Obrigkeitsstaat* became the object of pride and admiration.

In the final analysis, the German authoritarian state survived neither by accident nor through the strength of its traditions, nor even because of the support it received from key groups such as the intellectuals. Quite simply, it was very successful. Under the aegis of Prussia unification was achieved; the country prospered and entered successfully the ranks of major industrial producers. By the turn of the century Germany was taking her place as a world power. Why jeopardise those achievements?

Tensions in German society
Ideas of the 'unpolitical' German who either shunned the contamination of politics or else enthusiastically supported all the claims of the state are convincing as a picture of German society.[3] But we have to be on guard against accepting it as true of all classes. The industrial age brought with it a new proletariat which in the trade unions and in the Social Democratic Party (SPD) became a large and cohesive force. The organised working class was perceived as a threat to the established order and it was an additional reason for the middle classes to accept the *status quo*. Constitutional advance might easily have resulted in the Socialists winning power. They, apparently, were bent on promoting a socialist revolution and they were also renegade 'anti-nationals' – *vaterlandlose Gesellen* – who threatened to undermine the unity of the Reich and the German nation.

The traditional state had no way of resolving these endemic conflicts, nor – with the growing power of the trade unions and Social Democracy – could it easily resort to repressive action. The period before the First World War was marked by increasing social ferment and the political mobilisation of the working class continued apace. Since the authoritarian state was incapable of bringing about its own reform, its rulers looked increasingly outwards, wooing national unity at home by engaging in external policies – including the build-up of military power – which ultimately led to war. In one sense at least those policies were successful: at the outset of the war in 1914 the German people were united in their support of the emperor and the Reich.

Long before the defeat of Germany in 1918 the conflicts which had been suppressed in the initial enthusiasm for the war flared up openly and as the authoritarian system weakened, they became more intense. The German Revolution of November 1918 brought an end to the Empire and established a republic, but it did not remove the causes of conflict: the Weimar Republic came to resemble a spacious battleground for warring classes and conflicting interests. The republican institutions were founded on the principles of liberal democracy, which assumed a political competence that proved to be lacking. During the years of the short-lived republic the German failure to develop a 'liking' for parliamentary politics became apparent.

Those on the nationalist right hated the new republic for the ideals it represented, but too much had changed for the 'old order' of the Empire to be restored. National Socialism provided one alternative in the later years of the republic. Its attraction was to combine a distinctly modern programme with an appeal to nationalist traditions. The Nazi emphasis on the German *Volk* and the promise of the unity of a *Volksgemeinschaft* looked backwards, whilst the remedies promised for Germany's economic and industrial plight gave hope for the future. The compound of the old and the new – the paradoxical idea of 'going forward into history' – was an attractive alternative to an apparently unworkable democratic model. Once established, the Nazi regime took on a pace and direction which possibly not many Germans had expected, but at its commencement the dictatorship was widely welcomed: totalitarian 'anti-politics' may at first have seemed to resemble the style of the *Obrigkeitsstaat*.

Ultimately the Nazi 'mutation' failed, and in post-war Germany there was no option but to accept the dictates of the allied victors. In Western Germany that meant the establishment of liberal democracy. Yet the manner in which parliamentary institutions have taken root in the Federal Republic shows conclusively that there was no absolute barrier to the development of a 'liking for politics'. The experience also exposed the weakness of seeking to explain political development in terms of an immutable 'national character' – Thomas Mann's version is only one.

A study of the actual terms of historical development is likely to be more rewarding. A concise formulation which would express the distortions that occurred in the German case may be misleading, but it is clear that there were substantial differences between Germany and other West European states in the way in which fundamental issues were presented and resolved – those concerning the creation of national unity, the terms of industrialisation, rights of citizenship and political participation. Unlike other countries, which had the benefit of a slower evolution and which could resolve one issue before the next crisis built up, the situation in Germany was that of a 'belated nation' and the problems became inextricably interwoven. In consequence, the establishment of political democracy involved much more than the securing of institutional reforms. There are still aspects of the West German political system which remind us of the past upheavals; it remains to be seen whether the 'democratic problem' has finally been solved.

The Terms of Political Progress

For a brief period in 1848 and 1849 the Frankfurt Parliament gave the numerous party factions considerable freedom and the illusion of power. The permanent parties which subsequently developed had to adjust themselves to a much weaker position in the assemblies of the various German states. Even though, as in Prussia, the assembly gave the parties a base from which they sought to increase their influence, they were held at arm's length from the exercise of governing power.

The development which took place in Prussia proved later to be the model for the Reich as a whole. By the terms of the constitution granted by the Prussian monarch in 1852, the scope for democratic intervention was kept to a minimum. The Prussian minister-president was appointed by the king and was responsible to him alone. Popular representation in the elected assembly was severely distorted by the electoral system, the *Drei-Klassen Wahlrecht*, which divided the electorate into three tax classes, each with equal representation – with the result that a few wealthy individuals had a quite disproportionate influence on the choice of representatives. The chamber of deputies did have legislative and budgetary powers, but it was also checked by the second chamber, a nominated *Herrenhaus*. Both the 'three-class' franchise and the upper house were retained until 1918.

A decisive trial of strength between the elected assembly and the government occurred in 1862, when the chamber rejected the army estimates. As the crisis deepened, Bismarck was appointed minister-president by the king. His tactic was simple and effective: he blithely ignored the challenge, arguing that the constitution was silent on how a conflict between parliament and government should be resolved. His theory that there was a 'hole' in the constitution allowed him to argue that the needs of the state should take precedence. Government – and the collection and disbursement of taxes at their previously agreed levels – continued as usual.

Non-responsible government and the parties
Bismarck's victory in that confrontation was of importance for
later constitutional development. It meant that it was impossible
to develop a method of exacting governmental responsibility. The
fact that the assembly could not bring a government to account
meant that the parties were unable to enforce a *political* responsibility. There was an alternative which applied in theory at least:
governments were supposed to be responsible in law. Unfortun-
ately the mechanism for a legal enforcement by the courts did not
exist. The *Rechtsstaat* could provide redress against administrative
action but stopped short of providing a general sanction against
governments. As a result, the Prussian government was strictly
non-responsible in both a political and legal sense.[4]

Bismarck was able to use his interpretation of the constitutional
position to make himself impregnable to attacks from the parties,
and the style of government he first perfected in Prussia was later
carried over to the Reich. Bismarck was also a past master in the
art of manipulation. At times he found it expedient to rule with the
concurrence of the parties, at others he ruled against them, but he
was careful never to rule *through* them. In the absence of responsible government, it was scarcely surprising that a 'responsible'
party system did not develop either. The fragmented party system
was inclined to behave in ways which confirmed the negative views
of the role taken by the parties in relation to the state.

A simple extension of the argument to justify the separation of
state and society could be applied to the relationship of state and
government to the parties – for they were one expression of social
forces. The social factions represented in the parties illustrated the
dangers of minority power – the *Gewalt Weniger* – which were
inimical to the welfare and unity of the state. In the constant
struggle between the positive value of the state and the divisiveness
of party forces, the conservative thinker, Lorenz von Stein, put the
question: 'Who would not be on the side of freedom in this
struggle? The parties serve to make an objective policy impossible.
Their influence, indeed the influence of society on the state and in
the state, is not legitimate.'[5] August von Rochau in his *Grundsätze
der Realpolitik* of 1853 conceded that the political parties were of
greater relevance to modern conditions than the archaic system of
estate representation, but with strong qualification: 'Every party
must be one-sided and short-lived in comparison with the univers-
ality and duration of the state. The most fitting fate (*das schönste
Schicksal*) is for a party to dissolve once it has gained its ends.'

Constitutional dualism

A contemporary observer described the constitutional structure of imperial Germany as 'an artfully created chaos'. Perhaps only Bismarck, its chief designer, fully mastered the system. But in essence its aims were simple enough: to maintain the cardinal principle of the separation of state and society and to ensure that Prussian influence in Germany remained paramount. In practice they amounted to the same thing.

The constitution of the Reich in 1871 contained a surprising juxtaposition of two apparently contradictory elements: a generous concession to democratic representation alongside a commitment to the 'monarchical principle'. The best way to descibe the theory behind this arrangement is as a form of 'constitutional dualism', founded on two sources of legitimate authority. The monarchical principle was an assertion of the divine source of the emperor's authority; the emperor was endowed with a personal *Obrigkeit*, a basis of authoritarian power. The Reich itself was established as a compact between the rulers of the German states, not as a union of the German people, and for this reason the claim to *Obrigkeit* was unaffected by the presence of the constitution – its abrogation by the emperor was at all times conceivable.

The other source of authority was the Reichstag, which was democratically elected on a franchise that was considerably more generous than those of all other European states at the time. The Reichstag had important legislative and budgetary powers which the parties used to the full: the military budget in particular represented an area of continually shifting conflict and compromise between the assembly and the government. The parties were intent on extending the authority of the Reichstag, but they failed to achieve parliamentary government, being able neither to enforce governmental responsibility to the Reichstag nor to supply and control the personnel of government. The chancellor was appointed by the emperor and was responsible to him alone, and whilst the chancellor duly appeared before the Reichstag – the only minister to do so – and was generally answerable to it in justifying the policies of the government, neither he nor any member of his government was dependent on receiving the support of the Reichstag.

Within this constitutional structure of the Reich, Prussian predominance was secured in various ways. The ruling monarch of Prussia was at the same time the German emperor; he controlled the government of the Reich through his chancellor and also took supreme command of the German armed forces – an authority vested in him and not in the government. Prussian power was further strengthened within the federal structuring of the state through the composition of the Bundesrat which directly represented the governments of the constituent states, twenty-five in all. The Bundesrat was a key element in the system, since it combined legislative and executive functions. The legislative powers of the Bundesrat were, in fact, superior to those of the Reichstag, and the large vote that Prussia held in the Bundesrat – justified, since she was by far the most populous state – meant that the Prussian government was in a leading position. Furthermore, the minister-president of Prussia was also chairman of the Bundesrat, and since the chancellor normally held the Prussian post as well, it was possible for him to use the Bundesrat as a co-ordinating body for the government of the Reich as a whole. Finally, since Prussia itself was immune from the danger of popular control, thanks to the 'three-class' franchise, constitutional stability was guaranteed.

In the eyes of its apologists, the system of government adopted for the Reich was a 'unique' German solution. The combination of democratic elements and regard for traditional German values secured a 'balancing of powers'. It is true that there was a balance of authority between the Reichstag and the government, and Germany did enjoy long periods of stable government. It may also be the case that over the years the influence of the Reichstag increased. But the dualistic structure was exceptionally rigid; pressures for radical change were successfully resisted until Germany faced defeat in 1918, then all cohesion vanished.

The party system in the Empire

The democratic aspects of the Reich encouraged the formation of parties. Around a dozen were represented at the elections held from 1871 until 1912; some were small, especially those representing the various national minorities within Germany. A 'core' of some six parties represented the major divisions in German society. The table below shows how they fared in the contest for Reichstag seats. However, it is important to note that there was a steady bias against the representation of industrial and urban areas and that the electoral system used – the second ballot with a run-off election or *Stichwahl* – also distorted results.

Even though the SPD became the largest party in the Reichstag as a result of the 1912 election, it was still underrepresented. In

Reichstag Elections, 1871–1912:
Distribution of Seats in Selected Years

	1871	1877	1881	1887	1893	1903	1912
German Conservatives	55	40	50	80	72	54	43
Free Conservatives	39	38	28	41	28	21	14
Christian-Socials	—	—	—	1	16	11	3
National Liberals	155	128	47	99	53	51	45
Catholic Centre	63	93	100	98	96	100	91
Progressives	46	35	106	32	37	30⎱	42
German People's Party	1	4	9	—	11	6⎰	
Social Democrats	2	12	12	11	44	81	110
National minorities	21	34	45	33	35	32	33
Others	—	13	—	2	5	11	16

Notes

The results shown are for alternate election years; the 1912 elections were the last held in the Empire. In 1871 there were 382 seats in the Reichstag, but there were 397 for all subsequent elections.

The Christian-Socials were also known as the Anti-Semite Party. The 'Progressives' include two separate Liberal-Progressive parties for most years. 'National minorities' includes representatives of the Poles and the Danes and Alsace-Lorraine, as well as the Welfists, later Hanoverians.

1887 the party won a plurality of the *votes* for the first time, yet only twelve Reichstag seats. Not only did the SPD suffer from the bias of the electoral districts in favour of rural areas, it was also at a disadvantage in the *Stichwahl* – other parties often formed alliances at the second ballot to ensure the defeat of the SPD candidate. These handicaps were compensated by the unity of the party. Of the others, only the Catholic Centre was able to avoid the fragmentation which affected the party system: free from responsibility for government, the parties were especially prone to splintering.

The Liberals were by far the worst affected. The National Liberals were those who had unswervingly supported Bismarck and who had identified themselves with his 'national' successes, whilst the label of 'Progressives' covers the Liberal groupings which abhorred Bismarck's methods of rule and sought genuine constitutional advance. These radicals or Left-Liberals were constantly affected by their own internal divisions and were usually represented by more than one party. Whilst at the beginning of the Reich the various Liberal parties held a large share of the vote, by the First World War they were a declining force: German Liberalism failed to anchor itself in the middle classes. Making up the core of the party system were the two Conservative parties, their presence reflecting the division between the Prussian and largely Protestant

'Free Conservatives' who supported Bismarck, and the German Conservatives who, in the remainder of the Reich, sought to protect particularist interests.

As far as future development was concerned, the two most important parties were the Centre and the SPD, for they were to be the mainstay of parliamentary government in the Weimar Republic. Both bore the stigmata of the formative years of the party system in imperial Germany. Roman Catholics were stunned by Bismarck's crusading *Kulturkampf* and the SPD had to contend with the disabilities imposed by the Anti-Socialist Laws which were in force from 1878 until 1890. The *Kulturkampf*, seen by Bismarck as a trial of strength between Church and State, made it certain that the Centre Party would develop primarily as a defensive organisation, concerned to uphold the interests of the Catholic Church and the Catholic section of the electorate, a large minority in the Reich as a whole. The Centre was consistently successful in mobilising most of the Catholic vote, but that success was also a limitation. The party became a 'closed' one, unable to widen the basis of its appeal. How the Centre should escape from the 'tower' which it had built for itself was a source of anxious debate, but even later, in the Weimar Republic, it failed to make a connection with the Protestant Churches. The creation of a 'Christian Democratic' movement had to wait until 1945. The Centre Party thus remained a special element in the party system until the end of the Weimar Republic. Undoubtedly the Centre was a moderating political force, but the suspicion that its paramount concern was to protect Catholic interests was never entirely dispelled.

The charge originally made against the Catholic Church in Germany, that it constituted 'a state within a state', was one which was later levelled at the SPD. The 'exclusion' which Bismarck and later chancellors sought to practise against the organised working class had the effect of making the SPD and its related organisations an almost self-sufficient form of social integration for a large part of the German working class. The SPD was not only strikingly successful in electoral terms; the party also built up a huge membership – reaching a million prior to the First World War – which helped it to become wealthy and to engage in a variety of activities. Shorn of a connection with political power, the SPD concentrated on developing a powerfully organised movement, and the revolutionary ideology proclaimed by the party was perceived by the others as a menacing threat to the German state.

Yet there was a very wide gap between the revolutionary theory adopted by the SPD and its real nature: its Marxist orientation expressed one tradition, but there were other roots as well. The original *Allgemeiner Deutscher Arbeiterverein*, founded by Ferdinand Lassalle in 1863, had no Marxist pretensions: it was concerned with securing social advance through the state, aimed at political rather than economic goals, and was if anything 'romantically nationalist' in character. These Lassallean features of the later SPD were partly hidden by the fusion with the radical 'Eisenachers' in 1875 and still more so by the adoption of a fully Marxist platform in the Erfurt Programme of 1891. What resulted for the SPD was the creation of a 'revolutionary myth' and the perpetuation of an 'heroic' image gained in the period of the Anti-Socialist Laws.

There was intense controversy within the SPD concerning the ideological character of Social Democracy, and the arguments were fuelled by the heresy of 'revisionism' in the late 1890s. Eduard Bernstein maintained that the SPD had become wedded to Marxist predictions which were obsolete, founded on the erroneous belief that German capitalism was fast approaching a final crisis. Marx's 'scientific socialism' implied that socialism was inevitable, but for Bernstein socialism was essentially an 'ethical task', and hence neither its final nature nor the means to be employed could be slavishly determined in advance. Revisionism required the SPD to recognise the realities of German society, to abandon revolutionary socialism in favour of evolutionary socialism.[6]

The revisionist wing of the party was joined by the more pragmatically inclined 'reformist' groups, but the debate within the SPD remained unresolved. The first real test of the party's position came with the outbreak of war in 1914. As it then rallied to the cause of the Fatherland, the shallowness of the party's commitment to its ideological pretensions was sharply exposed.

Problems of government leadership
It may be supposed that with the divided condition of the parties and their inability to impose their will on governments, the task of the German chancellor would be simplified. Whilst it was not necessary for him to forge stable alliances having the force of a 'coalition', nor did he have to win the confidence of a majority in the Reichstag, it was still important for the government to pass its legislation, and in this respect the Reichstag could not be ignored. At times it was possible to rely on different combinations of support, particular 'majorities for the occasion'; at others there were attempts to forge consistent pro-government alignments, a *Block-*

politik. Increasingly, however, the chancellor became the focus of the struggle of the Reichstag parties to increase their limited power.

Beneath the stability of the imperial system there was an underlying constitutional malaise which was reflected in the position of the chancellor. His difficulties were apparent: appointed by the emperor and responsible to him, a chancellor had no final authority of his own, nor could he expect to obtain it from the parties. The hapless incumbent was caught between the two pressures, that exerted by the Reichstag and that which resulted from the independent authority of the state (the wilful intervention of the emperor and the high-handed demands of the military elite), neither of which the chancellor could hope to control.

Exclusive concentration on this constitutional difficulty may divert attention from related weaknesses in the system. Max Weber in his political writings saw the problem in terms of supplying political leadership for the Reich, and it is significant that in this connection he compared Germany unfavourably with Britain, which had developed a refined system of parliamentary government. His approval was directed not so much at the democratic content of the parliamentary form, but rather at the process of leadership selection which it entailed: strong leaders could arise through the medium of party competition, and a successful leader was able to set the seal on his authority by becoming 'a dictator of the election battlefield'.[7]

Weber saw that this line of evolution in Germany had been blocked in Germany, but not only on 'constitutional' grounds. Bismarck had been a political leader of genius, but no subsequent chancellor in the Wilhelmine era had risen above a competent mediocrity, nor could anything be expected from the 'dilettante' emperor, Wilhelm II. But where was the requisite leadership to be found? The absence of a strong and independent middle class was without doubt an important factor in Weber's view. The unification of Germany, and its transition to a modern industrial state, had been effected by the traditional Prussian elites, the backbone of which was the landed *Junker* class. That original leadership had made an historic contribution, but its impetus had waned without the middle classes assuming control. Germany had reached the modern era without a fundamental social modernisation; from a later perspective Germany before 1914 had the appearance of an 'industrial-feudal' society. The bourgeois parties reflected that continuing subordination, and whilst Weber conceded that Social Democracy represented the rise of a powerful social movement, his view of the SPD itself was largely negative: it was a blinkered, sectarian and bureaucratic structure, not a party to be entrusted with the leadership of Germany or able to justify its place as a world power. Weber saw no easy way out of the predicament. The interlocking of constitutional and social problems had led to a stunting of the German parties, the system could hardly be renewed from within, and by default the deadening power of the bureaucracy could prove to be the alternative to political leadership.

In the event it was the military bureaucracy which assumed control. As the 1914–18 war progressed, the country slithered towards military dictatorship. Nominally responsible to the emperor, the German High Command became increasingly contemptuous of any restrictions on its power. Whilst Germany was engaged in fighting a patriotic war, the parties in the Reichstag found it difficult to oppose the demands of the military leaders, and they for their part regarded neither the Reichstag nor the chancellor as serious rivals – indeed, they came to treat the chancellor as virtually their own nominee.

Faced eventually with the overwhelming superiority of the allied powers, the inevitable prospect of defeat in the field and the extreme war-weariness of the German people, the High Command at length realised that it would be necessary to sue for peace and that only a civilian government would be suitable for the purpose. A sudden desire for self-effacement overtook the military. Coolly, General Ludendorff took the initiative: 'The Supreme Command does not regard itself as being a power in politics . . . and is therefore without political responsibility.'[8]

With the aid of this neat formulation, it was suddenly found expedient to hand over all political power to the parties. They were to have the prime task of negotiating an armistice. The parties had no real option but to accept the invitation; a broadly based coalition was formed and the Parliament Act of 1918 was passed. Almost overnight Germany was transformed into a parliamentary democracy. The 'constitutional revolution' for which generations of radicals had struggled in vain became a reality – in defeat and as a gift from the unreformed (and unrepentant) military elite.

Weimar: Innovation and Breakdown

The German Revolution
Neither the social chaos which accompanied Germany's capitulation, nor the events surrounding the German Revolution which created the republic in November 1918, altered the essential fact

of the constitutional advance secured in the last weeks of war. But its reality was briefly obscured in the turbulent months following the collapse of the old regime: from a hopeless passivity endured in the final year or so of the conflict, the German people – and large sections of the armed forces – were suddenly galvanised by the possibility of creating an entirely new political order.

Only the slender authority of the provisional government formed by the SPD stood in the way of the disintegration of the German state, for in the general collapse the 'pillar of the state', the armed forces, proved to be just as much affected – the High Command no longer had a significant number of reliable units at its disposal. A line of constitutional legitimacy was preserved: Prince Max von Baden, the last imperial chancellor, entrusted the continuance of the Reich government to Friedrich Ebert, the leader of the SPD, for Prince Max realised that only the SPD was capable of asserting authority in the revolutionary situation. Yet at the same time the SPD took it upon itself to declare the creation of a republic and thus made a decisive revolutionary break. On the one hand 'Chancellor' Ebert represented the shaky continuity of the Reich; on the other hand the government of 'People's Commissars' which he led was a negation of the former system.

At least on the surface that appeared an entirely contradictory position, but it soon became apparent that the SPD was intent on bringing the revolutionary movement under tight control and diverting it to a constitutional path – and that Ebert's government was prepared to use all means to that end. The SPD was committed to bringing about fundamental social and political changes but, despite the party's revolutionary ideology, only by majority consent. Hence Ebert's priorities took the following sequence: the restoration of order, the holding of free elections, the institution of a constituent assembly, the establishment of a responsible government – dominated, it was to be expected, by the SPD – and finally the implementation of the party's programme. Those priorities were not shared by the extreme left, which correctly judged that the opportunity to make drastic changes would quickly pass: the euphemism of 'restoring order' effectively meant the strangling of the revolution. The aim of the revolutionaries was to overthrow the existing social and political system, using the Russian Revolution as their model. A confrontation was inevitable.

The seeds of confrontation had long existed within the SPD, but had remained at an academic level of ideological debate until the First World War. The pressures inside the party then became intense and led to the first split in Social Democracy with the formation of the USPD in 1917, the 'Independents'. The USPD was partly an expression of hostility towards continuing support for the war, but the breakaway movement also represented the left wing of the party, and it was from the USPD that the more extreme Spartakus movement sprang, eventually to become the KPD. The Independents at first participated in Ebert's provisional government but then withdrew in December 1918, at a point when they considered Ebert and the SPD were engaged in repressive action, not furthering the revolutionary cause. The climax came in January 1919 with the crushing of the Spartakus 'uprising' in Berlin. With no forces of its own for the purpose, the SPD government made use of the *Freikorps* (irregular detachments of former soldiers and officers) to put down the extreme left. In the desperate bid to maintain its authority, the government did not hesitate to call on the 'class enemy' for assistance – for the members of the *Freikorps* had no sympathy with the SPD or the republic it had created, only an 'interim loyalty' towards the provisional government.

After that episode the rift in the working-class movement became absolute, but it was also evident that the general revolutionary impulse had waned. The three months of turmoil in Germany had changed little beyond what had been almost undisputed at the outset: the creation of a parliamentary republic. Ebert had succeeded in asserting his priorities, and elections to a constituent National Assembly duly took place in January 1919. The parties which favoured a 'moderate' republican course, the SPD, the Centre and the liberal German Democrats, between them controlled about three-quarters of the seats in the new assembly. These three parties were in a position to decide the nature of a constitution for the republic and to form the first regular government, the 'Weimar Coalition' headed by the SPD. But the SPD failed to gain the absolute majority which it had sought, thus putting paid to any hope that the party would be in a position to implement its social programme. The time for retrenchment had come, for the SPD's partners were just as much against any extension of the German Revolution as they had been in favour of the parliamentary republic.

The Weimar constitution

The mainspring of the constitution drawn up in Weimar was naturally 'party government', parliamentary government based on the regime of the political parties. Yet the constitution departed in important ways from instituting an undiluted expression of parliamentary power by introducing a system of 'checks and balances' involving the Reichstag and the chancellor, together with the innovation of a popularly elected president. Max Weber was not involved in framing the constitution, but in providing for a president who was to act as a kind of *Ersatzkaiser*, and in making him subject to direct election, its provisions were consonant with the views he had expressed. Weber had advocated the creation of a strong *Führerdemokratie*, by means of which the stultifying influence of the parties would be dispelled: 'Only the popular election of the president could operate as a filter for the selection of leader personalities, whilst now the old professional politicians play their traditional game and shut out all really able leader figures.'[9]

Yet the parallel should not be taken too far. Whilst Weber visualised the president as possibly the major political force, the Weimar system took a half-way view: the president's power and popular authority should be held in reserve for use in crisis, but it was not expected that he would be a mainly representative figurehead either – for there could be no illusion that Germany would develop the habits of stable majority rule or that the threat of civil strife would disappear.

Although his direct election gave the president an authority independent of the parties, they saw no threat to their position. The parties assumed that in putting forward their 'own' candidates they could ensure that presidential policies were in harmony with their views. What actually transpired was rather different. The innovation succeeded in blurring the clear lines of responsibility which parliamentary government requires but without instituting a fully presidential system or even a *Führerdemokratie*. Unwittingly, the final evolution of the constitution took a form similar to the 'constitutional dualism' of the former Reich – the dualism of president and parties corresponded to the distinction between state and society in a new guise.

That implication was not immediately apparent. The first president of the republic, Friedrich Ebert, was chosen directly by the parties in the National Assembly. Although Ebert frequently had to make use of the presidential powers in the first difficult years from 1919 until 1923, he was primarily a 'party man' with no desire to extend his own authority. Only later did the presidential element in the constitution loom as a force in its own right.

The problem of balance

In the sense that governments were made unconditionally responsible to the Reichstag, the party basis of government was apparently
assured by the constitution. As long as parliamentary majorities
could be fashioned, workable governments could be formed – even
though the coalitions were generally short-lived. But the president
did have substantial opportunity for intervention. The constitution
gave him the right both to appoint and to dismiss the chancellor,
thus placing the latter in a position of double responsibility (the
same threat of being caught between two fires as under the imperial
system). In addition, the president could authorise emergency
decrees of sweeping effect under Article 48 of the constitution, a
power which could be used to subvert the authority of the

The Balance of Powers in the Weimar Constitution

President	Chancellor	Reichstag
Article 25 Power to dissolve the Reichstag	*Article 50* Dissolution requires counter-signature of chancellor	*Article 25* New election within 60 days; dissolution for 'same cause' not allowable
Article 53 Power to appoint and to dismiss chancellor	*Articles 53, 54* Responsibility to president (53) but must have confidence of Reichstag (54)	*Article 54* Negative vote of Reichstag unseats chancellor
Article 48 Power of decree and full powers of emergency	*Article 50* Measures taken require counter-signature of chancellor	*Article 48* All measures could be rescinded by Reichstag on simple negative vote

Reichstag. Even though the parties and the president ultimately
drew their authority from the same electorate, the final crisis of
the republic in the years from 1930 until 1933 showed that the
unity imparted to the political system by popular sovereignty was
quite illusory.

It may be thought that the Weimar constitution was deficient in
failing to give sufficient attention to possible eventualities. Yet
there was a careful distribution of power, a number of interlocking
devices with a final weighting in favour of the parties and,
ultimately, the electorate. Moreover, in the quieter middle years
of the republic, between 1925 and 1929, the constitution worked
well enough. Criticism is based on the experience of the closing

years of the republic, and then the constellation of circumstances exposed limitations in the constitutional safeguards. How the 'institutional interlocking' was conceived can be appreciated by extracting the major provisions which affected development.

We can see that two of the president's fundamental powers could only be used with the consent of the chancellor or at his request. In addition, the Reichstag had its own blocking powers, especially important in relation to the president's use of his emergency powers. In the key matter of the appointment of the chancellor it may appear that the president could bring in anyone of his choice. That was true, but a person coming to office solely with the president's blessing would not long survive a hostile Reichstag. Ultimately the force of Article 54 was superior to that of Article 53: sovereign power in relation to the chancellor lay with the Reichstag, even if its assertion were to be delayed through a dissolution and the holding of an election. In theory at least an encroachment on parliamentary authority should not occur.

Progress of the party system
The initial strength of the parties making up the original Weimar Coalition in 1919 was not maintained and the SPD, far from being able to determine the course of the republic, found that it was simply one party amongst others. The right-wing parties won favour again with the electorate, notably at the expense of the German Democrats (DDP). The complexion of governments changed from centre-left to centre-right, the Centre Party itself being the pivot of almost every coalition. The trend, however, was towards a moderate conservatism, since the forces of the extreme right had only a minute electoral following until 1930.

The general picture which emerges of the party system until 1930 is of one without any dramatic trends. The 'conservative consolidation' was marked by the election of Field-Marshal Hindenburg to the presidency in 1925. That event was not in itself a challenge to the parliamentary republic, and in some ways it opened the possibility for a reconciliation. It was significant, too, that the German Nationalists (DNVP) participated in broadly based governments from 1925 until 1928. Nor was the trend all one way, for the SPD came back into government following its election success in 1928. All the same, coalitions were unstable for the most part; paradoxically, the Great Coalition led by the SPD from 1928 until 1930 was the most durable of all, directly preceding the failure of the parliamentary system.

Reichstag Elections, 1919–1933

	1919	1920	1924 (May)	1924 (Nov)	1928	1930	1932 (Jul)	1932 (Nov)	1933
Turnout (per cent)	82.7	79.1	77.4	78.8	75.6	82.0	84.0	80.6	88.7
Votes (millions)	30.4	28.2	29.3	30.3	30.8	35.0	36.9	35.5	39.3
				percentage of votes cast					
NSDAP	—	—	6.6	3.0	2.6	18.3	37.4	33.1	43.9
DNVP	10.3	15.1	19.5	20.5	14.2	7.0	5.9	8.8	8.0
DVP	4.4	14.0	9.2	10.1	8.7	4.5	1.2	1.8	1.1
Z/BVP	19.7	17.8	16.6	17.3	15.2	14.8	15.7	14.8	13.9
WP	0.7	0.8	2.4	3.3	4.5	3.9	0.4	0.3	—
DDP/DStP	18.6	8.4	5.7	6.3	4.9	3.8	1.0	0.9	0.9
SPD	37.9	21.6	20.5	26.0	29.8	24.5	21.6	20.4	18.3
USPD	7.6	18.0	0.3	0.1	—	—	—	—	—
KPD	—	2.0	12.6	9.0	10.6	13.1	14.6	16.8	12.3
Others	0.8	2.3	6.1	4.2	9.4	10.1	2.2	3.1	1.6

Notes

'Others' include: the Deutsch-Hannoversche Partei, Christlich-National Landvolk, Christlich-Sozialer Volksdienst, Konservative Volkspartei, Deutsch Bauernpartei, the Bauern-und Weingärtnerbund, in addition to a number of others which were generally not represented in the Reichstag.

The system of proportional representation by party list was based on thirty-five very large electoral districts. Approximately 60,000 votes in any one electoral district was sufficient to win a seat. A party could be represented in the Reichstag with as little as 0.2 per cent of the national vote, but the exact percentage depended on the distribution of support within the Reich as a whole.

Neither the bare record of how the various parties fared at elections nor the details of coalition formation gives a sufficiently clear impression of the changes that took place in the party system. The nature of these changes can best be appreciated by examining the possible 'coalition' alignments throughout the life of the republic, taking the numerous permutations that were available for all the parties represented in the Reichstag.

The 'progress' of the party system, from relative cohesion to diffusion and thence to fragmentation, can be traced through the fortunes of the different alignments. The impossibility of finding any conceivable governing majority in the Reichstag after the 1930 election shows the extent of fragmentation, and from 1932 onwards the 'anti-system' parties had their own 'wrecking' majority. Finally, in 1933, a government based on a Reichstag majority did emerge – to crush the republic for good.

Chancellors and Coalitions in the Weimar Republic

February 1919	Scheidemann (SPD)	SPD, Z, DDP
June 1919	Bauer (SPD)	SPD, Z, DDP
March 1920	Müller (SPD)	SPD, Z, DDP
June 1920	Fehrenbach (Z)	Z, DDP, DVP
May 1921	Wirth (Z)	Z, SPD, DDP
November 1922	Cuno (non-party)	DDP, Z, DVP
August 1923	Stresemann (DVP)	DVP, SPD, Z, DDP
November 1923	Marx (Z)	Z, DVP, DDP/BVP
January 1925	Luther (non-party)	DVP, DDP, Z, BVP/DNVP
May 1926	Marx (Z)	Z, DVP, DDP, BVP, DNVP
June 1928	Müller (SPD)	SPD, DVP, BVP, Z
March 1930	Brüning (Z)	Z, DVP, DDP/DStP, and others
June 1932	Papen (non-party)	non-party, DNVP
December 1932	Schleicher (non-party)	non-party, DNVP, Landvolk
January 1933	Hitler (NSDAP)	NSDAP, DNVP, non-party, Landvolk

Party Alignments in the Weimar Republic

	'Left' parties	Weimar Coalition	Great Coalition	Right-Centre	National Oppositon	'Anti-system'
1919	45	76	81	54	10	8
1920	42	44	58	57	15	20
1924a	34	40	49	56	26	20
1924b	35	46	56	60	24	12
1928	41	37	55	53	17	13
1930	38	40	45	43	25	31
1932a	36	35	36	26	43	52
1932b	37	33	35	29	42	50
1933	31	30	32	26	52	56

Notes

The figures in the columns refer to the percentage of votes won at successive Reichstag elections by parties making up a particular grouping, regardless of whether or not they were in formal alliance, obviously not in the case of the 'anti-system' aggregate. The National Opposition existed only for the last years of the republic, but the constituent parties contested earlier elections.

'Left' parties were the KPD and the SPD as well as the Independent SPD for the first few years. The combination is of theoretical interest only, since the KPD and SPD were antagonists.

The Weimar Coalition consisted of the SPD, the German Democratic Party and the Centre Party.

The Great Coalition included the 'Weimar' parties and Stresemann's German People's Party (DVP).

Right-Centre coalitions involved various combinations, always with the Centre Party and ranging from the liberal German Democrats to the right-wing German Nationalists (DNVP) with the inclusion of small conservative parties.

The National Opposition was made up of the DNVP and the National Socialists. They first joined forces in the referendum on the Young Plan in 1929 and formed a coalition in January 1933.

The 'Anti-system' total is based mainly on the aggregation of the National Socialist and Communist share of the vote, but for the first two elections the USPD is included.

The role of proportional representation

It has frequently been argued that the adoption of a generous system of proportional representation in the Weimar Republic was a key factor in the disintegration of the party system and of particular help to the Nazis. If, for example, a relative-majority electoral system had been adopted, it is claimed, it is possible that the vote would have been concentrated in a few large parties and that the National Socialists would have been unable to become established in the party system.[10]

There are flaws in this line of argument. In the first place, it is doubtful whether multi-partism by itself creates instability in a political system, nor does the reduction in numbers always imply a gain in cohesion. Secondly, the second ballot system in pre-war Germany – a variant of the relative-majority type – maintained a flourishing multi-party system, and it is reasonable to suppose that those 'party traditions' would have been sufficiently resilient to survive. Finally, it is not the case that proportional representation led to a disproportionate increase in the number of parties represented in the Reichstag. Even though the ballot papers listed a bewildering profusion of parties, the great bulk of the vote went to half a dozen large parties, and the share of the vote taken by the very small ones declined sharply in the last, critical elections.

The other part of the argument relates specifically to the role of proportional representation in the rise of the National Socialists. It is undoubtedly true that unless a high 'qualifying' percentage is set, proportional representation makes the establishment of a new party much easier than under a relative-majority system, and the 'anchoring' of the NSDAP in the Reichstag from 1924 onwards supports that view. But the later advances of the Nazis, from 1930 onwards, had little to do with the nature of the electoral system, nor would the adoption of a relative majority system necessarily have held the party back. Nazi support was unevenly distributed in Germany as a whole. It was weak in some areas, strong in others – precisely the conditions which foster a rapid rise in representation in the relative-majority type with single-member constituencies. The phenomenon of National Socialism was too powerful to be contained by a simple electoral device.

Party characteristics

The lack of cohesion displayed in the Weimar party system arose more from the basic qualities of the individual parties than from the effects of proportional representation. The arrival of party government required them to exercise a co-operative responsibility, but the disposition of the parties had not changed at all: the characteristics which they had acquired in their formative years after 1871 remained. Their evolution had been determined by the prevailing form of non-responsible government which in the Weimar Republic developed into 'irresponsible' politics: governments were expendable, since party principles and interests came first.

As the crisis of the republic deepened, the underlying characteristics of the parties became more pronounced: each promoted a particular *Weltanschauung* and each represented special interests. The parties were all bound to their own clientèle, each with its own *Spezialvolk*, and the deterioration of political life was marked by the accentuation of sectional interests. In the later years of the republic there was a proliferation of very tiny 'interest' parties which, although not electorally important, were symptomatic of the ills of the political system. The larger parties concentrated on preserving their own sectional support: heavy industry, farming, trade unions, Catholic voters. It is against that background of social disintegration that the appeal of National Socialism came to be regarded so positively. In the place of the unedifying spectacle of the jostling of party interests in the Reichstag, the Nazis promised to create political unity and to restore social values which, they argued, the parliamentary system had debased.

It is significant that ideological rejuvenation in the Weimar Republic should have been confined to the two 'anti-system' parties which were absolutely committed to the destruction of the republic, the NSDAP and the KPD. But whilst the Nazi movement was able to make alliances and to harness the right-wing, nationalist vote, the KPD fought from a position of isolation. Thus there is a fairly precise correlation in the decline of the German Nationalist (DNVP) vote from 1930 and the rise in Nazi support. The transfer of allegiance was made easier by virtue of the 'common front' tactics pursued by the Nazis, which enabled Hitler to become the spokesman for the nationalist forces. The technique was used with success in the co-operation of the NSDAP with the DNVP and other groups on the occasion of the referendum against the Young Plan in 1929.

In contrast, the KPD was always in the position of waging a war against all the other parties. Its hostility to the SPD was based primarily on the experience of the SPD's role in the provisional government from 1918 until 1919 and in particular on the defeat of the Spartakus movement from which the KPD sprang. However, the two parties were diametrically opposed in their views on strategy: the KPD treated the existence of the republic as a barrier to the goals of the party, whilst the SPD regarded the republic as an essential step in working-class advance and therefore to be defended at all costs. The 'isolation' of the KPD is illustrated by the course it followed in the presidential election of 1925. It is at least arguable that if the KPD leader, Ernst Thälmann, had stood down at the second ballot, the 'Weimar' candidate would have defeated Hindenburg.

First Presidential Election, March/April 1925

	First ballot		Second ballot
	(votes in millions)		
Ludendorff ⎱ right-wing	0.28	Hindenburg	14.65
Jarres ⎰ parties	10.41		
Marx (Z)	3.89		
Held (BVP)	1.01	Marx	13.75
Hellpach (DDP)	1.57		
Braun (SPD)	7.80		
Thälmann (KPD)	1.87	Thälmann	1.93

Note
Absolute majority required in first ballot, relative majority in second ballot.

Even after the Nazi threat had become manifest, the Communists continued their war of attrition against the republic and the SPD in particular. Thus the leading KPD newspaper, *Die Rote Fahne*, in its issue of 17 November 1931 argued: 'Social Democracy is our major enemy. It is against the Social Democrats that we are mounting our leading assault in the current phase of the class struggle.' According to the strategic thinking of the Communists, the Nazis were actually the lesser evil, for a fascist regime would be merely a transitional stage – 'After the Nazis our turn will come!'

The stages of decline
It is impossible to show at what point parliamentary government in the Weimar Republic failed. In retrospect, the break-up of the Great Coalition led by the SPD in 1930 can be treated as a decisive turning-point, since that marked the end of majority government. The term 'Great Coalition' merely indicated the wide span of the parties participating, exploiting the maximum feasible reach in the

party system. Inevitably, therefore, the fall of the coalition – caused by the withdrawal of the SPD – meant the formation of a minority government, but that development of itself did not threaten the republic.

The new government, led by Heinrich Brüning of the Centre Party, because of its minority status, was forced to rely on the president's power to authorise decrees in order to push through its essential measures to attempt to deal with Germany's deepening economic and financial crisis. But Brüning was powerless to prevent a majority in the Reichstag from rescinding the presidential decrees. Accordingly, the Reichstag was dissolved in an attempt by Brüning to produce a majority for the Centre and its allies through an election. The move went sadly wrong. The result of the election held in September 1930 was of benefit only to the extremist parties, the Nazis and the Communists. Whilst the KPD recorded a relatively modest advance, the Nazi increase was spectacular (from a mere 2.8 per cent in 1928 to 18.3 per cent in 1930), raising its status to that of the second largest party in the Reichstag.

After that *débâcle*, the moderate parties were in a difficult position. The hope of restoring majority government had receded and a further contest might only help the anti-republican forces to strengthen their hold. The SPD in particular was forced to change its tack. Instead of outright opposition to Brüning's minority government, the SPD adopted a passive 'policy of toleration', fearing the consequences of the fall of the government. The new *Tolerierungspolitik* meant that the moderate parties had to accept the style of government which Brüning himself was forced to adopt – reliance on presidential authority.

There thus occurred a subtle change of emphasis: from being dependent on the Reichstag, the chancellor became increasingly reliant on the goodwill of the president instead. In the circumstances the shift was inevitable, and even though President Hindenburg had been elected in 1925 as the candidate of the rightist and therefore basically anti-Weimar front, the republican parties had had little to complain of in his behaviour in office. Hindenburg stood for the traditional values of the military establishment, values to be identified with the German state, not the parliamentary republic. But there had not been an open contradiction between the two. Their coexistence was apparently more than confirmed in 1932 when Hindenburg was 'adopted' by the republican parties to run as their presidential candidate to meet the challenge of Adolf

Hitler. The curious alliance worked, even though Hindenburg, narrowly missing the required absolute majority in the first round, was forced to a second ballot.

Second Presidential Election, March/April 1932

	First ballot		Second ballot
	(votes in millions)		
Hindenburg (all republican parties and DNVP)	18.65	Hindenburg	19.36
Hitler (NSDAP)	11.34	Hitler	13.42
Thälmann (KPD)	4.98	Thälmann	3.72
Other candidates	2.67	—	

As an immediate result of Hindenburg's re-election, the republic was saved for a while. But the consequence of retaining Hindenburg in office was less happy. With the new injection of popular authority, the president could afford to treat 'his' chancellor as expendable; after all, Brüning only headed a minority government. From Hindenburg's point of view and, perhaps more important in the opinion of his informal *camarilla* of advisers, Brüning was 'unreliable' and he was dismissed (more correctly, forced to resign) in May 1932.

The departure of Brüning broke the last link with parliamentary government. From then on presidential rule, guided by the *camarilla*, became undisguised. The new chancellor was Franz von Papen, a political unknown with no pretence to a parliamentary following, whom Hindenburg personally favoured. Since Papen was understandably anxious to avoid facing the Reichstag where his defeat would have been a foregone conclusion, a new election was called. The result was predictable: the size of the extremist vote increased enormously – the NSDAP and the KPD won over half the votes between them. The chancellor had to resort again to the expedient of dissolving the Reichstag immediately it reconvened, but the November 1932 election scarcely changed the overall strength of the 'anti-system' vote.

By the end of 1932 the Reichstag had ceased to be a support for democratic politics and the parliamentary system was entirely discredited. The following the Nazis had won in the country and in the Reichstag made Hitler's insistent demand for the chancellorship appear irresistible. The twists and turns of the presidential *camarilla*, authoritarian and anti-republican rather than pro-Nazi, became increasingly desperate; no longer was it a question of keeping Hitler out, but of the terms on which he should be allowed in. The replacement of Papen by General Schleicher in December 1932 brought no relief, but it gave Papen the chance to conduct secret negotiations with Hitler and eventually a formula was agreed. Hitler was to become chancellor with Papen as his vice-chancellor, and the Nazis were content to have only two ministerial posts; in addition, Hugenburg of the DNVP was brought into the government (that alliance was critical for Hitler to be able to command a majority). Hitler became chancellor on 30 January 1933. Whatever hopes Papen may have nursed that the arrangement would somehow 'control' Hitler, the National Socialists had no intention of sharing power with anyone else. However debased political life had become up to that point, thereafter the chance of taking any other direction disappeared: there was no alternative at that stage to dictatorship.

A constitutional fault?

Even though the system of parliamentary government failed over an extended period rather than at any particular point, perhaps the critical event was the dismissal of Heinrich Brüning. The slide from parliamentary to presidential rule was thereby completed. It is here that the constitutional position is important – the 'double responsibility' placed on the chancellor. The unrestricted right of the president to appoint *and* to dismiss the chancellor was a latent threat to the parliamentary system. Had the president only had the power to remove a chancellor with the positive concurrence of the Reichstag, then the agreement might have been withheld in Brüning's case. At all events, Brüning would have had an additional source of authority and Hindenburg might have wished to avoid a confrontation. Even though it can be argued that the chancellor's responsibility to the Reichstag (Article 54) took precedence over the president's power of dismissal (Article 53), that interpretation did not help Brüning.[11]

It is worth noting that the Reichstag defeated a motion of no-confidence in Brüning tabled in May 1932. This suggests that had Brüning remained in office, he might have been able to attract consistent support from the moderate parties – and possibly for an indefinite period, since a further election need not have been held until 1934. By that time the economic crisis had passed, and the National Socialist vote declined at the end of 1932. The Nazi storm might have been ridden out.

This chain of reasoning may be too speculative, but it is evident that the position of the president in the Weimar Republic was one of its least satisfactory features. There was an evident danger in his ability to acquire an authority superior to that of the chancellor. In this respect the provision for his direct election was equal in importance to his particular powers – as the aftermath of the 1932 presidential contest showed. The constitutional balance was tipped too far in creating a 'third force' independent of parliament and government. That objection would not apply if an unalloyed presidential form of government had been planned from the beginning. Even with the 'mixed' system, if the president had been elected by the Reichstag (as with Ebert) then he would have acted as a unifying force, working with the parties rather than against them.

A telling argument against the relevance of constitutional niceties is that they take too little account of the realities of political power. Thus it can be maintained that if Hitler's way to a legal accession to power had been blocked, the impetus of his movement was such that there would have been an extra-constitutional assault, against which the republic would have been equally helpless. But that view neglects the sanction which legal norms still carried, and Hitler was aware of the fact. The failure of his *putsch* in Munich in 1923 convinced Hitler of the necessity of adopting a 'constitutional' strategy in the future: he could not risk a second abortive coup. Repeatedly he made the claim that he was determined to come to power by legal means. Furthermore, the presence of the *Reichswehr* on the sidelines prompted caution. The benevolent neutrality adopted by the military leaders towards the Nazis held good as long as the legal forms were observed, but there was no guarantee of their continued aloofness in the case of armed insurrection.

However, Hitler's choice of a constitutional path to power has to be seen as one element in a wider 'double strategy'. The approach through legality brought the Nazis into the arena of normal party politics and electoral competition, but the other element in the strategy was based on the threat of force: parades of paramilitary units, violence in the streets, intimidation of political opponents, the techniques of terror. To argue that in the end Hitler came to power by legal means involves an arbitrary separation of the two parts of the 'double strategy', legality and force. The two methods were not alternatives, nor were they in competition; they complemented one another. Used in combination, they were devastatingly effective: the 'constitutional' ploy glossed over the essentially lawless nature of National Socialism; in turn, the display of force showed that the Nazis were not just one more party playing out the political game. Hitler's formulation in the paradox of a 'legal revolution' precisely captures the seemingly contradictory combination. Once power had been won, the two parts of the strategy were fused: the reign of 'legalised terror' began.

The appeal of National Socialism

The largest question mark of the Weimar Republic hangs over the attraction of National Socialism and the ability of Hitler to raise several million Germans to a high pitch of enthusiasm and intoler-ance. It is easier to show who responded to the appeal than to demonstrate why the response was forthcoming and why it was so massive. Support for the NSDAP was strongly biased towards certain categories of the population. The Nazi vote was middle-rather than working-class, Protestant rather than Catholic, younger rather than older, rural and small-town rather than urban and large-city, located in northern rather than in southern Germany. A composite picture of the typical Nazi voter would include all these attributes, but the party's following was obviously more hetero-geneous than these broad labels suggest. The sheer size of the Nazi vote – some fourteen million in 1932 – shows that there was a genuine mass mobilisation at work.[12]

It is also true that at no time did the Nazis obtain for themselves the support of a majority of those voting. The vote of the Centre Party stood up well, and the same applies to the SPD and the KPD (excluding the election of March 1933, which was held under the duress of the dictatorship). It is notable that these three parties were all ones which, through the medium of the Catholic Church and the organised labour movement, could supply a much more thorough form of 'social insulation' for their supporters than other parties. The more 'exposed' parties were those which broadly represented middle-class interests: the conservative-national DNVP, the liberal-conservative DVP and the liberal-radical DDP. The DDP was the first to fail, well before the rise of the NSDAP, but both the DNVP and the DVP lost a considerable amount of support directly to the Nazis from 1930 onwards.

The ideal-typical Nazi voters were present in large numbers, but it is important to bear in mind the diverse nature of groups which were attracted: farmers, industrialists, owners of small businesses, unemployed workers, and so on. There was also an important mass-elite admixture in the support for National Socialism. Nazi influence was widespread within many key groups: leaders of industry, the universities (the middle-class students as well as the academic staff), officers of the *Reichswehr*, officials of the state bureaucracy. The movement did attract the rag, tag and bobtail, but it also exercised a fascination over respected professional people, even though they may have felt some distaste for the activities of the Nazi stormtroopers.

If we have a reasonably clear picture of which social groups were inclined to give the NSDAP their vote, there is no simple explanation of why they did, when they did. We can refer to the pressure of conditions at the time, to the positive content of Nazi programme and ideology and to the personal hold which Adolf Hitler was able to exercise on a large part of the German population. These are only three areas of explanation and none is likely to be sufficient in itself.

Of the objective conditions ruling at the time, the economic depression which began in 1929 was by far the most important – the Nazi vote rose in line with the growth in unemployment. It is also significant that the first Nazi successes occurred earlier, in 1928, in rural areas which were first affected by a down-turn in agriculture. The depression affected business confidence in Germany, as was the case for many advanced countries, but the whole edifice had already been undermined by the experience of the great inflation of 1923. That catastrophe had been overcome, but it had left in its wake a large and disgruntled section of the middle class, insecure and eager for strong remedies to meet the new crisis.

Also to be taken into account, along with the economic factors, are those of a less measurable kind but which were nevertheless perceived in the same way: the humiliation of the defeat in 1918, the harsh conditions of the Versailles Treaty. Whatever misfortunes had befallen Germany and particular classes, the blame was laid at the door of the parliamentary republic, and its inability to supply remedies or even to provide decisive majority government at the time of crisis was the last straw. By 1930 a large part of the electorate was ripe for a radical mobilisation.

The Nazi programme naturally offered all the necessary means to eradicate the causes of German weakness and dishonour: Jews,

Communists, Social Democrats were to be the obvious casualties. Behind the specific threats and promises, however, there was the much more nebulous attraction of National Socialist ideology. Its central tenet was German national unity, from which flowed many of the particular aspects of the creed: the racialist myths, the exclusion of 'un-German' elements, the rediscovery of the *Volk*, the vision of a *Volksgemeinschaft*. Many of the implications of National Socialist ideology were probably lost on Nazi supporters, but it promised to end the traditional divisions of society and the polarisation of class conflict.

Perhaps one should not look too closely for a coherence in Nazi ideology. Indeed, one aspect of the appeal of Germany under National Socialism was simply that it would offer 'the opposite of what we have now'! Nor was the Nazi hierarchy over-anxious to specify too closely the content of the revolution: it was much easier to play on fears and hopes than to show how many not-easily-reconcilable differences of interest would be resolved. That ambiguity applied particularly to the future of the economic system – it soon became clear that 'National Socialism' by no means meant the end of capitalism.

Neither the programme nor the ideological basis of National Socialism can be considered of critical importance in their own right: they were instrumental to the acquisition of power. The credibility of the Nazi message was open to question, but Hitler himself was its unifying force – indeed somehow its personification. Essentially the Nazi ideology was concerned with the assumption of absolute power: Hitler was to wield that power. The presence of Hitler invited adulation but also a total subordination.

It is not possible to distinguish which of the appeals of National Socialism predominated. Without Hitler's contribution, the movement may not have held together; equally, without the particular circumstances of the time, Hitler's impact might have been no more than that of the averagely unsuccessful demagogue. Attempts to explain the rise of German fascism by referring to one particular feature alone must be inadequate. That applies to explanations which point to the strong continuities in German thought, to the suggestion that Nazism, in its return to national mysticism, was simply a throwback to the past. It is just as contrived to seek a purely 'economic' explanation, to take the economic crisis as the sole determinant and, in isolating the reactionary features of German capitalism, to show that German fascism was simply a result of 'the capitalist crisis'.

Discontinuity in the Political System
In its consequences for German society, the impact of the Nazi dictatorship was the most profound of all the upheavals in German history. But it is insufficient to take the year 1933 by itself as standing for the whole era, and the wider effects of the dictatorship have to be taken into account along with particular acts of policy. Nor should the regime itself be considered in isolation from the manner of its passing in 1945, nor even from the consequences of its collapse. The years from 1933 until 1945 and later constitute a whole period, a multiple fracture rather than a simple break.

The two fractures
The first break was signalled by Hitler's accession to power in January 1933: from that point onwards the Nazis were free to implement their revolution and to dismantle the institutions of the republic. The election held in March 1933 was fought under the shadow of political terror, and it is difficult to suppose – had the Nazis failed to control a majority in the Reichstag as a result – that they would have been prepared to relinquish their hold. Once the majority was available, the general enabling law, the *Ermächtigungsgesetz*, which required a two-thirds majority, gave the government an unrestricted decree-making power. There then followed the various steps towards totalitarian rule: the abolition of the trade unions and their incorporation into a state-controlled *Arbeitsfront*, the dissolution of the parties, leaving only the NSDAP, and then the proclamation of the 'merging' of state and party. Only President Hindenburg remained as a vestige of the republican order, and on his death in 1934 Hitler combined the two offices of chancellor and president into that of the omnipotent Führer controlling the state, the government, the party and the German people. Hitler stood at the head of an entirely new type of political system.

   The Nazis were not content to have a total political control but sought, through the policy of *Gleichschaltung*, to achieve a total subordination of society as well. The application of *Gleichschaltung* was general but erratic. In principle it was aimed at all expressions of pluralism: political institutions, trade unions, the universities, the mass media and cultural life. The intention was to disarm all potential opponents of National Socialism, to make any form of organised resistance impossible, to create a totally regimented society. But the effect was uneven: it was deemed expedient and sufficient just to keep the Churches on a short rein;

the economic order, the private ownership of the means of production, was retained intact. Thus the process of *Gleichschaltung* was carried as far as was adequate for the purpose: the economic system was operated under the directives of a 'command economy' and made subordinate to the primacy of 'political will'. 'Why,' Hitler asked, 'should we socialise the banks when we have socialised the people?'

The political and social institutions of pluralism were the obvious targets of *Gleichschaltung*, but National Socialism also challenged – and subjugated – the traditional elites of German society, the ones which had never accepted the Weimar Republic and which still survived. There still existed an 'unmodern' sector which was untouched by the German Revolution: the state and certain social elites. A whole network of political and social connections persisted, their unity expressed in the mystique and values attached to the state and their apotheosis found in the *Reichswehr*, which preserved its independent status throughout the Weimar Republic. Yet they were not spared under Nazi rule, nor were their backward-looking values in any way sacrosanct. The subordination of the *Reichswehr* took place gradually but it was thorough. The attempt to assassinate Hitler in July 1944 can be seen in that light as the dying act of revenge on the part of a vanishing elite.

Once those elements lost their leading position in society, the effect was irreversible. Ralf Dahrendorf describes the fundamental change as 'the inextinguishable social revolution of National Socialism', and we can appreciate that this 'social revolution' had largely unintended consequences: by obliterating the lingering features of Germany's past uneven development, National Socialist rule helped bring about a basic modernisation of German society.[13] Disastrous as the experience proved to be for Germany, the weight of the dictatorship broke the complex lines of the existing social structure. The 'modernisation', in its immediate effect, brought about an equality of subordination, equal deprivation as a '*Volksgenosse*', under Hitler.

That rendering is incomplete unless the scale of the defeat in 1945 is added to the development: the collapse signified not only the end of the Nazi era but its complete evaporation as well. The regime, the apparatus of the dictatorship, National Socialist ideology, all indissolubly tied to the person of the Führer, vanished with him. Yet the removal of Nazi power exposed a curiously altered society beneath, not an incipient alternative structure of authority but a 'vacuum of social power'. That situation was necessarily transient; even so, it showed that future evolution would not be bound by the former patterns.

The year 1945 also marks a sharp rupture, but it is an essential complement to what had gone before. Just as the breaks caused by National Socialism have to be treated together, so too must the impact of allied occupation be treated in conjunction with the disintegration of the Nazi system.

Restoration or renewal?
Despite the total nature of allied occupation, it is easy to exaggerate the extent of the change brought by the Western powers to Germany. There are grounds for arguing that in Western Germany an actual 'restoration' took place; not, naturally, a reversion to the immediate past but the re-establishment of a *status quo ante* – essentially a resurrection of the conditions of pre-Hitlerian Germany. An implication of that argument, and one which is frequently advanced by left-wing critics of the Federal Republic, is that the features and tendencies which had led to Fascism as the successor of the first republic are still present to contaminate the second republic. In consequence, political debate in Western Germany carries additional colouring: a preoccupation with the chances of an actual 'fascist revival'.

The criticism gains in force through the contrast made with the German Democratic Republic: the occupation of Eastern Germany by the Soviet Union ensured that an entirely new basis for social and political development was created. But in Western Germany a parallel 'revolution' did not occur. It soon became evident that the Western allies had no intention of making – or permitting – radical changes in the economic order, whilst the Soviet Union went ahead with its version of creating a socialist society. Not unnaturally, the Western powers regarded the re-establishment of a market economy with favour, since their own economic systems were similarly based. The important point was that the National Socialist regime had not interfered at all radically with the pre-existing economic structure. A straight line of continuity was maintained: Western Germany had its direct antecedents in the Weimar Republic.

There was also a political resurrection. The first generation of political leaders in the Bonn Republic was largely composed of survivors from the Weimar Republic. Those politicians took the first republic as their natural point of reference. They owed their favoured position in the initial post-war period to the occupation authorities who were concerned to establish a liberal-democratic political system. The Weimar Republic had not been a good advertisement for liberal democracy, but it was the only model Germany had: the Bonn Republic was inevitably a revamped edition of its Weimar forerunner.

Both on 'economic' and 'political' grounds the argument for continuity is plausible, and with it the contention that the unhealthy characteristics of the past became embedded in the Federal Republic. But is the argument properly based?

One obvious defect is that it fails to take into account the extent of the changes brought about by National Socialism. If the 'legal' and 'social' revolutions had been only superficial, the chances of a restoration would have been high. But their effect was fundamental: the Nazi 'transformation', with its unintended consequences, made the need for a further post-war liberal-democratic *revolution* largely redundant.

The modernisation of German society under National Socialism provided the setting for a post-war renewal, to use Dahrendorf's expression: the opportunity for a 'rejuvenated' German capitalism, freed from the constraints of the 'industrial-feudal' society. If that formulation is correct, it implies that the Federal Republic runs no *greater* risk than other West European states of lurching towards a fundamental social crisis.

Nor can it be convincingly argued that the 'political resurrection' was a retrograde step, that the reinstatement of the Weimar generation meant the imposition on the country of men who had 'learned nothing' through their experience of National Socialism. They were at least aware of the pitfalls that should be avoided in creating a new liberal democracy. The same applies to the leading representatives of social organisations, in particular the churches: they were aware just how much they had ducked their responsibilities in failing to offer a proper resistance to National Socialist doctrines.

The West German renewal was incomplete, for there is plenty of evidence to show that inherited attitudes persisted in the Federal Republic and that 'old Nazis' made a habit of turning up in leading positions of state and society. The question is whether isolated occurrences really lend substance to the charge of 'restoration' or whether West German society is qualitatively different from the past.

There is no real need in this respect to make comparisons with the East German state. Both parts of Germany now have their own history, and both have been subjected for a long period to the powerful influences from the trans-national societies of which they are parts. The link they have with each other may be traced back to the 'frozen' German Revolution of 1918. For its long-delayed conclusion we have to look beyond the Weimar Republic and past the Nazi dictatorship: the completion of the revolution can be seen in its two alternative forms – the antagonistic social and political systems of the present two German states.

The parties and the occupation
The fundamental changes brought by National Socialism, war and defeat, along with the post-war occupation, represented a cumulative transformation which can be related to the specific case of the party system. Gerhard Loewenberg in his essay on 'The Remaking of the German Party System' makes this connection: 'The social changes which Nazism brought to a head had been going on for half a century without basically affecting the party system. Only the destruction of that party system under totalitarian coercion *and* the establishment of new ground rules for party competition by the occupation regime permitted social change to work its political effect.'[14] Loewenberg's argument stresses the importance of the purely political factors which were operative in the post-war period: the basic social changes wrought by the Nazi dictatorship were in themselves insufficient to ensure which direction would finally be taken. If, as after the First World War, Germany had been left to itself, then the final political form would have been difficult to predict.

    We do not have to look far to ascertain the nature of the purely political factors: the claim of the allied powers to exact an unconditional surrender on Germany led to their assumption of a *total* responsibility for Germany's political future. The unlimited jurisdiction they wielded (the absence of any German government or state power) meant that a German political system ceased to exist. Even though the allies were committed to restoring democracy to Germany, their rule was initially authoritarian. The Potsdam Agreement of July 1945 did require that the separate zones into which Germany was divided should be treated uniformly, but in practice each occupying power was free to 'restore' democracy according to its own lights. There were similarities: they all engaged in the close regulation of political activity; they all adopted a basically autocratic attitude; and they all followed the identical procedure of 'licensing' only those parties with a democratic potential. This active intervention, 'democracy under licence', resembled the old *Obrigkeitsstaat* in a modern form.

Active discrimination was practised most determinedly in the Soviet Zone. Even though the parties, similar to those in the Western zones of occupation, were permitted to operate, the KPD was placed in a favoured position from the outset. Yet it was apparent that the Communists were not well served electorally – the Party ran at best a weak second to the SPD. Since the Soviet Union had no use for the nice rules of liberal democracy, other means had to be found to ensure Communist hegemony. One device was the creation of an 'anti-Fascist bloc' composed of all democratic forces through which the KPD could exercise power. Another was the use of controlled political ancillaries – trade unions, youth movements and other mass organisations – as supplementary control mechanisms. The third means employed proved decisive: in April 1946 a shot-gun marriage took place between the KPD and the SPD in the Soviet Zone. The merger of the two parties to form the Socialist Unity Party (SED) ensured that the winning of elections would present no great problem, and the SED soon became an orthodox Communist party of Marxist-Leninist persuasion. The other 'bourgeois' parties were retained, thus sustaining the spurious impression that a party system continued to operate. The formation of a 'National Front' of the parties and mass organisations provided the umbrella for all political activity, and elections took the form of the prior allocation of seats in the *Volkskammer* on the basis of a single list of candidates, with the guarantee that the SED and its appendages would always constitute the majority.

Such purposive control was not evident in the Western zones. The Western allies were bound by their own norms of liberal democracy and the revival of party competition was regarded as valuable in itself, not as a means of exercising subtle supervision. Nonetheless some reservations have to be made. The Western allies were not prepared to tolerate all parties, regardless of their creed. They were concerned to ensure that the emerging political system in Western Germany was to their liking (it is a matter for speculation what course they would have adopted had they been faced by dominant parties which opposed their policies). Moreover, the period of occupation was not a brief interregnum. There was ample opportunity for the Western allies to influence the outlook of the major parties in ways favourable to their own strategic concepts, and from those postulates other consequences for the party system flowed: a state built up as an integral part of the Western defensive system against the Soviet Union was bound also to reflect that hostility in the nature of its domestic concerns.

A rather ambiguous relationship developed between the West German parties and the occupation authorities. They were granted increasing freedom to determine the main lines of policy, at first locally and then in the *Länder*, but whatever their responsibilities, they were conditional and restricted. It meant that although their co-operation was usually forthcoming, the final responsibility rested with the occupying powers. In this way the parties avoided the dangers which were evident in the Weimar Republic – those associated with apparently taking full responsibility and yet in reality having to follow the dictates of the victors.

The manner in which sovereignty came to the West German state – by instalments – was arguably the most favourable condition for the secure establishment of the party system. The initial *Land* elections were held in 1946, and later, with the fusion of the British and American zones in 1947 and the Frankfurt Charter of 1948, the parties assumed control of economic affairs. The Basic Law itself, which provided the instruments of government for the Federal Republic, was made subject to the higher 'law' of the Occupation Statute. Even after the republic was created in 1949 the West German state was kept in a subordinate position until becoming a member of the North Atlantic Treaty Organisation in 1955.

This layering of sovereignty can be likened to a protective cocoon: when it was finally shed the parties and the political system were firmly established. The limited nature of the competitive party system during the occupation provided a moderate degree of polarisation between the parties, a 'democratic distance', which in the absence of radical alternatives aided popular identification with the political system. It was no accident that the major parties which first took root, the old SPD and the new CDU, were the ones which maintained a dominance thereafter. The West German party system which to begin with had a synthetic quality had already become apparently indigenous by the time the Federal Republic came into being.

Fig. 1 Germany: the zones of occupation in 1945 and the Eastern territories

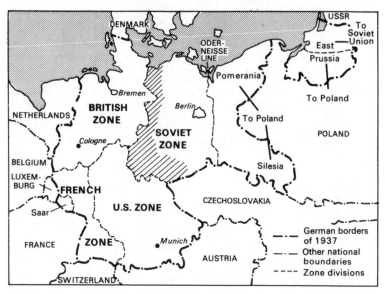

Notes

The shaded area, principally parts of Thuringia and Saxony, indicates occupation by the American and British forces until they withdrew at the end of June 1945.

The city of Bremen was an enclave of American occupation within the British Zone.

The Saar, although occupied by French forces, was treated separately from the French Zone.

Notes and References

1. F. Gilbert, 'Political Power and Academic Responsibility' in L. Krieger and F. Stern (eds.), *The Responsibility of Power*, Macmillan, 1968, pp. 411–13.
2. Quoted by H. Kohn, *The Mind of Germany: The Education of a Nation*, Macmillan, 1961, p. 159.
3. See Fritz Stern, 'The Political Consequences of the Unpolitical German', *The Failure of Illiberalism; Essays on the Political Culture of Modern Germany*, London: Macmillan, 1972.
4. For a discussion of the missing 'keystone' of the German *Rechtsstaat*, see Otto Pflanze, 'Juridical and Political Responsibility in Nineteenth Century Germany', in Krieger and Stern, op. cit.
5. Quoted by Otto von der Gablentz, *Politische Parteien als Ausdruck gesellschaftlicher Kräfte*, Berlin, 1952, pp. 5–6.
6. On the debate within the SPD, see Peter Gay, *The Dilemma of Democratic Socialism*, Columbia University Press, 1952.
7. There is a collected edition of Max Weber's political writings: *Gesammelte politische Schriften*, Tübingen: Mohr, 1958. See also, D. Beetham, *Max Weber and the Theory of Modern Politics*, Allen and Unwin, 1974.

8. Quoted in R. M. Watt, *The Kings Depart: The German Revolution and the Treaty of Versailles*, Penguin Books, 1972, p. 163.
9. Quoted by W. J. Mommsen, *Max Weber und die deutsche Politik, 1890–1920*, Tübingen: Mohr, 1959.
10. The classic case against the use of PR in the Weimar Republic was made by F. A. Hermens, *Democracy or Anarchy?* (1938), reprinted in H. Eckstein and D. Apter, *Comparative Politics*, Collier Macmillan, 1965.
11. Arnold Brecht (amongst others) has argued for the precedence of the Reichstag in securing the responsibility of the chancellor: *Prelude to Silence: The End of the German Republic*, New York: Oxford University Press, 1944.
12. On support for the National Socialists, see A. Milatz, *Wähler und Wahlen in der Weimarer Republik*, Bonn: Bundeszentrale für politische Bildung, 1968; S. M. Lipset, *Political Man*, Heinemann, 1960; T. Childers, 'The Social Bases of the National Socialist Vote', *Journal of Contemporary History*, October 1976; J. Noakes, *The Nazi Party in Lower Saxony*, 1921–33, Oxford University Press, 1971.
13. R. Dahrendorf, in *Society and Democracy in Germany*, Weidenfeld and Nicolson, 1968, forcefully (and paradoxically) argues: 'While the social revolution of National Socialism was an instrument in the establishment of totalitarian forms, by the same token it had to create the basis of liberal modernity; the counterrevolution on the other hand can be understood only as a revolt of tradition, and thus of illiberalism, and of the authoritarianism of a surviving past.' p. 412.
14. G. Loewenberg, 'The Remaking of the German Party System', in M. Dogan and R. Rose (eds.), *European Politics: A Reader*, Macmillan, 1971, p. 279. See also his excellent concise essay cited in the further reading below.

Further Reading

K. Adenauer, *Memoirs*, Weidenfeld and Nicolson, 1966.
K. Bracher, *The German Dictatorship: The Origins, Structure and Effects of National Socialism*, Weidenfeld and Nicolson, 1973. (Bibliography.)
A. Bullock, *Hitler: A Study in Tyranny*, Penguin Books, 1964.
L. D. Clay, *Decision in Germany*, Heinemann, 1950.
G. A. Craig, *Germany: 1886–1945*, Oxford University Press, 1978.
R. J. Evans (ed.), *Society and Politics in Wilhelmine Germany*, Croom Helm, 1978.
J. Fest, *Hitler: A Biography*, Weidenfeld and Nicolson, 1974.
J. A. Gimbel, *The American Occupation of Germany: Politics and the Military, 1945–1949*, Stanford University Press, 1968.
H. Grebing, *Geschichte der deutschen Parteien*, Wiesbaden: Franz Steiner, 1962.
L. Krieger and F. Stern (eds.), *The Responsibility of Power*, Macmillan, 1968.
G. Loewenberg, 'The Development of the German Party System', in K. H. Cerny (ed.), *Germany at the Polls*, Washington: American Enterprise Institute, 1978.
E. Litchfield (ed), *Governing Post-War Germany*, Cornell University Press, 1953.
G. Mann, *A History of Germany since 1789*, Penguin Books, 1974.
P. Merkl, *The Origins of the West German Republic*, Oxford University Press, 1963.
A. Milward, *The German Economy at War*, Athlone Press, 1965.
G. L. Mosse, *The Crisis of German Ideology*, Weidenfeld and Nicolson, 1966.
S. Neumann, *Die Parteien der Weimarer Republik*, Stuttgart: Kohlhammer, 1965.
A. Nicholls, *Weimar and the Rise of Hitler*, Macmillan, 1968.
K. J. Newman, *European Democracy between the Wars*, Allen and Unwin, 1970.
T. Nipperdey, *Die Organisation der deutschen Parteien vor 1918*, Düsseldorf: Droste Verlag, 1961.
H. Plessner, *Die Verspätete Nation*, Stuttgart: Kohlhammer, 1969.

G. A. Ritter (ed.), *Die deutschen Parteien vor 1918*, Cologne: Kiepenheuer und Witsch, 1973. (Bibliography.)

A. Ryder, *From Bismarck to Brandt*, Macmillan, 1973. (Bibliography.)

T. Schieder, *State and Society in Our Times*, Nelson, 1962.

D. Schoenbaum, *Hitler's Social Revolution: Class and Status in Nazi Germany*, Weidenfeld and Nicolson, 1967.

J. P. Stern, *Hitler: The Führer and the People*, Collins/Fontana, 1975.

W. Treue, *Die deutschen Parteien: Vom 19 Jahrhundert bis zur Gegenwart*, Frankfurt: Ullstein, 1975.

S. Verba, 'The Remaking of the German Political Culture' in L. Pye and S. Verba (eds.), *Political Culture and Political Development*, Princeton University Press, 1965.

S. J. Woolf (ed.), *The Nature of Fascism*, Weidenfeld and Nicolson, 1968.

2 The Constitutional Framework

The Status of the Basic Law
The spectre of the Weimar Republic is not easily laid to rest in Germany. Even though the Federal Republic has a reputation for stability, any slight faltering of the political institutions immediately provokes an air of intense crisis: the ever-present fear that a pronounced failure would show, after all, that liberal democracy does not work in Germany. This insecurity may help to account for the marked reliance on the constitution and on legal norms: they provide a measure of reassurance and certainty in the face of the dangerous vagaries of politics. Yet it is surprising that the Basic Law should have achieved its high status as the pillar of the republic despite its inauspicious origins.

The genesis of the constitution
Once the decision to create a separate West German state had been taken, its realisation followed rapidly. The London Conference of June 1948, consisting of the three Western occupying powers and the Benelux states, authorised the calling of a German constituent assembly to draft a 'democratic constitution' which would provide for 'a governmental structure of the federal type which is best adapted to the re-establishment of German unity . . . and which will protect the rights of the participating states, provide adequate central authority, and contain guarantees of individual rights and freedoms'. That invitation led to the setting up of a German Parliamentary Council, composed of elected representatives from the *Land* assemblies in proportion to party strength. The Parliamentary Council approved the Basic Law in May 1949 and, after

ratification by the *Länder*, the constitution came into full effect with the holding of a federal election in August 1949.

Nowhere in the Basic Law was any reference made to the restricted nature of the sovereignty accorded to the new state. In fact, the Western allies retained several powers under the Occupation Statute, issued in April 1949, and they were sufficiently numerous to make the Basic Law appear a subordinate document. The 'reserved powers' included questions of disarmament, reparations, decartellisation, foreign affairs, foreign trade and exchange. Moreover, at the outset any amendment to the Basic Law required sanction from the allies, who also retained powers of emergency – in effect, the authority to suspend the constitution if necessary.

These restrictions hardly gave the new constitution an impressive standing. Nor, perhaps, was it thought necessary in the conditions ruling at that time. Even though the creation of two German states made reunification immediately more difficult, the general supposition was that an all-German government would be formed at some stage, and that would render the Basic Law inapplicable, as was made explicit by Article 146: 'This Basic Law shall cease to be in force on the day on which a constitution adopted by a free decision of the German people comes into force.' Anyway it was only because they believed they were engaged in a limited, provisional enterprise that the parties were willing to participate at all. They were also unwilling to give the state the permanent hallmark of a constitution, hence the adoption of the term 'Basic Law' – *Grundgesetz* rather than *Verfassung*. It is relevant too that at no stage were the West German people themselves directly consulted, neither whether they desired a separate state nor whether they approved the terms of the constitution. Instead, all decisions were taken by the parties and their representatives in the *Länder* governments: the sole link was through the elections to the *Land* assemblies, elected on a quite different mandate.

With all these handicaps it must have seemed difficult to attach great importance to the Basic Law: it was neither an expression of sovereignty nor obviously based on the will of the people, let alone expressing their enthusiasm and commitment. On the other hand, it did meet the needs of the moment, a stop-gap contrivance which was a reaction to a growing international crisis and to the problems of providing competent government in a divided country. The significance of that context was shown in the work of the Parliamentary Council, which moved towards fairly swift agreement despite the even balance between the major parties: of the sixty-five voting members, the CDU and SPD had twenty-seven seats each, with the remainder distributed amongst the minor parties, including the FDP and KPD. Only the Communists and the Bavarian CSU voted against the final draft, and all the *Land* assemblies, with the exception of Bavaria, ratified the Basic Law. Some provisions were strongly contested in the Parliamentary Council, especially those concerning the distribution of powers within the proposed federal state, but the extent of the final consensus is the more important fact.

The whole venture could hardly fire the imagination, but there were benefits in the way the Basic Law was introduced. The perils of an electoral contest were avoided and with it the danger of the appearance of a wide gulf between the CDU and the SPD. The timing was also important: had a constitution been drawn up immediately after the war, it would have been a different document, reflecting the social dislocation of Germany. But already by 1949 the worst difficulties had passed, and the currency reform of June 1948 promised a brighter economic future. The worsening relations with the Soviet Union, culminating in the blockade of West Berlin, convinced any waverers that the provision of a workable government for West Germany was the essential priority.

By the time the Federal Republic came into being its main features were already determined: it was a state founded in opposition to the influence of the Soviet Union, based on the requirements of a market economy, and already showing the impress of a particular type of political party. The Basic Law confirmed the course of post-war evolution: it was devised by – and, in a sense, for the benefit of – those parties which had achieved a dominant position during the occupation.

Learning from Weimar

If we ask how it was that the Basic Law not only managed to survive long after the Federal Republic ceased to be a 'provisional state' but also assumed a central importance for political development, then a partial answer is forthcoming: the high status of the constitution is related to the fact that it has faithfully reflected the balance of power in post-war West Germany, a balance that has not materially altered since that time.

But that answer must be incomplete. It does justice neither to the content of the constitution nor to its elevated position in the political system. The Basic Law has shown itself to be a sensitive and ingenious constitutional mechanism in its specific arrangements, and at the same time it is a powerful statement of liberal-democratic constitutional theory. Those claims may appear to be large, especially considering the circumstances in which the Basic Law was drafted, but how else can we explain the way in which its normative values have acquired an almost independent sanction within the Federal Republic?

In devising the new constitution the almost overriding preoccupation of the delegates was to avoid the 'mistakes' of the Weimar Republic; the Basic Law reflects a sustained attempt at rectification rather than a desire to construct a visionary democratic order. It was felt sufficient to concentrate on two leading problems: to remedy the errors of the Weimar constitution and to ensure that there would be no erosion of the law, no return to the totalitarian lawlessness of Nazi Germany. Both problems are obviously closely related, but there is a difference in emphasis. One involves a concentration on what may be called the 'instruments of government', whilst the other is concerned with raising the law to a position of authority above the uncertain eddies of politics.

The constitution of the Weimar Republic had sought to achieve a balanced distribution of power amongst the various organs of state, but the weighting had proved to be unsound. In particular, the creation of a strong president, who was largely independent of both parliamentary and party control, resulted in two distinct sets of legitimate authority, supported by the separate 'constituencies' of the president and the Reichstag. That division is quite compatible with a presidential system of government but not with a parliamentary one. The Weimar constitution constructed a formal balancing of powers by juggling with several potentially 'active' pieces, but that method finally led to a total fusion, not a balanced division.

Constitutional balance in the Federal Republic was secured by quite different means. Instead of maintaining an ambiguous relationship between the presidency and parliamentary government, the Basic Law opted unequivocally for the latter form. Concentration on parliamentary government ensured that there could only be a single source of political leadership, issuing from, and based on, the parliamentary parties. The Weimar Republic only succeeded in grafting a 'parliamentarised' system of government on to a much older tradition. In the Federal Republic the steps taken to 'demote' the president effectively removed one source of challenge to parliamentary authority. The president's opportunities to intervene actively were drastically reduced, and the method adopted for his election – by a 'Federal Assembly' (*Bundesversammlung*) consisting of the members of the Bundestag together with an equal number of electors from the *Land* assemblies – guaranteed that he would be both a parliamentary and a party nominee. The dominance of the parties ensures that, unlike the position in the Weimar Republic, the 'will' of the electorate may not be set against itself.

Ultimately the single source of political leadership is expressed in the person of the chancellor, now placed in an elevated position. He wields power through the control of a parliamentary majority and, by the same token, the line-up in the Bundestag is the most important constraint affecting his authority. In that respect the position of the West German chancellor is akin to that of a British prime minister who can 'normally' expect to control a parliamentary majority. But the parallel is inexact, since the West German system imposes a variety of constraints which do not affect the operation of British government but which act as important modifications to the concept of unqualified parliamentary sovereignty in the Federal Republic.

German federalism

One of the most significant modifications occurs through the operation of the federal system adopted for the republic. The federal structure is possibly one of the most underrated of West German political institutions, often treated as quite ancillary to the parliamentary system. Some importance may be attached to the allied demand that the new state was to be organised on federal lines to counter centralising tendencies which the Americans in particular were anxious to avoid. The parties were divided in their views. The CDU favoured a federal solution, partly because it was an extremely decentralised party and also because it did not expect to be the controlling force in the central government. With its centralist traditions, the SPD desired a unitary state, believing that it would be the dominant party and naturally not wishing to have its power thwarted by stubborn governments in the *Länder*.

Those wranglings may distract attention from the importance of federalism as a tradition of government in Germany, even though it has never appeared to be of special significance in the balance of power. The federal form of the Reich of 1871 was a cover for Prussian hegemony, and in the Weimar Republic the constituent

Fig. 2 The *Länder* of the Federal Republic

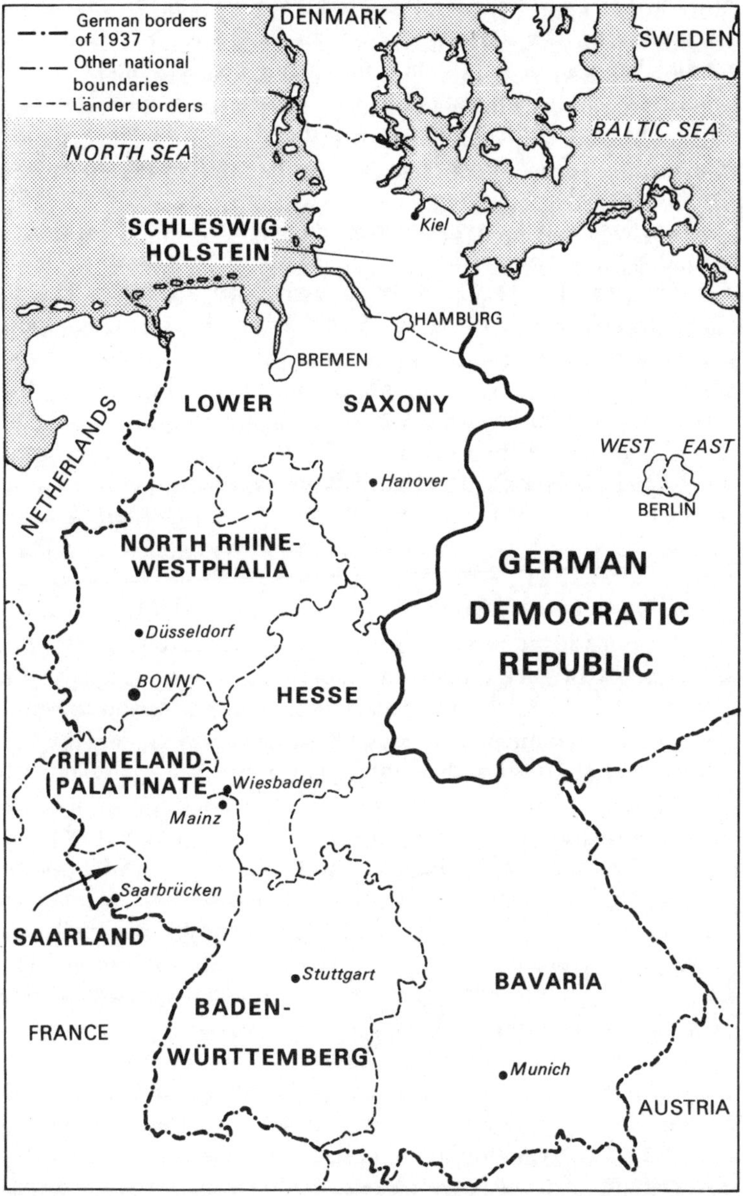

Note

Originally there were eleven *Länder* in addition to West Berlin. The present *Land* of Baden-Württemberg was formed in 1952 by an amalgamation of the three *Länder* of Baden, Württemberg-Baden, and Baden-Hohenzollern. The Saarland acceded to the Federal Republic in January 1957, thus bringing the total to ten.

states – without their old rulers – were even less important. Ironically, the power of Prussia in imperial Germany was one reason for strengthening the central government in the republic, with the result that Papen was able to use the presidential power of emergency decree to oust the elected Prussian government in July 1932 and place Prussia under the direct administration of the Reich. One of the remaining bastions of republican loyalty was thus destroyed.

The apparently subsidiary nature of German federalism is confirmed by the terms of its re-establishment in 1949. None of the *Länder*, with the exception of Bavaria, had a strong claim to historical continuity, and Bremen and Hamburg, although supported by their Hanseatic traditions, were no more than small city-states. The artificiality of the present system is underlined by the great variation in the size of the states and by the lack of popular identification with their existence. On the other hand, they drew some strength from the fact that they were there before the Federal Republic came into being, and by 1949 the *Länder* parties (and, just as important, the bureaucracies) had a vested interest in their continued survival.

The existing ten *Länder* – exclusive of West Berlin, which remains outside the jurisdiction of the Federal Republic – have the full panoply of governments in miniature. They are headed by a minister-president, they have their own constitutions and constitutional courts, administrative systems and civil service, and they all follow the pattern of parliamentary government responsible to an elected assembly. Such attention to form may appear wasted, considering the extent of their powers (the *Länder* have only a few 'original' powers left to them by the Basic Law – mainly police, local government and cultural affairs). The Basic Law either gives the federation exclusive right to act in certain fields or spells out powers to be exercised 'concurrently' by the federation and the *Länder* – but in this latter area federal legislation takes precedence over that of the states.

How, then, can the West German system be justified? The answer lies in the peculiarity of the relationship between the *Länder* and the federal government: in a wide range of matters they act as the responsible administrative agents for the federal government. Thus Article 83 reads: 'The *Länder* shall execute federal laws as matters of their own concern in so far as this Basic Law does not otherwise provide or permit.' Article 84 empowers the *Länder* to establish 'requisite authorities' to that end, and

Article 85 makes it clear that the question of their establishment is to be the concern of the *Länder*.

It is this administrative competence of the *Länder* which gives German federalism its strength. The division of power which is involved differs sharply from that in the conventional model of federalism, where the demarcation between the states and the federation rests on the allocation of specific powers to one or the other, so-called 'co-ordinate federalism'. That distribution can best be represented as a 'vertical' division of authority, whilst the German approach follows a 'horizontal' line: overall direction and legislative authority resides with the federation, but implementation with the *Länder*.

In following the 'horizontal' principle – from which, of course, such matters as defence, foreign affairs and currency are excluded, as being the sole responsibility of the federation – the *Länder* have considerable administrative resources at their disposal. Each *Land* has its own civil service, and the extent of decentralisation means that the federal service is relatively small. In addition, the *Länder*, if by no means in a position of financial autonomy, nevertheless do have substantial powers of taxation and an important voice in the allocation of revenue. Even though ultimately the *Länder* are not free to go their own way, their administrative authority in practice gives them discretion as to means and priorities. 'Horizontal' federalism results in a curious form of 'administrative politics', typified by the interaction of the two administrative hierarchies through which political differences are expressed and by virtue of which the *Länder* governments are able to maintain a 'bargaining capacity' in relation to the federal government.[1]

The key place of the Bundesrat

It would be an unequal match if there were no other supports given to the *Länder*, for there would be little to prevent a steady accretion of power and responsibility shifting in favour of the federal government. The Basic Law stems this drift in two ways. In the first place it provides a number of constitutional guarantees: the inviolability of the federal principle, guarantees of revenue and taxation powers, and the protection given by the Constitutional Court. The second method of promoting the interests of the *Länder* is through their collective representation at the federal level in the Bundesrat. This second chamber is one of the most potent of all the constitutional checks and balances.

The place of the Bundesrat in the Federal Republic follows

earlier precedents closely: the Reichsrat in the Weimar Republic and the Bundesrat under the imperial system. More remotely, it has links with the idea of 'princely representation' of the states in the Holy Roman Empire. The genesis is important: instead of the 'democratic' practice of making its composition dependent on direct and popular election, the post-war Bundesrat reverted to the traditional form. It was composed exclusively of delegates from the *Länder* governments, the size of each delegation depending very approximately on the size of the *Land* population. The Bundesrat is therefore a permanent 'conclave of governments' rather than merely a second legislative chamber. It is also a direct expression of the will of the governments concerned, since the individual delegations vote *en bloc* according to the instructions of their *Länder* governments.

It is clear that with this special form of representation the Bundesrat could never become just a pale reflection of the Bundestag. What the Bundesrat loses in not being directly elected is more than compensated by giving a platform to the *Länder* governments, even though only the Bundestag has authoritative power over the federal government. The Bundesrat does have considerable influence over federal legislation, as well as the federal budget, taxation and constitutional amendments. The Basic Law specifies that in those areas which directly affect the competence of the *Länder*, the consent of the Bundesrat is mandatory – the related laws are *zustimmungsbedürftig*. Constitutional changes require a two-thirds majority in both the Bundesrat and the Bundestag. On all matters which do not require its specific assent, the Bundesrat still has a considerable say. After the reconciliation procedure has been exhausted (the function of the joint committee of both chambers, the *Vermittlungsausschuss*), the Bundesrat may still raise an objection (*Einspruch*) to a bill. The *Einspruch* amounts to a qualified veto: if it is based on an absolute majority in the Bundesrat, it can be overcome by a similar majority in the Bundestag; a two-thirds vote against in the Bundesrat requires a two-thirds majority in the Bundestag if the will of the federal government is to prevail.

The possibilities for, and occasions of, direct confrontation should not be exaggerated. Certainly, the intention in the Basic Law seems to be to secure a co-operative relationship between the federal government and the *Länder*. That emphasis is evident in the wide competence given to the Bundesrat as a co-ordinating body: Article 50 stipulates that the *Länder*, through the Bundesrat,

Fig. 3   The Federal Legislative Process

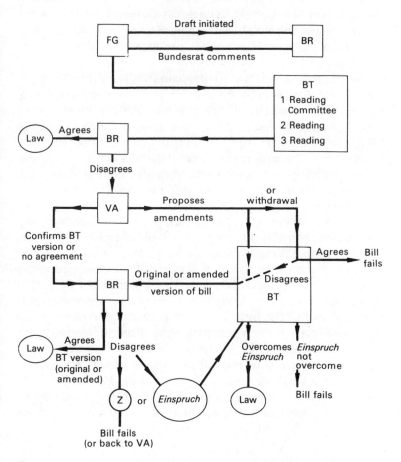

Key

FG = Federal Government; BR = Bundesrat; BT= Bundestag;
VA= *Vermittlungsausschuss* (equal numbers from BR and BT);
 Z = *Zustimmungsbedürftige Gesetze* (laws requiring consent of BR);
Einspruch = objection by Bundesrat based on absolute or two-thirds
majority, overcome by similar majority in Bundestag.

are to participate in the administration as well as in the legislation of the federation. This feature again draws on German tradition and was present in imperial Germany as well as the Weimar Republic – the Reichsrat had an important administrative function in the republic when the parliamentary system became unstable.

The Bundesrat is a significant administrative nexus setting the federal government and the *Länder* on the same level. In all legislation the Bundesrat is first consulted whilst bills are in draft form before being submitted to the Bundestag. The federal government is represented in the Bundesrat, and there is ample scope for an administrative reconciliation: the committees of the Bundesrat are largely composed of senior *Land* civil servants, and they will seek adjustments with their opposite numbers from the federal ministries.

The administrative gloss protects the Bundesrat from becoming overwhelmingly politically oriented, and the intention in the Basic Law was evidently to provide an adequate defence for *Länder* interests. But the party-political composition has emerged as the really decisive factor in determining the relationship of the Bundesrat with the Bundestag and the federal government. It is at least evident that the Basic Law was extremely generous in giving the *Länder* the powerful counter-weight of the Bundesrat. Once that balance came to be interpreted in straight political terms, rather than in the constitutional style of the *Länder* interests 'as such', then a whole dimension of potential conflict was revealed. The result is an amalgam expressed by the idea of 'party federalism', the impact of which we shall need to examine at a later stage.

The supremacy of law

The Basic Law describes the Federal Republic as a *Rechtsstaat*, not as a hopeful or symbolic gesture but as an indication of the normative requirements placed on the organs of state and on political life more generally. In fact, the sovereignty of the law is the prime principle of the constitution, to which all other aspects have to be adjusted: the powers of the constitution have to be exercised within the framework of the law. But that aim could only be realised if two conditions were met: first, that all the provisions of the constitution should be subject directly to a legal enforcement and, second, that means of supplying an authoritative interpretation of the Basic Law should be available.

Those conditions are both fulfilled by the existence of the Federal Constitutional Court which can adjudicate on any aspect of the Basic Law. Such third-party interpretation is essential for a federal state, and the Constitutional Court performs a normal balancing function between the *Länder* and the federation, as it does in regulating the competences of all the organs of state. The Court is also concerned with the supervision of the basic individual freedoms as they are set out in Articles 1 to 19 of the Basic Law. These are chiefly the 'liberal' freedoms – those of speech, assembly, association, choice of employment, political asylum, as well as the security of the person, the home and the family.

It is in its capacity as guardian of individual freedoms that certain other implications of the Basic Law become apparent. The result of raising the Basic Law to a pre-eminent position by making the *Rechtsstaat* directly enforceable has not been simply to place the constitution above politics but in an important way to make it a determinant of politics. That slant is evident in the view that the Basic Law imposes certain constitutional tasks (*Verfassungsaufträge*) which require fulfilment, in a somewhat programmatic sense.

These 'tasks' are frequently held to be embedded in the clauses setting out individual rights: the liberal freedoms may be more widely interpreted to imply social obligations as well. That follows from the argument that the social preconditions must be established if the constitutional freedoms (say, 'free choice of occupation' or 'equality before the law') are to be given substantive meaning. Even though the Basic Law is almost silent on the question of 'social rights' – content with implying the social responsibilities of the state in the expression *sozialer Rechtsstaat* – this deficiency has not prevented a body of social criticism from using implied constitutional norms as the basis of argument. Nor has the Constitutional Court kept entirely out of the arena: faced with innumerable cases requiring its ruling, the Court has had to take account of the social and political contexts and implications of its judgements.

In advancing the supremacy of the law as a powerful check on political institutions, the Basic Law has also acquired political authority. A rather contradictory twist is evident. Whilst the Basic Law belongs to the classic statements of 'limited government', the framework of law and its interpretation has involved the state in a host of legal obligations.

Parliamentary Government

One key provision of the Basic Law determines the parliamentary character of government in the Federal Republic: Article 63 requires that the chancellor shall be *elected* by the members of the Bundestag. In other words, the head of government can only enter office by securing the active support of the assembly and that – normally – by means of an absolute majority at the commencement of a new legislative term. West Germany is exceptional in requiring a formal process of election, but the principle is the same for all parliamentary systems: an incoming government has to aim to win the support of a parliamentary majority.

In the West German case, the explicit stipulation of 'election' was a deliberate attempt to remove any possibility of ambiguity. With the precedent of the Weimar Republic in mind, the authors of the Basic Law were concerned to avoid a similar regression to the unrestricted exercise of presidential power. They were also disinclined to trust in the growth of constitutional convention to reinforce the parliamentary system, since there was a risk that a political crisis might allow a quite different type of government to be foisted on the young republic.

The elevation of the chancellor

As the crisis of the Weimar Republic had shown, the chancellor could easily become the sacrificial victim of both the Reichstag and the president. It was therefore to be expected that the Basic Law would concentrate on increasing the chancellor's authority. That was achieved in part by down-grading the position of the president and by making the chancellor the main beneficiary of the president's former estate. The experience of the first four presidents in the Federal Republic shows that the office can only maintain a representative figurehead who could not become a serious contender for power. The four – Theodor Heuss, Heinrich Lübke, Gustav Heinemann and Walter Scheel – were all chosen as sound party men, at best respected personalities rather than widely influential leaders. Whilst it is true that the president still has some residual powers, they are insufficient for him to develop a power base of his own. (At one time Adenauer considered relinquishing the chancellorship to stand as president, but soon gave up the idea when he realised how little he would be able to intervene in government.) The 'emergency laws' do allow the president to take an active role, but his powers are far more restricted than they were under Article 48 of the Weimar constitution. A president also has some discretion over the dissolution of the Bundestag, and that may apply in the situation in which the Bundestag is unable to elect a new chancellor by an absolute majority; even so, the president has no means of imposing his own candidate on the assembly.

Parliamentary government in the Federal Republic depends entirely on the relationship between the chancellor and the Bundestag. In the provision made for the initial election of the chancellor a premium is placed on the Bundestag giving him continuing support. The position can be stated more forcefully: there is a clear *constitutional expectation* that, once elected, a serving chancellor will stay in office for the whole four-year term of the Bundestag, until a new Bundestag first meets and elects, or re-elects, a chancellor.

No constitution can absolutely guarantee governmental stability without at the same time substantially modifying (or damaging) the freedom of a parliament to choose and change governments. Still less can the parties be regulated so as to make them uphold the government unquestioningly. But the 'presumption' in favour of government stability in the Federal Republic does indirectly enforce responsibility on the party system. Article 67 of the Basic Law stipulates that the Bundestag is only able to express its lack of confidence in the chancellor by electing a successor – a simultaneous process. This constitutional novelty, termed the 'constructive vote of no confidence', was introduced to avert the threats to governments from the formation of purely negative – and possibly transient – hostile majorities, similar to those which in the end made the parliamentary system of the Weimar Republic unworkable. In fact, the procedure has never been fully operative and only once initiated – in 1972, when the CDU–CSU opposition came within an ace of unseating Willy Brandt. But the indirect effect has nevertheless been to enhance the position of the chancellor.

His stature was further raised by the leading place accorded to him within the government. The Basic Law, under Article 65, makes the chancellor alone responsible for the general lines of government policy. (In parliamentary systems such questions are treated as a matter of collective responsibility, but this is not the case, in theory, for the West German one.) This power to determine policy, the *Richtlinienkompetenz*, makes it necessary for the chancellor to bear the responsibility for the government before the Bundestag and places him head and shoulders above his colleagues in government, an elevation which is supported by his exclusive right to nominate federal ministers.

It may appear that, armed with his constitutional powers, the chancellor is in an almost impregnable position. But that conclusion loses sight of political realities. It would be unrealistic to suppose that the chancellor can easily defy the factions within his own party, ignore the interests of his partners in coalition or ride roughshod over the considered opinions of his ministers. What can be concluded is that a new chancellor at least starts with an injection of constitutional authority. That may be insufficient to create a strong chancellor, and he may fail dismally in office, but as long as he is there the chances of the emergence of a rival authority are considerably diminished.

Alongside the 'chancellor principle', the Basic Law does give some recognition to two other theories of governmental responsibility, without, however, spelling out their consequences. One is the doctrine of individual ministerial responsibility, and the other, the idea of the collective 'cabinet system'. They modify the impression that the chancellor carries the whole weight of governing authority. Thus Article 65, whilst giving the chancellor sole responsibility for the determination of general policy, empowers the other ministers to conduct the business of their own departments 'autonomously', and assuming their own responsibility. Individual ministers are presumed to have a free hand within their departments, and the Basic Law in this respect echoes a German tradition: ministers tend to be valued for their technical competence and gain authority through the expertise which they bring to departments. As specialists, they are inclined to stay with one department; they are also inclined to 'hold on' to office. There is a relatively low turnover of ministers, few dismissals, and still fewer resignations caused by disagreements on policy (features more evident when the CDU was in office than under the SPD administration). Individual ministerial responsibility therefore does not conflict at all with the general authority accorded to the chancellor, who is further strengthened by his power of appointment and by the responsibility which he bears absolutely to the Bundestag. Furthermore, the development of the Chancellor's Office, the *Kanzleramt*, as an overarching 'policy ministry' enables the chancellor to bolster his *Richtlinienkompetenz* considerably.

There is a third principle of government contained in the Basic Law, somewhat surprisingly left largely implicit: the idea of the cabinet system and of collective responsibility. Perhaps the lack of emphasis was deliberate, given the desire to boost the chancellor's authority. Thus the Basic Law imposes the sole requirement that the Federal Government – the chancellor together with the federal ministers – should decide on disputes arising between individual ministers. The 'collective' character of the government is also ensured by making its life dependent on the chancellor's tenure of office – although the collectivity thus expressed is rather one of subordination.[2]

Clearly, the full operation of a cabinet system (in the sense of a collective equality) would run into head-on conflict with a forceful application of the 'chancellor principle'. Nevertheless, we have to bear in mind that whatever the strict interpretation of the constitutional position might seem to imply, it is the actual power relationship within government that is likely to be decisive. The real constraints affecting the chancellor are those which are not specified in the Basic Law.

The question of chancellor democracy

These real constraints are to be found in the political forces which operate both within and without the government. A chancellor's stature among his own party, his relative ability compared with possible rivals, the number and character of factions within the ruling party, its strength in the Bundestag in relation to the others – all these factors play a part in fashioning the standing of the chancellor. But there is an additional dimension supplied by the exigencies of coalition politics: the need to attract and maintain the support of a coalition partner. This factor has, if anything, grown in importance during the life of the Federal Republic: even though the number of parties has declined – perhaps because it has – the dynamic of coalition potential is undiminished. If the line-up of parties in relation to government formation was always a foregone conclusion, then a chancellor would not be faced with much uncertainty in dealing with a coalition partner.

In the mid-1950s, the heyday of the Adenauer era, it did appear that the political institutions of the Federal Republic were developing along different lines from parliamentary democracy, towards a system in which the chancellor was the key figure – for which the apt description of 'chancellor democracy' was coined. The experience of short-lived governments in the Weimar Republic brought the unexpected stability of the Federal Republic into even sharper relief. Konrad Adenauer's exceptionally long hold on office (continuously from 1949 until 1963) raised the position of chancellor to a level which could scarcely have been envisaged by those who framed the Basic Law. With the support of his constitutional powers, Adenauer lost no time in setting his stamp on government.

Adenauer never infringed the rules of parliamentary government, but the strict requirements of the Basic Law simply did not act as a limiting factor on his authority. Basic to Adenauer's success was the power of attraction he exerted over the electorate, so much so that at the height of his popularity the results of elections (in 1953 and 1957) could be read almost as personal votes of confidence, with incidental approval given to the CDU. As a result, the CDU in the Bundestag resembled a mandated college of electors, pledged to Adenauer. A similar tendency was evident within the government: the chancellor's authority was supreme for the members of the cabinet, and the smaller coalition partners appeared as appendages to Adenauer's personal government.

With the benefit of hindsight, it is comparatively easy to see that the 'chancellor democracy' of the Adenauer era was made possible by a constellation of factors, a pattern of features in the development of the Federal Republic which is unlikely to recur. Of major benefit to Adenauer was the nature of the CDU in its early years: he was in a position to build up the party as a federal force at the same time as making his place within it practically unassailable. The outlook of a large section of the electorate was also important: many people first came to terms with democratic politics through the medium of his slightly paternalistic and authoritarian style. It was a manner which appealed to sentiments unused to the cut and thrust of party politics at the time, but, once the reconciliation was effected, the 'Adenauer effect' became redundant.

A third significant factor in the formative years of the republic was the international status of West Germany. Adenauer was able to make the decisive contribution in determining how the Federal Republic would align itself, and his commitment to the Western alliances and to European integration enabled him to win a unique position in post-war politics. The 'rehabilitation' of West Germany, her growing international standing, gave Adenauer the stature not just of a successful chancellor but of a statesman.

It is no accident therefore that, with the 'primary conditions' no longer obtaining, subsequent heads of government have had to take a more modest view of their constitutional position. The 'retreat' applied to Adenauer's two immediate CDU successors, Ludwig Erhard and Kurt-Georg Kiesinger, both anyway scarcely forceful personalities. The two SPD chancellors, Brandt and

Helmut Schmidt, had much more political presence, and in their different ways both set their own imprint on government, but the traditions of the SPD are much less conducive to allowing a chancellor an unquestioned dominance of the party. Even if later chancellors show outstanding flair, they are unlikely to be able to recreate the conditions which permitted 'chancellor democracy' temporarily to flourish. Adenauer was in power sufficiently long to experience the changing conditions for himself: he came up against the barrier of a more sceptical electorate, felt the tug of restive factions in his own party, found the limits of his own foreign policy, and finally had to accept the impositions of a recalcitrant coalition ally.

The coalition requirement may have been the most important long-term force limiting a chancellor's authority. Since 1961 only three parties (four with the CSU) have been represented in the Bundestag, but the balance of party strength has continued to exact on governments a high degree of collegiality. But that need not strengthen the hold of the cabinet directly – the important issues and lines of policy have to be settled by direct inter-party agreement, and the forum for that activity may be found in an *ad hoc* or permanent coalition committee, at a point where the junior coalition partner has to be treated virtually as an equal.

What then remains of the legacy of 'chancellor democracy'? Adenauer's example inevitably sets some kind of standard by which other chancellors will be judged, even if any attempt to follow his footsteps would now be widely regarded as an unjustified usurpation of parliamentary government, not a return to a healthy tradition. Possibly the sporadic call for a 'strong man' might hark back to Adenauer, but another precedent is probably intended. There remains the knowledge that the Basic Law allows and even encourages the emergence of an authoritative chancellor. To that extent a penumbra of uncertainty remains: it is conceivable that a large shift in the relative strength of the parties could lead to a reassertion of the chancellor's power.[3]

But the constitution has had one permanent effect which stems particularly from the requirement that directly after an election the Bundestag itself chooses the chancellor. It is a natural corollary that the parties should enter the election campaign with a suitable chancellor candidate ready for presentation to the electorate. This prior commitment is not at all obligatory, and the practice took hold gradually in the case of both major parties. For the first election in 1949 the parties still operated in the context of a multi-party system, and it was anyone's guess who might eventually be chancellor. The CDU for the next four elections – 1953 until 1965 – was in the happy position of seeking the return of the serving chancellor, and only for the elections from 1969 onwards has the party had to resort to a process of selection, each time with a different chancellor candidate. The SPD adopted a candidate for the first time in 1961. Brandt was unsuccessful then, but the party continued with his candidature both in 1961 and 1965. The parade of the party's chancellor candidate is now an integral feature of the electoral strategy, and federal elections are consciously fought on the merits of the rivals involved. To that extent elections to the Bundestag do have a plebiscitary character, since the electorate is involved in a direct choice of a personal almost as much as a party nature. As one result, the successful contender is bound to enjoy added prestige within his own party.

Yet it may be incorrect to read this development too much in constitutional terms – or even to use the additional argument that the stipulation of election by the Bundestag has been instrumental in bringing about a fundamental change in the party system. That train of reasoning sees in the electoral impact of the choice between rival candidates for office a drive which favours the larger parties, for only they can put up candidates with a serious chance of success. Since this factor has become a leading function of elections, the advantage to the larger parties is cumulative, to the lasting detriment of smaller parties. But it is more reasonable to suppose that the growing dominance of the CDU and the SPD in the party system was the causal factor; their growth allowed them to exploit the possibilities of the chancellor candidate.

In the final analysis, the role taken by the chancellor in the Federal Republic has to be judged in relation to the working of the parliamentary system as a whole: the stability of parliamentary government, the ability of the parties to act as a source of political leadership and to supply cohesive coalition formations, the part played by the Bundestag in maintaining a live relationship between parliament and government. If Adenauer had succeeded – wittingly or not – in weakening the parliamentary basis of government, then these questions would have become irrelevant: 'chancellor democracy' would have to be judged on quite different criteria.

Parliamentary control
The stability of West German governments has been exemplary. No chancellor has fallen to an adverse vote in the Bundestag and

only once has it been necessary to seek an early dissolution. Except for brief intervals, governments have been able to rely on a consistent parliamentary majority, and there have been few difficulties in replacing one government by another or in finding an alternative coalition formula. These indicators could be interpreted as evidence of the subordination of the parliamentary parties to government, but, although true for a part of Adenauer's rule, it would be wrong to regard the Bundestag as a docile instrument of government power.

The three cases of premature retirement of a chancellor indicate the importance of party pressures in the Bundestag. Adenauer's eventual retirement in 1963 was finally forced on him by a combination of unrest in his own party and the demand of the Free Democrats. Erhard, after less than three years in office, fell in 1966 because of intense dissatisfaction with his leadership – rife inside his own party – and the refusal of the FDP to continue to serve in his government made Erhard's departure inevitable. Brandt's resignation in 1974 had no immediate parliamentary or party-political connection, since it occurred as a result of the 'Guillaume Affair', the discovery of an East German spy employed on the chancellor's personal staff. There was no constitutional reason for Brandt to resign, but it had also become increasingly evident that he had lost his grip on government and that leading figures within the SPD, in the cabinet and in the Bundestag, were actively opposed to Brandt continuing in office.

Had any of the three attempted to remain, then the consequences for party and coalition unity would have been acute; their departure was enforced as a latent form of parliamentary control. It is against the background of political reality that the guidelines set by the Basic Law have to be judged: the formal rules determining parliamentary control tell only a part of the story.

German parliamentary traditions also affect the relationship between the Bundestag and government, for they developed in the nineteenth century at a time when governments were not responsible to the legislature, which precluded the fusion of powers and personnel which occurred in Britain. Even with the arrival of full parliamentary government in the Weimar Republic, the essential divide between government and parliament persisted, and the practice is still recognisable in the Federal Republic: the government is a distinct entity within the assembly, a fact which is illustrated by the separate seating and by procedure in plenary debates, whereby government ministers present their case separately and in addition to the spokesmen for the governing parties.

An additional consequence of the separation of government and assembly was that German parliaments fastened on to the legislative function as the best means of establishing their authority. This conception of the 'work' of an assembly has persisted in the idea of an *Arbeitsparlament*, or 'working parliament', which is in contrast to the British *Redeparlament*, the role of the House of Commons as a debating forum. The difference is also notable in the comparative neglect of plenary sessions in the Bundestag, with only about one-third of the total British allocation.

The emphasis on legislative competence has led to a reliance on the committee structure of the Bundestag. Less contentious legislation is frequently not considered at all by the full Bundestag, since the main legislative work takes place in the specialised committees which mirror the functions of the major government departments.

The tradition of 'assertion through legislation' also colours the behaviour of the parliamentary opposition. An opposition party will produce its own 'shadow' bills, detailed proposals duplicating the measures introduced by the government, even though the labour goes quite unrewarded. Members of the Bundestag are valued by their parties for the degree of expertise which they bring to their office, and their major contribution may be in one or other of the specialised committees, not on the floor of the Bundestag. This process of 'professionalisation' is marked in the Federal Republic; a high proportion of the members of all parties have an 'administrative' background of one kind or another, often a legal training, and are increasingly the products of the higher education system.

Occupations of Bundestag Members

	SPD	CDU	CSU	FDP
	percentage of party *Fraktion* in 6th Bundestag			
Career politicians, trade unionists and other officials	44.2	38.3	28.7	32.3
Civil servants	24.1	16.4	28.6	6.4
Professions	21.2	15.5	18.3	28.9
Employees, manual workers	3.4	1.0	2.0	3.2
Business, independent means	3.4	16.0	12.2	9.6
Farming	0.4	10.9	10.2	16.1
Others	3.0	2.0	—	3.2

(Adapted from Heino Kaack, *Geschichte und Struktur des deutschen Parteiensystems*, Opladen, 1971, p. 600.)

These characteristics all tend to pitch parliamentary control in a lower key than that of the British system, which, in the style of the *Redeparlament*, constantly underlines the polarisation of Government and Opposition in the manner of a continuous election campaign. The Bundestag is also geared to a four-year term, and whilst there is the possibility that the coalition will change, the chances of a snap election being called are fairly remote. But it would be wrong to assume that for these reasons the control is less adequate or that the competitive aspect is weak, for the survival of only two major parties has necessarily brought about a clearer polarisation than is evident in a multi-party system.

There remains the question of whether the Bundestag is the most important of the available 'sites' for the control of government. In the British case it is clear that there is no alternative to the control exercised by the parties in the House of Commons. The system of checks and balances in the Federal Republic, however, is much more widely dispersed: both the federal structure, including the Bundesrat, and the provisions for constitutional jurisdiction have to be treated as important supplements to a purely parliamentary form of control.

The Party State
The idea of the 'party state', or *Parteienstaat*, has a special connotation in German politics, deriving from the chequered history of the parties and from the doctrine that the state stood for a system of values and obligations independent of society. The gulf between the state and the parties was such that the concept of a party state would have seemed a contradiction, an abomination even, to many nineteenth-century theorists. In the Federal Republic the conjunction still raises important questions: What should be the limits of party influence? What are the implications for the parties and for society?

The parties in the state
These questions involve much more than the consideration of 'party democracy' – a representative democracy with party government. The distinction first became apparent in the Weimar Republic: party democracy was established but not a party state. To have created the latter, it would have been necessary to supplant the values of an independent state tradition and to expel the leading elites identified with those values. Neither the German Revolution nor the constitutional system of the republic succeeded in the task,

and party democracy coexisted uneasily with the old traditions. Through the 'social revolution', as it affected the state, the dictatorship laid the foundations for the new era.

It is not too fanciful to represent the post-war parties as entering an empty 'house of power'. Under the friendly aegis of the occupation, they enjoyed a new freedom: there was no state establishment to resist their authority, no counter-elites to contain them, nothing to redeem the German state tradition. It would have been strange in those circumstances if the parties had not gone beyond the simple re-creation of a party democracy. They proceeded to make their position secure, as they had to, in order to overcome their historical denigration, their failure in the Weimar Republic, their ignominious dissolution in 1933.

For this reason there is no exaggeration in saying that the Basic Law was written 'by and for the benefit of' the post-war parties. That was not an explicit aim, but the fact was that the constitution was drawn up in conditions which placed the political elite in almost complete isolation from external pressures. Yet it is best to appreciate the Basic Law as symptomatic of the party state, as one expression of the changed relationships, rather than as itself creating the conditions for the supremacy of the parties.

The Basic Law does not bristle with references to the parties; their supremacy is best inferred from the nature of the parliamentary system that was established, making any alternative source of authority or challenge impossible. However, Article 21 sets out the functions and legitimate nature of the parties:

1. The political parties shall participate in forming of the political will of the people. They may be freely established. Their internal organisation must conform to democratic principles. They must publicly account for the sources of their funds.
2. Parties which, by reason of their aims or the behaviour of their adherents, seek to impair or abolish the free democratic basic order or to endanger the existence of the Federal Republic of Germany, shall be unconstitutional. The Federal Constitutional Court shall decide on the question of unconstitutionality.

One reading of these provisions is that they were framed as an entirely pragmatic response to past and present problems. But much more is at stake. The recognition accorded to the parties in the Basic Law does not merely endow them with a legitimacy which they had previously lacked, for the fact of constitutional recognition places the parties on a level with other organs of state: they have constitutional functions to discharge. Thus, far from being merely the tolerated representatives of the pluralist order, the parties have a special relationship with the state: they bear to it a responsibility, and they can also expect its support, manifest in the substantial state financing of the political parties, which is entirely justified by Article 21. Their participation in 'forming the political will of the people' (*politische Willensbildung*) is a constitutionally imposed task for which the wherewithal has to be found.

The exclusion of those parties which endanger the state is a natural extension of the privileged position which the parties enjoy, the price that has to be paid. In principle, it is not a question of the extent of the perceived danger, but the sheer incompatibility of their principles with the precepts of the constitution. Thus the Basic Law leads to the establishment not so much of a party state 'in general' but a certain type of party state, effectively one which is identified by the Basic Law.

That the terminology used in the constitution was not accidental is shown by the later Party Law of 1967, which filled in some of the requirements of Article 21. Thus the Party Law states: 'Parties are, in constitutional law, a necessary component of the free democratic basic order . . . Parties shall participate in forming the political will of the people in all fields of public life.' The wording is important. By anchoring the parties in constitutional law, they are given an elevated and protected position – the Constitutional Court has ruled that the parties should be regarded as *Staatsorgane*, literally 'organs of the state'. Their role in 'forming the public will of the people' imparts a superior 'educational' function, and their participation 'in *all* fields of public life' justifies their presence in the state and throughout society. Far from the constitution and the Party Law merely securing the place of the parties within the pluralist order, the prevailing norms may actually restrict that order – which amounts to the imposition of a form of 'party pluralism'. On the other hand, the effect may be to debilitate the parties, to 'officialise' party activity in a way which is contrary to their original nature as expressions of self-regulating and competing forces in society. If the parties have 'captured the state', there is also a sense in which the state has captured the parties.

It is easy to exaggerate both characteristics, but it is undeniable that the parties in the Federal Republic have a standing unthinkable in the past. Critics have seen their rise to predominance as a move away from parliamentary democracy towards an oligarchy of the party state. In losing their previous strong attachment to ideology, the parties have emphasised that they are *Volksparteien*, parties of the whole people. Yet in so changing they have subtly altered their character as 'representatives of the people'. As Gerhard Leibholz expressed it: 'The parties show a tendency to identify themselves with the people . . . They make the claim *to be the people*'.[4]

The political role of the bureaucracy

The extension of party influence in the Federal Republic has to be related to the 'sub-constitutional' area of the administrative hierarchies, the bureaucracy and more generally the public service. It is of particular importance that a whole class grew up in the nineteenth century coloured by the mystique of 'service to the state', regarding itself as above politics and the parties. That tradition has to be examined with an eye on the post-war transformation to see how the adaptation – the grafting of the party state on to the previously independent one – was effected.[5]

The governmental system of imperial Germany is not too incorrectly described as a form of *Beamtenherrschaft*, rule by permanent officials. These 'ruling servants' enjoyed a reputation for professional expertise and scrupulous severity, personified in the figure of the *Landrat* who, as the appointed agent of the central government, made the will of the state apparent even in the smallest village. The servants of the state shared the privileged status of *Beamte*, and there was a peculiar injection of status-honour involved, *Amtsehre*, which had some association with the concept of honour in military service. It was not a fortuitous connection: the civil arm of the Prussian state service was a product of a state organised on quasi-military lines. The army wore uniforms, whilst the civilian administrators did not. Thus civil servants were not simply public employees but one expression of the authority of the state. They shared a common social outlook, and their unity was further strengthened by codes of conduct, administrative procedures and a special *Beamtenrecht*, the bureaucratic mirror image of the *Rechtsstaat*.

All these attributes of state service helped to underpin the belief that the administrators wielded a unique authority in society. They were the visible representatives of the state, and in practising their statecraft they could use the plea of 'reasons of state', *Staatsraison*, to protect themselves from a wider accountability. Merely to superimpose a 'party democracy' on the administrative structure, as occurred in the Weimar Republic, only masked the underlying characteristics. The dictatorship, its consequences, and the subsequent collapse of the German state proved to be a vital process of dethronement. There was a 'discontinuity', confirmed by a later ruling of the Federal Constitutional Court, which held that there had been a *Traditionsbruch* in May 1945, a breach in continuity for the state service, which put civil servants in the Federal Republic on an entirely new footing. The judgement implied that public servants did not serve the state as a living and permanent continuity but the constitutional order which obtains at the time. A further implication was that a serving official should consider his actions carefully, for he would no longer be able to rely on the permanent protection of the state.

The *Traditionsbruch* has to be regarded largely as a symbolic break, but it is essential to an understanding of the changed relationship of the parties with the state and the bureaucracy at large. The practical consequence in the Federal Republic has been the overt politicisation which has taken place throughout the public service. Its extent has been remarkable, but the potential for such a development already existed, since it was recognised that German civil servants did already have an inherent 'political capacity'. The nature of earlier authoritarian rule meant that they inevitably took active part in public affairs at the highest levels as ministers or state secretaries. Furthermore, they were often prominent members of elected representative assemblies, for there is no tradition in Germany that public servants should be politically 'disabled'. Their involvement did not necessarily signify a democratisation of the state – and it may have served to protect its interests – but in the era after 1945 the question of political competence helped the parties to invade the state service, a reverse flow of influence from society to the state. It is as though, robbed of the 'protection of the state', the bureaucracy now looks to the protection of the parties.

Party infiltration
Party politicisation mainly affects the senior ranks of the federal civil service, the levels of state secretary and *Ministerialdirektor*, or departmental head. The long domination exercised by the CDU over the federal government meant that influence came from one direction, and only after the entry of the SPD into government was there any marked reshuffling of senior appointments – a policy which involved the promotion of officials known to be sympathetic to the party to key positions and the shunting off of others to

remote sidelines if they were judged to be lukewarm or hostile to government policies. Inevitably, the return of a CDU government would entail further changes. There are good reasons for ensuring that a party's control of government should not be thwarted by the bureaucracy, and to that extent the practice adopted in the Federal Republic is quite defensible and accords with the position in other countries. Political control has been additionally strengthened by making appointments from outside the service, 'political' state secretaries, who are more or less successfully grafted on to the existing administrative hierarchy. A further development, since 1967, has been the creation of a number of parliamentary state secretaries, effectively junior ministers, which has reinforced the position of the minister and the party in the departments concerned. All of these changes in German practice can be judged positively, since they help to ensure that the bureaucracy does not remain aloof from society. The old stereotype of the German *Beamte* has been finally shattered.

What applies to the state service at the federal level is equally true for the *Länder*, and it is especially important in view of the high degree of dispersal of state activity and the public service. Indeed, the scope for politicisation is probably much greater in the *Länder*, for the parties have multiple points of access, which is encouraged by the extremely wide definition in Germany of what constitutes 'state service'. It is also apparent that party influence reaches deep into the administrative structure. There are innumerable gradations of the public service, which includes the judiciary, the schools and the universities, but there is an additional range of public activity involving direct or indirect participation by the *Länder*, including such institutions as public broadcasting and the *Länder* banking authorities. These bodies require the appointment of officials and the setting up of supervisory boards. The need for political control is undisputed: the scope for party patronage is immense.

In some *Länder* the formation of government depends largely on one party, and its control over the administration inevitably colours the public service and the choice of personnel. In others some balance is achieved by alternation in power or by the changing composition of coalitions. But initial appointment or promotion may depend on having known sympathies with, or even membership of, a particular party: the party card, the *Parteibuch*, may prove to be the indispensable passport. Except in the bastions of one-party supremacy, as Bavaria is for the CSU, there will emerge some proportionality of influence, an allocation in accordance with party strength reminiscent of the Austrian *Proporz* principle. Such *Proporz*-sharing takes place federally in the case of high judicial appointments and is especially relevant to the Federal Constitutional Court; the parties make no bones about pushing the claims of their favoured candidates. A similar procedure operates for the public broadcasting authorities, where the networks are primarily the responsibility of various *Länder* governments. It is considered natural that the leading party should have the major say in senior appointments, but a share of subordinate posts will be controlled by the other parties. In addition, each network makes provision for supervisory bodies which (on healthy democratic grounds) are charged with the oversight of programmes and related matters concerning radio and television output. Nomination to such boards is almost entirely controlled by the parties on a 'shared' basis.[6]

The examples of the Constitutional Court and broadcasting can be used to show that a proper 'democratic balance' is maintained: the full participation of the parties, in competition with one another, ensures that the 'public interest' will not be neglected. At least we can be sure that the parties will scrutinise the activities of their opponents closely: control is not left to happy chance. But the method can preclude other interests from being properly heard, and it also constitutes a denial that there can be such a thing as an impartial public service or that some kind of neutral 'establishment' could be vested with the power of arbitration. In the Federal Republic the 'public interest' has to be equated with the enlightened self-interest of the parties.

There is an awareness of the dangers which can accompany the unrestricted influence of the parties; a realisation too that it is not only the lines between the bureaucracy and the parties which may become blurred but also those between the state and the private sectors. The pervasive nature of the party state encourages the spread of a host of party 'connections' to the trade unions and the business world. The three layers – party, bureaucracy and the private domain – become wedded or 'felted' together. The latter term corresponds to the German *Verfilzung*, which was coined precisely to express the undesirable intimacy of the relationship especially between the SPD in some *Länder* and the trade unions, although in principle the idea of *Verfilzung* can be applied to other parties and other types of association. The financial scandals which have occasionally rocked a *Land* administration and its leading party show that the disquiet is not misplaced and that a reliance on the accountability of the parties does not entirely resolve the problems of democratic control. However, fears that this style of government could lead to a new form of domination (*Filzokratie*) do appear exaggerated. What can scarcely be disputed is that the interpenetration of state and society has proceeded too far to be reversible, whether we are concerned with appointments to the Constitutional Court or with the political sympathies operative in the selection of the director for a local '*Staatstheater*'.

The implications of patronage in the gift of a ruling party is one shadow-side of the party state, but there are other ramifications as well; if it is to be supposed that public officials do have definite political leanings and loyalties, then we should expect them to be displayed. One positive consequence is that state employees are not disbarred from political activity: a significant proportion of the Land assemblies and the Bundestag membership is made up of people employed in state service. A negative consequence is that the freedom to hold political views is accompanied by an active discrimination against those whose leanings are deemed to be 'extremist' – antithetical to the 'free democratic basic order' – which is an administrative parallel to the constitutional injunction against certain types of political party.

The West German party state thus displays ambivalent features. It enforces a form of democratic control over the state but at the same time becomes entangled even more with the problem of deciding on the content and the limit of that democratic influence. It is not difficult to point out the defects in the West German system, but is is less easy to propose an obvious alternative. Had the parties 'stood back' in the formative years of the state, then they would have been open to the charge of allowing the old state values to be preserved and of inviting the traditional elites to re-establish themselves. Nor is it necessary to assume that the party state is entirely monolithic: party competition does provide a balance, and the parties themselves are not in a position to rule without regard to other institutional constraints. Moreover, it would be mistaken to suppose that the individual parties always succeed in presenting a united front. These restrictions are uneven in their application (they are at their weakest in *Länder* with a history of one-party dominance) but whether they obtain or not, one of their effects has been to discredit belief in an 'independent' state served by a special class of dedicated officials.

Acceptance of the Republic
Ultimately the value of the constitutional framework, the 'legitimacy' of the Republic and its institutions, has to be judged by the
extent of its popular and elite acceptance. There is no one test for
discovering how far West Germans are committed to the Federal
Republic; the fact that there are various ways of approaching the
question of legitimacy no doubt accounts for the opposing views
that are held. One line of argument cites the undoubted evidence
of political stability, but there are others which in varying degrees
emphasise a pervading 'crisis of legitimacy'.

If we base an opinion solely on the rapidity with which parliamentary institutions were adopted in Western Germany, it is
tempting to conclude that liberal democracy was given an
immediate and enthusiastic greeting and that subsequent stability
has shown the welcome to be permanent. That rendering is too
facile for several reasons. One is that the nature of the initial
acceptance by no means allows a straightforward interpretation.
Another is that a distinction that has to be made between passive
toleration and active commitment. A third reason for caution lies
in the 'object' of legitimacy – whether it is accorded to the state, to
the regime with its institutions and personnel, or more generally to
the social and economic structure of the republic.

Initial acquiescence
It is salutary to look back to the conditions of the immediate
post-war years and to appreciate how little they had to do with the
positive attractions of liberal democracy. Three factors help to
explain why the new system was acceptable. One was the setting
supplied by the Western allies: their presence made it difficult to
resist the democratic lead. A second was the 'negative reinforcement' presented by the Soviet Union, a threat fostering a West
German consensus which might otherwise have been absent. The
third draws attention to the kind of relationship which most West
Germans maintained with the emerging political system: it was a
limited acceptance, prompted by their primary concern – how to
cope with the pressing needs of daily life. At best they suspended
judgement.

Possibly the aggregation of these factors adds up to an excessively
negative view of post-war Germany. But it is important not to
obscure the extent of disorientation which prevailed, even after
the West German state had come into existence. It would anyway
be a distortion to suppose that the rejection of National Socialism

was complete, just as it would be to believe that the majority of Germans were busily engaged in reassessing the course of German history – as, for instance, Friedrich Meinecke attempted in *The German Catastrophe*. Those were not their preoccupations, nor were Germans prepared to write off the past. An early survey of public opinion captures the mixed feelings of the population.

Post-War Opinion on Germany

Question 1:	*When in your opinion was Germany best off in this century?*	
Answers:	During the Empire period	45%
	Between 1920 and 1933	7%
	Between 1933 and 1938	40%
	Between 1939 and 1945	2%
	After 1945	2%
Question 2:	*When in your opinion was Germany worst off in this century?*	
Answers:	Between 1914 and 1919	3%
	Between 1920 and 1932	7%
	Between 1933 and 1938	2%
	Between 1939 and 1945	8%
	Between 1945 and 1948	70%
	From 1949 until 1951	8%

(Allensbach Institut für Demoskopie, 1951)

Even allowing for the fact that distance may have enhanced the view, the responses are revealing. Admittedly, the terms 'best off' and 'worst off' gave an economic bias to the answers, but the political implications are apparent. Ordinary Germans were inclined to compare their situation in the years after 1945 unfavourably with any other period they could recall, and a large section of the population probably looked back to the dictatorship with some nostalgia, to the time when Germany was 'best off'. It is also evident that there was no general agreement about a 'preferred past' to which a return might be made. This disorientation has to be seen in the context of a divided nation and of a German state which had ceased to exist.[7]

Absence of a positive consensus, the difficulty of displaying one at all, meant that the system of liberal democracy was tolerated: it satisfied the needs of the moment. Those needs were primarily economic in character and were increasingly satisfied through the outstanding performance of the Germany economy in the 1950s and 1960s. Indications that a recovery was possible became evident in the immediate consequences of the currency reform of 1948, and by the early 1950s the 'economic miracle' had transformed the popular outlook. The ruling CDU was quick to seize the advantage and demonstrate that economic well-being was directly linked to its doctrine of the social market economy, *soziale Marktwirtschaft*, which released the forces of productive enterprise through the operation of market forces – in contrast to the rigidities and shortages which the CDU claimed would be the chief result of the SPD's policy of planning the West German economy.

The integrative mechanism

Above all, the CDU was able to demonstrate to the electorate the effectiveness of democratic politics: the party therefore acted as the major agent of political and social integration. Its electoral successes throughout the 1950s owed much to the cardinal economic connection, and the process of integration is nowhere more strikingly shown than amongst that section of the West German population variously described as 'refugees' or 'expellees' – all those who originated from other parts of the former Reich. A large proportion came from the 'lost provinces' of East Prussia, Pomerania and Silesia; in addition, there were the Sudeten Germans expelled from Czechoslovakia, and the continuous flow of East Germans to West Germany, a movement which continued apace until 1961. The extent and impact of this non-indigenous 'refugee' element should not be underestimated. Thus in 1960 the total population was around fifty-two million; of these something under ten million were 'expellees', mainly from the lost territories, and a further three million were voluntary immigrants from East Germany. The former group amounted to over 18 per cent and the latter to over 6 per cent of the total population – in aggregate between a fifth and a quarter. That proportion becomes all the more significant when account is taken of the economic plight and social dislocation which affected the newcomers. Their presence represented a powerful potential for a complete social disintegration. Even though they were bound to favour West Germany in preference to the regimes they had left behind, their rapid assimilation was by no means a self-evident development. The economic recovery was decisive in giving the dispossessed and the uprooted a stake in West German society.

The power of attraction, or *Anziehungskraft*, of the social and economic system developing in the Federal Republic was mediated through the parties, primarily through the CDU and its identification with economic success. The national and 'homeland' claims of the many 'refugee' groupings were as unsatisfied as ever for they could not return, but their place within the republic was assured. It also followed that they were inclined to accept the form of a parliamentary democracy and to identify themselves with the major parties. Whilst the CDU reaped the major benefit, the contribution of the SPD should not be neglected, for it was in a position to make a renewed appeal to those who had supported the party up to 1933, even though they had meanwhile moved into Western Germany. Between them the CDU and the SPD succeeded in 'mopping up' the bulk of a possibly volatile and potentially radical vote.

What applied to the new arrivals in West Germany was also true for the rest of the population: through the process of economic recovery there followed a more general integration and a reconciliation with parliamentary institutions. If at any time during the 1950s the economic miracle had ceased to work, the apparent reconciliation might have turned to active discontent. In the final analysis legitimacy depends on effectiveness, and the experience of the Federal Republic is a convincing case study in the importance of the economic factor in defining 'effectiveness'.

Yet a distinction has to be drawn between legitimacy as expressed by 'acceptance' and the stronger form of 'attachment', from passive acquiescence to active support. Thus the 'vote of confidence' accorded to the CDU in the years of its greatest popularity is quite compatible with the view that West Germans on the whole took an instrumental view of the political system. Studies of post-war attitudes confirm 'instrumentality' as an apt term. Thus Gabriel Almond and Sidney Verba in *The Civic Culture* portrayed an electorate which was politically well informed and showed a degree of 'subject competence' in being able to deal with – and have confidence in – those exercising political or administrative authority.[8] But on other counts the picture was negative: West Germans also showed a marked detachment from politics, an unwillingness to become involved and an inclination to take a restricted and formal view of the political system and their obligations towards it. Those reservations were reinforced by the 'objective' situation of the Federal Republic, a provisional state lacking a national focus. To them we should add the whole weight of inherited values and attitudes, precisely the ingredients of the 'democratic problem' in Germany. Aversion to political conflict or at least the difficulty of regulating it and handling the slippery idea of parliamentary opposition are part of that problem. The Weimar Republic had shown how quickly a degeneration could come about – and that was the only relevant example to take. Nor was there any great historical landmark which could serve as a rallying point for good democrats. Neither 1848 nor 1918 was appropriate: the German people lacked the catharsis of a successful democratic revolution and that deficiency was not remedied after 1945. Liberal democracy could only make muted claims.

All these reservations – the instrumental regard for the political system, the nature of the German political culture, the absence of a strong democratic precedent – contribute to the difficulties of assessing the extent to which the Federal Republic was securely legitimised, even though political stability was its most prominent feature. Thus a high level of formal participation, measured by a large turnout at elections, with the vote overwhelmingly in favour of the 'pro-system' parties, could not by itself be treated as sufficient evidence. Indeed, it was not entirely specious to argue that the opposite was true in the case of West Germany: the apparently overwhelming consensus could be interpreted as a form of hyper-stability, a malfunctioning of the democratic process!

Crisis of legitimacy?
Even though observers could hardly dispute the factual evidence of a working parliamentary system, their critical standpoint was justified on the basis of a longer-term view of the outlook for the Republic: would the thin 'democratic reserves' prove adequate to survive a fundamental crisis? Such a crisis – mounting international tension, a showdown over reunification, severe unemployment and economic disruption, weakness or *immobilisme* in government – might lead to a sudden evaporation of support. In its stark form at least, the question did not have to be answered; various particular crises had to be surmounted, but none proved to mark a critical juncture or a fundamental test of loyalty.

Despite the non-arrival of an ultimate challenge – perhaps precisely because of its continuing absence – a sense of impending crisis has been a feature of political life in the Federal Republic. Comparatively minor upsets are frequently interpreted as fore-shadowing much more radical disturbances to come. Thus whatever the impression may be for a detached observer, the internal picture has often resembled that of a crisis-ridden and beleaguered democracy. Internal dissension exposes a raw historical nerve. A hint of inflation evokes memories of the collapse of the currency in 1923. Debates on the *Ostpolitik* were spiced with furious accusations concerning the historical behaviour of one or other of the parties. Any indication that a new party might be formed and gain a modest electoral success leads to immediate speculation about a disintegration of the party system. All parallels with the Weimar Republic are treated as wounds which can easily open once more.

These tendencies to over-reaction highlight a central paradox in the matter of legitimacy: the sense of insecurity which is embedded in the stable political form. They may also be related to surviving aspects of the German political culture: the aversion to political conflict and the desire for synthesis. If that resolution is not immediately attainable, then there must be a drastic fault in the arguments put forward by opponents.

Several tests of the cohesion of the Republic – national, economic and political – have promoted consolidation and have increased German self-reliance. The 'national issue', together with the whole question of West Germany's alignment within Europe, have been disturbing features at successive stages, but the eventual outcome has been to stabilise the republic. The German attitude to the economy is now much more relaxed than it was in the past. The hectic growth of the later 1950s could not be maintained indefinitely, but whilst it persisted, fear of an inevitable down-turn was sufficient to set the parties in disarray. That obsessional concern has abated: continuing economic expansion is no longer a prerequisite for political allegiance.

A not-dissimilar pattern is evident in some aspects of party competition. The attempt to give the 'refugee' vote a permanent expression was initially successful, but that petered out after the 1957 election. More important, the career of the right-wing extremist National Democratic Party (NPD) represented the high point of an electoral challenge in the late 1960s. Attempts to read into the party's vote indications of a neo-Nazi resurgence are probably misleading, and the NPD's rapid decline after failing to gain representation at the 1969 election supports the view that its fleeting success was due to a 'protest' vote – against the federal coalition of the CDU and SPD, against government – as a result of the economic recession.[9] What the episode of the NPD did demonstrate was the long-lasting integrative power of the CDU – as long as that party kept its distance from the SPD.

Yet the 'crisis' of legitimacy offered by party challenge by no means exhausts the possibilities of political upheaval. The phenomenon of the *Ausserparlamentarische Opposition* (APO), as its own title suggests, was a specific rejection of conventional electoral politics and of the parliamentary system. The movement was therefore explicitly 'revolutionary' in character and constituted a denial of the legitimacy of the republic. From its base in the universities (where the p.incipal demand was for an end to the archaic system of 'professorial rule') the APO sought to achieve a 'democratisation' of German society. Yet the movement – a motley of groupings, not an organised power – failed to make wider social and political connections; in particular there was no hint of a positive response from the industrial labour force. The APO began its life in the 1960s, and remained, the preserve of a middle-class, university elite.

Nonetheless, the movement which the extra-parliamentary opposition set in train were of more lasting significance for the attack on parliamentary democracy. One line of development was the move away from 'peaceful confrontation' towards the use of violence. Several clandestine groups of an anarcho-terrorist character were formed, and for a decade they waged their private war against the state. Their revolutionary myths, built up around the persons of Andreas Baader and Ulrike Meinhof, and the so-called Baader-Meinhof Group, set the precedents in the practice of terror, becoming as much an end in itself as a means. The tactic of political assassination was aimed at provoking reaction and thus exposing the repressive nature of the state, and the chosen victims were taken as representatives of the prevailing order. The long-drawn-out trials of those members caught and charged, their incarceration, and the deaths of some of the leaders in prison, helped to maintain the faltering momentum of the movement, even though all coherent political direction had long since been lost.[10]

It can be questioned whether this violent episode can be construed as a serious challenge to the legitimacy of the state, for active involvement was restricted to perhaps a few hundred people. But, of course, the perceived threat was much greater than the extent of numerical support, and the nature of the reaction – the atmosphere of a state of siege and the passing of anti-terrorist legislation – has to be taken into account. Furthermore, although it was a 'private war', the movement was not entirely isolated, since there were many others who, whilst not always prepared to condone the violent methods employed, belonged to a broad category of 'sympathisers', sharing the same view of the state's repressive character.

That character was defined in Marxist terms and was thus in accord with the general left-wing critique of capitalist society. But the original debt to orthodox Marxism was supplemented in a rejuvenated West German form by a continuing fascination with the state as part of the German academic tradition. This type of questioning of the Republic's legitimacy was an intellectual preserve and naturally became an important preoccupation within the universities. In the hands of a well-placed intellectual elite, with resources for wider dissemination, the weapon of the legitimacy issue was used with effect.[11] At times, however, the modes of argument acquire unreal qualities. Thus it is quite feasible to set up models of legitimacy which, in postulating the conditions of a desirable legitimacy, resemble ideal-type constructs. It is another step entirely to 'demonstrate' the validity of those models in respect of existing social and political institutions and find a 'deficit of legitimacy'.[12] Forecasts of a 'crisis of legitimacy', imminent or even actually present, automatically follow, despite any evidence to the contrary. Such reasoning has a spurious attraction, but it may generate self-fulfilling prophecies and reinforce a climate of confrontation and insecurity which pervades the wider political arena.

For a significant proportion of the intellectual elite a negative relationship with the Federal Republic and its institutions is evident. But that is not the case for other elite groups in West German society. There is a sense in which the most important ones – the bureaucracy, the military and the business elites – have been 'depoliticised'. That process requires the breakdown of a separate 'elite identity', so that sectional political reactions and involvement are not dissimilar from those of the population at large: the elites do not propagate a distinctive set of values. An alternative rendering would be to say that the supremacy of the party state has made it impossible for other, opposed values to persist.

That is particularly true of the loss of a special 'state legitimacy' for the civilian and military elites in state service, and it contrasts with the situation in the Weimar Republic. In this respect the West German *Bundeswehr* bears no comparison with the former *Reichswehr*. The *Reichswehr* leaders in the Weimar Republic deliberately fostered the idea that the military was the repository of state and national values and the belief was supported by the existence of a social elite and a crusting of the old nobility. The West German *Bundeswehr* is on a quite different footing. Not only are the armed forces subject to firm political control, but the attempt has been made, perhaps not too successfully, to implant an idea of 'internal responsibility' (*Innere Führung*) as a counter-weight to the possible re-emergence of traditional values. That reversion is anyway less likely for an army which is based on the principle of conscription, and the presence of a military ombudsman, the *Wehrbeauftragte*, who reports directly to the Bundestag, helps to ensure that the political controls are maintained. (The present incumbent is a long-serving member of the SPD.)

Generally the military no longer enjoys the high social esteem of the past: service in the forces is a career, not a calling. Nor is the *Bundeswehr* in a position to advance its version of the 'national cause': the West German armed forces originated in the accession of the Federal Republic to NATO and grew up in the framework of its requirements and strategy, not as a national force dedicated, perhaps, to advancing its own solution for German reunification. These conclusions are not vitiated by the occasional unguarded remarks of 'old generals' or the nostalgic reunions of former *Waffen-SS* comrades: the presence of unreformed elements does not amount to the survival of an elite.

Finally, the leading groups in industry and commerce – although never, of course, a homogeneous elite – find themselves in absolute consonance with the political realm. We shall wish to examine the precise relationships between the parties and the economy at a subsequent stage, but it is evident that of all social groups, those in the economic sector have felt most at home in the Federal Republic. They have enjoyed the benefits and the protection of the social-market doctrine from the outset, and the SPD in government at no point threatened their position.

To speak loosely of a crisis of legitimacy is to neglect the standpoint of key sections of society; it is also evident that the wide elite consensus is joined by a substantial popular one. The broadest social indicators – patterns of voting, the absence of widespread social and industrial unrest – confirm that picture, although they do not provide much help in ascertaining the degree of attachment, nor do they indicate what may be termed 'the objects of legitimacy'. The peculiarity of West German development has been the difficulty, over a long period, of finding a secure object of attachment. The emergence of a 'state consciousness' in the Federal Republic was by itself insufficient as long as the possibility of reunification remained in the background. Only after Brandt's *Ostpolitik* came to fruition in the early 1970s did the process of 'self-recognition' emerge, which may by now have developed into a specifically West German national consciousness.

For this reason the onus of legitimacy was placed almost entirely on the parliamentary institutions of the Basic Law, which itself had to be tested. The test came relatively late in the Federal Republic, not until the first occasion when there was a substantial change of political power: until 1969 the acceptance of the parliamentary republic by a large section of the electorate depended on the apparently 'permanent' nature of CDU rule. Although the formation of the CDU–SPD coalition from 1966 until 1969 brought forth the largest wave of protest, the really critical phase may have been the initial period of SPD rule, when the issue was whether the principle of 'alternative government' would be allowed to operate.

Subsequent development, both in the idea of a West German attachment and in the strength of the parliamentary system, confirms that the legitimacy issue – a hump rather than a crisis – has been resolved. Another form of crisis was that associated with the attack on the state and its symbols by the anarcho-terrorist fringe, which reached a peak in 1977 with the abduction and subsequent murder of Hanns-Martin Schleyer who, as head of the German Employers' Confederation, represented an ideal target.

The surmounting of that crisis contributed towards the accumulation of legitimacy: the state did prove itself effective. Critics would argue that a price has been paid for the massive legitimacy which the Federal Republic enjoys. It involves the whole question of 'toleration' which we shall examine later. Criticism of the legitimacy of the West German state might take the form of suggesting that the Republic has become 'over-legitimised' – that it has moved beyond the scale of acceptance towards a zone of actual intolerance. However, that political judgement almost certainly overstates the case, and we should appreciate that the political dimension is only one source of legitimacy. In the longer term the more diffuse attachments secured through the economy and its performance are likely to be more important for ensuring the stability of the republic.[13]

Notes and References

1. On the different 'types' of federalism, see G. Sawer, *Modern Federalism*, C. A. Watts, 1969. Sawer's intermediate type of 'co-operative federalism', in which the states preserve a 'bargaining capacity' with the central government, fits the West German case.
2. For the change in the chancellor's executive role, see W. Kaltefleiter, 'Modernisation of the Bureaucracy: From the Chancellor Principle to the Cabinet Principle', *International Journal of Politics*, 1972.
3. It can be held that 'Chancellor democracy' does have a permanent significance for the Federal Republic. See K. D. Bracher, *'Die Kanzlerdemokratie – Antwort auf das deutsche Staatsproblem?'*, in *Zeitgeschichtliche Kontroversen*, Munich: Piper, 1976.

4. G. Leibholz, *Verfassungsstaat – Verfassungsrecht*, Stuttgart: Kohlhammer, 1973, p. 81. For a more detailed expression of Leibholz's views: *Strukturprobleme der modernen Demokratie*, Karlsruhe: Müller, 1967.
5. The most succinct account of party–state connections in Germany is to be found in K. Dyson, *Party, State and Bureaucracy in Western Germany*, Sage Publications, 1977.
6. For the structure and control over the German system, see A. Williams, *Broadcasting and Democracy in Germany*, Bradford University Press, 1976.
7. The range and movement of opinion in the early post-war years was monitored by the American occupation authorities; see A. J. Merritt and R. L. Merritt (eds.), *Public Opinion in Occupied Germany: The OMGUS Surveys, 1945–1949*, Urbana, Illinois, 1970. For a summary of changes in the 1950s, see G. Schmidtchen, *Die befragte Nation*, Freiburg: Rombach, 1959.
8. G. Almond and S. Verba, *The Civic Culture: Political Attitudes and Democracy in Five Nations*, Princeton University Press, 1963. That earlier version has been subjected to a critical re-examination: G. Almond and S. Verba (eds.), *The Civic Culture Revisited*, Boston: Little, Brown, 1979, with an appreciation of the changes in the West German political culture by David Conradt.
9. Whilst the NPD can be dismissed as an *electoral* force and its fate does accord with a typical 'protest' movement, the Nazi shades refuse to be entirely dispersed. For a well-documented survey, see E. Kolinsky, 'Nazi Shadows are Lengthening over Germany', in *Patterns of Prejudice*, Nov./Dec. 1978. For analyses of NPD fortunes: T. A. Tilton, *Nazism, Neo-Nazism and the Peasantry*, Indiana University Press, 1975; S. Warnecke, The Future of Rightist Extremism in West Germany, in M. Kolinsky and W. Paterson (eds.), *Social and Political Movements in Western Europe*, Croom Helm, 1976.
10. A readable account of the various terrorist activities, but without a sustained political analysis, is J. Becker's *Hitler's Children*, Michael Joseph, 1977. See also, M. Funke (ed.), *Terrorismus: Untersuchungen zur Strategie und Struktur revolutionärer Gewaltpolitik*, Bonn: Bundeszentrale für politische Bildung, 1977. (Part III, *Terrorismus in der Bundesrepublik Deutschland*.) The book contains a detailed chronology of terrorist activity in the Federal Republic and a bibliography.
11. See K. Sontheimer, *Das Elend unserer Intellektuellen*, Hamburg: Hoffmann und Campe, 1976. Also, 'Intellectuals and Politics in West Germany', *West European Politics*, February 1978.
12. Jürgen Habermas was one of the most influential writers concerned with 'legitimacy' and 'system crisis'. See his *Legitimation Crisis*, Heinemann, 1976; and *Protestbewegung und Hochschulreform*, Frankfurt: Suhrkamp, 1969.
13. 'Economic performance' accords with a 'social-eudaemonic' view of legitimacy in modern societies. See G. Poggi, *The Development of the Modern State*, Hutchinson, 1978, p. 134.

Further Reading

K. von Beyme, *Die politische Elite in der BRD*, Munich: Piper, 1971.
D. Conradt, *The German Polity*, Longman, 1978.
L. Edinger, *Politics in Germany: Attitudes and Processes*, Little, Brown (revised edition) 1978.
T. Ellwein, *Das Regierungssystem der Bundesrepublik Deutschland*, Opladen: Westdeutscher Verlag, 1973.
W. Hennis, 'Die Rolle des Parlaments und die Parteiendemokratie', in *Die missverstandene Demokratie*, Freiburg: Herder, 1973.

84   Democracy in Western Germany

N. Johnson, *Government in the Federal Republic of Germany*, Oxford: Pergamon, 1973.

M. Kriele, *Legitimitätsprobleme der Bundesrepublik*, Munich: C. H. Beck, 1977.

G. Languth, *Die Protestbewegung in der BRD, 1968–1976*, Cologne: Verlag Wissenschaft und Politik, 1976.

R. Leicht, *Grundgesetz und Politische Praxis*, Munich: Carl Hanser, 1974.

G. Loewenberg, *Parliament in the German Political System*, Cornell University Press, 1967.

K. A. Otto, *Vom Ostermarsch zur APO, 1960–70*, Frankfurt: Campus Verlag, 1977.

F. Pilz, *Einführung in das politische System der Bundesrepublik Deutschland*, Munich: C. H. Beck, 1977. (Bibliography.)

K. Sontheimer, *Grundzüge des politischen Systems der Bundesrepublik Deutschland*, Munich: Piper, 1978.

K. Sontheimer, *Die verunsicherte Republik: Die Bundesrepublik nach 30 Jahren*, Munich: Piper, 1979.

K. Sontheimer and H. Röhring (eds.), *Handbuch des politischen Systems der Bundesrepublik Deutschland*, Munich: Piper, 1977.

D. Southern, 'Public Administration in West Germany', in F. F. Ridley (ed.), *Government and Administration in Europe*, Martin Robertson, 1979.

Bibliographies

K. D. Bracher (and others), *Bibliographie zur Politik in Theorie und Praxis*, Düsseldorf: Droste, 1976.

A. J. Merritt and R. L. Merritt, *Politics, Economics, and Society in the Two Germanies, 1945–75: A Bibliography of English-Language Works*, Illinois University Press, 1978.

3   The Evolution of the Party System

Parties of a New Type

Germany and the West European pattern
European party systems have many features in common. There
are similarities which can be traced to the conditions affecting their
formation and development. Especially important was the spread
of industrialisation and the consequent rise of an urban-based
proletariat which was given full political effect by successive
extensions of the franchise in the nineteenth and early twentieth
centuries. There were other influences – typically those of religion
and urban–rural differences, as well as ethnic and national values –
but in most cases the party systems chiefly reflected the force of
class politics and led to the familiar scheme of a left–right
continuum for the political parties.

Germany did not differ in the main thrust of this development:
social class was the main polarising force. The parties were affected
by the peculiarities of non-responsible government, for it
exaggerated the primary characteristics of the parties – their ideology and their interest basis – and later the German party system
proved inadequate to bear the weight of full parliamentary government. But this failure did not make the parties essentially different
from their counterparts in other European countries.

The European pattern, once it was established, proved extremely
resistant to change: party systems developed a kind of inertia
based on a fixed ideological outlook and well-defined areas of
social support for the parties. Yet it was also true that the party
systems could not be frozen for all time: the gradual build-up of

changing social conditions was bound at some point to be expressed in the parties.

The force of the accumulation of new factors became apparent after the Second World War. Partly as a consequence of wartime pressures and dislocation, partly because of the later effects of economic growth and social change, a loosening of traditional social ties became apparent. West European society experienced a break-up of relatively closed communities, the weakening of religious and other special bonds. Above all, the economic changes created the opportunity for a greater social mobility, which made the rigid barriers of society appear increasingly redundant. All those observable changes led also to the supposition that the old style of 'ideological politics' had lost its relevance. A conclusion was that the fundamental alterations in West European society meant the end of ideology: the chief cause of ideological difference, class divisions, was waning in importance.

The implications for the old, established parties were profound, for a threat to their supremacy loomed. The future belonged to parties free from the ballast of ideology and able to appeal to diverse social groups. Parties which could successfully make a transfer would be able to win a wide following, perhaps control government almost permanently, whilst the old-style 'narrow' parties would languish in gentle decline and pine away in helpless opposition. The successful party of the new type would be the catch-all party.[1]

When we look at the developments that have taken place in West Germany since 1945, the theory of the 'transformation' of party systems applies to an almost uncanny degree. The rise of Christian Democracy, in the form of the CDU, was an entirely new phenomenon for Germany. Instead of insisting on its ideological purity and seeking a restricted and assured sectional support, the CDU took the field with the diluted *Weltanschauung* of Christian Democracy and made a virtue of the mixed following the party hoped to attract. The CDU was the model for a genuine *Volkspartei*, and the formula for electoral success lay in dealing with the multiplicity of social claims. Thanks to the rapid economic recovery of the new state, the CDU government was in a favourable position to meet the rising expectations of post-war society. The party sought, in fact, to be identified with that society.

The SPD was faced with a novel and disturbing choice. German Social Democracy had either to maintain its traditional outlook – a socialist ideology aimed at, and restricted to, the working class – or adopt a strategy similar to that of Christian Democracy. At first the former alternative was adopted, partly through conviction and partly from inertia; there was anyway insufficient evidence that the nature of post-war society had radically and permanently changed. But throughout the 1950s the CDU formula continued to work, and the SPD felt itself sentenced to permanent opposition.[2] Quite deliberately the party then set out to follow the CDU model of the *Volkspartei*. The effect, in electoral terms, was almost immediate: the West German party system was soon dominated by two major parties, and many smaller ones went to the wall; they had neither the opportunity nor the disposition to compete in similar terms. The logic of the victorious catch-all party was a catch-all party system.

In many ways West Germany was an exemplary demonstration of the transformation thesis at work, and yet important qualifications have to be made to the theory of a common trend in Western European party systems and Germany's place within it. From the perspective of the late 1970s the movement which seemed to be irresistible in the 1960s looks less convincing. Old sources of ideology have been replaced by new ones, and the former lines of social cleavage, if not restored to their pristine form, still have a salience for political allegiance. Party systems, too, have not been drawn ineluctably towards a two-party, catch-all type. Old parties have survived to be joined by new ones, party systems have expanded rather than contracted, and governments – contrary to the implication of the victorious catch-all party in office – have become less rather than more stable.

These developments at least cast some doubt on the validity of the assumption of a *general* trend and direction implied by the admittedly substantial nature of social change in Europe. But what is most strange is that the West German party system should have so exactly fitted the original model and – just as important – should have continued to do so. This 'deviance' leads to the questioning of what the prime causes determining the evolution of the West German party system actually were: greater weight has to be attached to the special post-war conditions, to the consequences of the dictatorship, to the defeat, to the division and occupation of Germany. Those factors may be just as important as the wider ones which affected Western Europe as a whole.

The reservations are given additional point in the argument that the original formulation of a common Western European trend relied too much on the West German case – an extrapolation which proved to be unjustified. The Federal Republic has retained all the features intact: two-party dominance, absence of proliferation, stability of government. It is evident that we have to examine West German development on its own terms.

The foundations of the CDU

Christian Democracy in post-war Germany was an expression of a movement common in several European countries, bred in the struggle of resistance to the dictatorships and united in its anti-fascism. Active German resistance had been weak, but the strength of aversion from National Socialism in the Churches and their members was sufficient for the new movement to gain initial impetus in 1945. There were barriers to communication between the different zones of occupation, but they did not prevent the formation of various zonal parties all under the banner of Christian Democracy; members of the clergy were also well placed to help the formation of a common party, even though from the outset the CDU was not in a narrow sense a 'religious' formation.

The German form of Christian Democracy differed substantially from its expression elsewhere, since it was a party of alliance between Catholics and Protestants, not simply a new style for political Catholicism. The alliance was essential to overcome sectionalism: the forerunner of the CDU, the redoubtable Centre Party, had mustered a large part of the Catholic vote, but that success was also a limitation, since Catholics were in a minority (about a third) in the Reich as a whole. Catholic politicians and Church leaders believed that the time had come to end Catholic isolation and to involve the Protestant Churches in a common venture.

A reconciliation was easier to effect in the wake of the dictatorship, for the Churches had suffered the same plight under National Socialism, and they shared a responsibility for the moral catastrophe of their failure to rally opposition. The Churches in 1945 were ready to take a part in rebuilding Germany on the basis of a democratic commitment.

If Germany had remained undivided, the subsequent fortunes of the CDU would have been different. With the preponderance of the Protestant vote in Germany, the CDU might well have fragmented, but that threat was removed: whilst the CDU in the three Western zones gradually moved together, the CDU parties in Berlin and the Soviet zone became increasingly detached. That development significantly changed the composition of the electorate: the Catholic population was concentrated in southern and western Germany, so that from their position as a minority Catholics reached approximate parity, taking the Western zones by themselves. An all-German CDU would have been in a much weaker position, its voting strength less reliable and the 'Eastern' CDU quite probably unwilling to accept the Catholic leadership of the West.

The cohesion of the Catholic vote, a legacy from the Centre Party, helped the CDU to build up stable support, but strenuous efforts were made to avoid a relapse into political Catholicism. Strict attention was paid to securing a balance of influence inside the party, especially in the allocation of party offices, with the result that a kind of confessional *Proporz* system operated. Nonetheless, the motor of the new party was Catholic, and the party's centre of gravity was the Catholic Rhineland; it was natural, though not inevitable, that North-Rhine Westphalia, the most populous *Land*, should supply the federal leadership of the party. Adenauer was a properly representative figure of the CDU.

The strong Catholic impulse within the CDU was important in other ways as well. The social involvement and teachings of the Church supported a social tradition which was expressed in various ways; its most advanced expression lay in Christian Socialism, which was an active force in the early years of the CDU. The impact of social Catholicism waned after the Federal Republic was established, but strongholds remain in the CDU, especially the influential *Sozialausschüsse* ('social committees') of the party. The presence of social Catholicism ensured that the CDU could never become a straight conservative party – a guarantee which would not have held if the religious balance had been different.

In mobilising a large proportion of the Catholic vote, the Centre Party set another pattern for the CDU: it provided for the possibility of achieving a wide social integration. Regardless of their class affiliations, practising Catholics had been encouraged to support the Centre Party. So on a limited scale the essence of a new-type party already existed, one that had been an embryonic *Volkspartei* in bridging the division between capital and labour.

Ideology and Christian Democracy
A succinct formulation of the CDU's new approach is the idea of a 'double compromise': the one between Catholicism and Protestantism, the other between capital and labour. Together the two compromises gave the CDU its claim to be a party of the whole

people. But beyond a general 'Christian' commitment and a concern with class reconciliation, German Christian Democracy showed no clear direction, and the vagueness was accentuated by the party's dispersed nature; it had no one centre of power, no organisation above that of the *Länder* parties, no agreed leader.

There was a conviction, common to all parties, that a completely new start had to be made in Germany to remedy those conditions in society which had encouraged the growth of National Socialism. That sentiment came to the fore in the Christian-Socialist wing of the CDU, and its influence was shown in the CDU's Ahlen Programme, adopted for the British Zone in 1947. There it was roundly argued: 'The capitalist economic system has not served the national and social needs of the German people adequately. After the catastrophic political, economic and social collapse – as a consequence of criminal power politics – only a basically new structure can follow on . . . no longer serving capitalist profit and power but solely the well-being of our people.' The favoured alternative was some form of *Gemeinwirtschaft* (a communal economy) but its detailed functioning remained obscure.

The Ahlen Programme was the high point of radical Christian Socialism, and once the CDU had managed to win substantial power in the *Länder* and on the inter-zonal authorities, the emphasis changed dramatically. By the time of the first federal election in 1949 the party's leading figures had been able to control the Frankfurt Economic Council and they had behind them the success of the 1948 currency reform. That experience convinced them that capitalism was not, after all, finished. The party leaders gratefully accepted Ludwig Erhard's recipe for a 'social market economy', combining the discipline of the market system with the ethos of social responsiblity. The CDU's 1949 programme gave the new doctrine a prominent place, and subsequently it became an article of faith for the party.

There were additional reasons for making the change. In 1947 the political lines were not quite so sharply drawn as they were even two years later. By 1949 it was evident that the major struggle for power would be between the CDU and SPD; that growing polarisation was joined by the increasing tensions between East and West. The CDU unhesitatingly identified its interests with those of the Western powers, and that standpoint necessitated unqualified support for the capitalist economic order.

How should the ideological status of the CDU be judged? We have seen that its 'Christian' component, although important for its unity, neither gives the party a combative spirit nor ties it to a single direction of policy; at most the inclusion gives a vantage-point from which particular developments can be judged, a *Weltanschauung*. Of greater importance is the party's anti-communist outlook, for this factor has a continuing importance indirectly for domestic politics as it has for foreign policy, seen both in the CDU's initial Western orientation and in its hostility towards the communist bloc. Then there is the party's belief in the sanctity of the social market economy. Together, the three elements help to characterise the party, but they fail to inject into its policies a strong ideological content which, say, nationalism would supply; that line was extinguished by the post-war position of Germany and was anyway sacrificed in taking the course of integration with Western Europe.

It may be argued that any one of these ingredients could suddenly become matters of contention, but the CDU has for long reflected the predominant ideology of the Federal Republic itself – not surprisingly, since the party moulded the Republic, summed up in the idea of 'the CDU state'. It is therefore a party concerned mainly to preserve the *status quo*, whether in government or in opposition. Within the party there is an agglomeration of view-points which have to be balanced; their unity cannot be taken for granted, but ideological dissension has never become of critical importance within Christian Democracy.

Leadership in the CDU

A common orientation towards political power is the binding force on the CDU. The concentration on winning or retaining govern-mental power as a sufficient aim is typical of a 'non-ideological' catch-all party, but increased strains emerge in other areas; in particular, the question of party leadership assumes a pivotal importance – the leader has to compensate for the absence of ideological appeal. The history of the CDU can quite adequately be recounted in terms of the leadership question: the original unification of the party, the ascendancy of Adenauer, the problems of succession, the continuing difficulties facing a CDU leader in asserting his position.

Adenauer's rise to power within the CDU and thence to federal government showed his supreme prowess in the techniques of party in-fighting. Adenauer first came to prominence as the chair-man of the CDU in the British Zone, and from that base he warded off challenges from the Berlin CDU and from other *Länder*.

He then gained further influence and prestige as president of the Parliamentary Council from 1948 to 1949, and that body, charged with drawing up the Basic Law, contained many of the leading parliamentarians from the separate *Land* assemblies. Prior to the 1949 election, and even immediately afterwards, there was no unified or formal leadership of the party. Adenauer managed to arrange a majority coalition (based on his insistence that the CDU should not share government with the SPD) which was just sufficient to secure his election as chancellor. He was then the *de facto* leader of the CDU, but he actually became party chairman subsequently in 1950.

Had the CDU not been in a position to form the government in 1949, the question of leadership could have presented serious problems, and the momentum of Adenauer's rise would have been checked. The fact that Adenauer did win power was sufficient to enable him to wield undisputed authority in the party; his chancellorship masked the situation within the CDU, for the exercise of governmental power hid the underlying instability of the party with regard to leadership and organisation. Adenauer was content with a rudimentary federal party structure, more in the nature of a loose co-ordination, and the post of party secretary – essential to secure federal direction – was not created until 1967. The system quite suited Adenauer's style: he had no wish to be hampered by a tight party organisation and he was far better placed as chancellor to impose his will on the party.

It is important to bear in mind the decentralised character of the CDU, for it is probably the most promising starting point for any examination of its later difficulties, especially the key question of party leadership. The origins of the party, built up from a number of largely autonomous centres of power in the *Länder*, dictated Adenauer's relationship with the subordinate units. His position resembled that of a feudal monarch: the powerful party barons in the *Länder* offered him their loyalty and tributes, but they retained power within their own fiefs.[3]

Adenauer's legacy to the CDU was laced with thorns. As long as he retained a firm hold on the electorate, the cohesion within the party was kept. But the spell was finally broken in 1961 and the problems of succession arose in an acute form. Ludwig Erhard, the acknowledged architect of the economic recovery, was apparently the obvious choice, since his popularity with the electorate was second only to Adenauer's. Yet his brief spell in office, from 1963 until 1966, and his ignominious departure provide an exact illustration of the problems which beset CDU leaders. Any successor to Adenauer would have had problems; Erhard's position was made more difficult by Adenauer's personal opposition, and Adenauer continued to snipe at Erhard after his own 'retirement', since he was still the chairman of the CDU. Even though Erhard led the CDU to victory in the 1965 election and was able to gain the party chairmanship for himself, his position was nevertheless insecure. He lacked the ability to consolidate his leadership of the party, and once things began to go wrong (an economic down-turn and a poor performance for the CDU in *Land* elections), the plotting in the party to replace him continued apace. Deserted by the Free Democrats and without strong allies in his own party, Erhard had no alternative but to resign.

Erhard's fall revealed the precarious nature of leadership within the CDU, and the whole subsequent development of the CDU has been affected by this concern. Erhard suffered from his own lack of political ability, but equally important was the absence of federal authority and organisational power vested in the leader; mere chairmanship of the party is insufficient, although clearly it is an essential step. The recent career of Helmut Kohl illustrates the importance of securing a firm base in *Länder* politics and thence moving to a control of the party, with the chancellorship as the – eventual – prize. Kohl first established himself as the CDU minister-president of the Rhineland-Palatinate. In 1971 he competed unsuccessfully for the party's federal leadership, but was elected in 1973. The next hurdle was to secure nomination as chancellor candidate, a struggle which lasted until 1975. Although Kohl won over the CDU to his side, the more difficult problem was to overcome the objections of the CSU to his being the joint CDU–CSU candidate. Under him, the CDU–CSU narrowly failed to win the 1976 election, but even so Kohl retained his authority in the party, since he had paid careful attention to the essentials of organisation and alliance structure in the CDU. Moreover, it is notable that Kohl himself was a provincial product: he had never held federal office or even a seat in the Bundestag. Only after the 1976 election did he finally take his place as the virtual 'leader of the opposition' for the parliamentary party.

Kohl undoubtedly learned much from the fate of his predecessors: Erhard, Kiesinger and Rainer Barzel. The last two sealed their fates by failing to win federal elections (Kiesinger in 1969 and

Barzel in 1972), but Kohl in 1976 was not at first affected: the 'revolt', when it came, was from the CSU, but it turned into a confrontation between the two parties, without, as it appeared, weakening Kohl's personal position. Yet the party does not easily forget an election failure, and Kohl's adroitness in controlling the various strategic bases in the CDU – including party organisation, through his nomination of the secretary-general – was at all times dependent on the promise of electoral success, with *Länder* elections as the immediate pointers. He had to be aware, as his own progress in the party showed, that any one of the *Land* potentates can regard himself as a potential chancellor: secure within his own party, and heading a *Land* government in his own right, he can sally forth to joust with the other party barons for the federal prize. A party leader has no easy way of controlling the powerful *Länder* leaders; there is no strict hierarchy and the parliamentary party is not a decisive arena. He must prove more adept than his rivals at forming alliances. In the end Kohl failed.[4]

It is ironic, after Adenauer's easy and unquestioned exercise of authority, that the CDU should have been plagued ever since with the problem of providing effective and stable leadership. But this position is not accidental or due simply to a partial vacuum at the top after Adenauer's departure. Nor should the inevitable concentration on personalities and the power struggle be allowed to obscure the character of the party. To have a convincing leader is vital for the CDU, in order to bring together the various streams of opinion and to compensate for its loose ideological position. Moreover, the rivalries between the *Land* leaders also have a function in expressing differences of tendency in the party – probably a more important channel than that provided by its federal structure or by the factions within the parliamentary party.

Schumacher and the SPD

In the conditions which prevailed in Germany immediately after the war, the SPD felt that it had a natural claim to lead the democratic forces and that it was the party most suited to govern. Its advantages over all other parties were considerable: the SPD had impeccable democratic credentials and was soon able to rebuild its organisation. A large proportion of early SPD members had been in the party before 1933, and the maintenance of a leadership cadre in exile made it easier for the SPD to start as a national party and reassert its centralist tradition. The party lost potential support through the division of Germany, but that did not significantly alter its pre-1933 position, and it was compensated by the inability of the KPD to offer serious competition in Western Germany.[5]

There was also an undeniable relevance of the SPD's brand of 'democratic socialism' to the condition of Germany. If the old mistakes were not to be repeated, society had to be rebuilt, and to do so it would be necessary to have a planned economy with active state intervention. Only the SPD, it appeared, could offer a new course for Germany – on the basis of democratic choice. The party also had a resolute leader, Kurt Schumacher, who, given the visible evidence of his suffering under the Nazis, could speak with authority for 'the other Germany'.

These positive auguries dictated the party's strategy. Convinced that the SPD was the rightful heir to the German political estate, Schumacher was determined to avoid too close an association with other parties and risk losing the initiative: the SPD should come to power on its own terms. Thus the party had to mount watch over two threats, the 'popular front' tactics employed by the Communists and the early successes of the CDU. Schumacher was powerless to prevent the enforced merger between the SPD and the KPD in 1946 as far as the Soviet Zone was concerned, but the SPD rejected the fusion in Berlin and there was no chance of the KPD being able to bring off a similar coup in Western Germany.[6] The more vexing problem turned out to be the strength of the new CDU and the question of how to determine the SPD's attitude towards it. Whilst there were good reasons for close co-operation in *Länder* government and administration, the SPD was not inclined to accept those coalitions as the future pattern unless it had the controlling influence.

Schumacher did not underestimate the problems of the party in seeking to gain majority power, nor the fact that it had to overcome a major historical handicap: the widely held belief that Social Democracy had always failed to put Germany's interests first. That reputation Schumacher sought to overcome by following a strong 'national' line. Opposition to the policies pursued by the Soviet Union went without saying, but the strategy required independence from the Western occupying powers as well. This time, unlike after the First World War, the party would not make the mistake of associating itself with a 'policy of fulfilment' and allow the 'anti-national' charge to stick. The SPD would only co-operate with the Western allies on a basis of equality – and then only if German national interests were not sacrificed.

A mistaken strategy?

A prime result was that Schumacher, and with him the SPD, quickly gained a reputation for another quality, awkward intransigence: he was seen to be unwilling to work with the CDU and often openly hostile to the Western powers. The SPD naturally found itself to be in an ambiguous situation – following a course of frequently bitter opposition and yet still sharing the same democratic values. As the party's oppositional stance became more marked, the CDU proceeded to rebuild the West German economy and to forge alliances according to Adenauer's ideas, whilst the SPD stood helpless on the sidelines.

A decisive step in the exclusion of the SPD occurred with the formation of the Bizonal Economic Council. The narrow lead held by the CDU and its allies forced the SPD into opposition, for Schumacher was unwilling for his party to take a subordinate role in the Economic Council's executive body. That line-up set the tone for the later formation of a federal government: Adenauer had no intention anyway of governing with the SPD if he could possibly find an alternative.

Left out of the first federal government, the SPD had to adjust itself to being in opposition. In Schumacher's view that meant seeking a definite polarisation, for only by offering itself as the sole alternative government could the SPD properly present its radical alternatives to CDU policies. Ample grounds for a polarisation were available. Adenauer's government, far from insisting on Germany's rights, appeared bent on accepting allied dictates – thus jeopardising the hope of reunifying Germany. But the CDU did not incur an immediate penalty; on the contrary, 'fulfilment' paid off: Adenauer received all the accolades, and the Federal Republic tangibly benefited.

The CDU also pursued its policy of the social market economy with vigour. As an egalitarian party, the SPD was bound to find the reliance on market forces an anathema to its principles. The SPD favoured planning, direct controls and nationalisation – none of which had a part in Erhard's schemes. The German economic system did not immediately take off under Erhard's guidance, and the SPD was hopeful that the electorate would soon show its preference for the socialist alternative, as it would for the SPD's stand on reunification. The process of polarisation was completed by the personal animosity that existed between Adenauer and Schumacher: it was a duel between two protagonists over the future of Germany. But the public antagonism did not help the SPD

much, whilst Adenauer was quite happy to use the SPD as his foil
and so gain political profile for himself and his party.

In retrospect it is easy enough to compile a list of mistakes
committed by the SPD. Yet both its case and its strategy were
entirely reasonable in marking out a new course for Germany.
One miscalculation was to assume that the West German electorate
was so dedicated to the national cause that this preoccupation
excluded all immediate concerns. Another error was to underestimate the recuperative power of the West German economy,
and once conditions became appreciably better, the SPD's
insistence on its old-style socialism, with all the paraphernalia of
government intervention, appeared not merely irrelevant but
downright harmful. Schumacher compounded the negative
electoral effect. He reminded people too much of the past – the
shades of National Socialism, of the Weimar Republic – whereas
Adenauer's whole approach held a promise for the future. Even
though Schumacher's contribution to the SPD was considerable
(in holding the party together in the first critical years, in blocking
off the Communist threat, in maintaining the electoral base of the
party intact), his style did not help the party to win over new social
groups. In his positive view of the German state and nation – he
has been called the 'last Lassallean' – Schumacher personified the
non-Marxist roots of German Social Democracy and was one of its
more forceful leaders. But his strategy for the SPD was probably
unsound. Instead of creating an intense, if still democratic, polarisation, the party might have been better advised to follow a deliberate policy of co-operation with the CDU. Adenauer would not
have welcomed the embrace, for he much preferred to have the
SPD in harmless opposition, but there were several leading figures
in his own party who took the view that the Federal Republic
should be governed by a broad coalition, including the SPD.

Above all, the weakness of the SPD was that it became trapped
in its own web of opposition. Opposition in principle to a range
of government policies – European integration, rearmament,
economic policy – was perhaps convincing at the outset. Yet
changing circumstances forced the SPD to drop absolute condemn-
ation and substitute a half-hearted acquiescence, later even a
grudging approval. Constantly the SPD found itself left behind as
events altered the context of the Federal Republic: the growing
intensity of the Cold War, the increasing improbability of any
immediate chance of reunification, the patent successes of the
initial steps in European integration, economic recovery, the rising

status of the Federal Republic. The SPD really had no choice in the end but to concede, for the party did 'accept' the republic: it was a state which the SPD had helped to create.

Until Schumacher's death in 1952 it was possible to believe that the SPD had a studied and complete alternative to CDU policies. With the party's defeat in the 1953 election, there was a loss in credibility and morale, and the absence of adequate leadership also became apparent. Schumacher's style hardly encouraged the emergence of other strong personalities; by default the central organisation of the party, the *Apparat*, took charge under the amiable but colourless Erich Ollenhauer. The fact that by the 1957 election the SPD had in practice dropped all its sharp alternatives to the CDU did not save it from another shattering defeat. The party was then in the weakest possible position: it lacked a leader with popular appeal; its programmes were pale amendments to the proven policies of the CDU; it had no experience of federal government; its philosophy of 'democratic socialism' appeared threadbare. The CDU was poised to rule for decades to come.

The imperative of reform

It was after the reverse of 1957 that the reform movement within the SPD made headway. To express the initiative as a contest betwen reformists and Marxists would be misleading, since it was much more a move against party traditionalism, which happened to be expressed in Marxist terminology, but which, as a matter of fact, had lost all radical commitment. The need to rethink the whole approach of Social Democracy was widely admitted; the alternative was indefinite stagnation, if not actual decline.

The reformist movement originated in the upper reaches of the party and was associated with people who enjoyed an authority and reputation independent of the executive, especially the influential '*Bürgermeister* Group', which represented the power that the SPD had been able to win at local and *Land* levels, in contrast to the federal weakness of the party. A focus for the new mood in the party was Willy Brandt, who was elected governing mayor of Berlin in 1957. (Berlin at that time was both symbolically and internationally the most important part of Germany.) Brandt also became a member of the SPD's central committee in 1958; that link was important in reinforcing both the reformist wing and for advancing the fundamental proposals in a new programme which was put before the party conference at Bad Godesberg in 1959. The Godesberg Programme of the SPD was the first definitive statement of the party's aims since the Heidelberg Programme of 1925. It was not so much concerned with detailed plans as with defining the place of Social Democracy in German society.

There can be no mistaking the radical nature of the redefinition which took place. Most striking is the extent to which the SPD disavowed any Marxist connection, whether as an indication of the ultimate aims of the party, as an explanation of history, or even as a critical perspective. That severance led the Programme to a quite eclectic view of 'democratic socialism': it was located in 'the Christian ethic, humanism, and classical philosophy'. Equally important was the rejection of any dogmatic belief or claim to a special understanding of society: the SPD was not a 'church or counter-church', nor did it feel called upon to 'explain the history of mankind'. In arguing that 'socialism is not a substitute for religion', the SPD was at the same time admitting the essentially pluralist nature of West German society and identifying itself with that pluralism. If Social Democracy was to give up all claim to primacy for the working classes, then it had to recognise the legitimate interests and values of *all* sectors of society, not just those of one class: the admission was made specific in the case of religion, thus breaking with the old, anti-clerical tradition of the party.

If Social Democracy was to become an integral part of the pluralist order, the need for the SPD to regard itself as a 'class party' no longer carried weight, for the class orientation implied a quite different view of society: not pluralism but class conflict. Thus the Godesberg Programme explicitly dropped the 'class' label and instead claimed to be a party of the whole people, a *Volkspartei*.

What the SPD lost in 'critical perspective' in adopting the new programme, it gained in flexibility in its attitude towards current issues. The pragmatic approach removed the last shreds of its opposition to the market economy, recognising that its capabilities were still great and that the German people could ill afford to dispense with its benefits. In effect, the SPD subscribed to a defence of the economic order, but with the important caveat that the proper balance of economic power should be maintained, thus allowing the party in government to intervene as much as necessary to preserve 'economic freedom' although not so much as to impose a socialist economy as an article of belief. There should be just as much planning as necessary. In other matters, too, notably the questions of defence and European co-operation, the SPD came very near to identifying itself with the established policies of the Christian Democrats.

In one sense the SPD was 'catching up with Bernstein', for 'the final goal' had been jettisoned. But the new SPD went further than Bernstein would have countenanced, since for him 'the movement' was everything, yet in 1959, at one stroke, the movement, the revered forms, the symbols and the traditions of the party were cast aside. It is true that all the reform destroyed was a set of 'revolutionary myths' which were only a handicap to the SPD in its bid to win over new voters, but exactly how was the party to replace them in rekindling enthusiasm?

The Godesberg Programme itself did not offer much scope, but at least its adoption did not lead to a split in the SPD, for it was finally accepted by 324 votes to 16. That result gave the party leaders cause for confidence in fighting future elections: their hands were not tied and they could compete more easily with the CDU by adopting a policy of *Annäherung*, which would minimise differences. Furthermore, the reform movement also brought Brandt to additional prominence in the party: the long interregnum (filled by Ollenhauer, who led the party to defeat in 1953 and 1957) was over. Ollenhauer remained party chairman, but Brandt was chosen as the party's chancellor candidate to fight the 1961 election.

Brandt's contribution of a new look to German politics – somewhat in the 'young Kennedy' style of the period – took the SPD out of the doldrums it had faced since the beginning of the republic. The near static vote (in percentage terms) which the SPD held prior to the 1959 reforms was transformed in subsequent elections. A rapport was found with new sections of the electorate which had previously mistrusted Social Democracy. Despite successive 'defeats' for the SPD in 1961 and 1965, the rising trend of popular support was unmistakable. In those circumstances, the place of both Brandt and the party programme was assured.

The real impetus – the imperative, even – behind the movement for reform was a determination to improve the SPD's chances of winning government power. The Godesberg reforms succeeded in two ways: by increasing the party's vote and by making the SPD more acceptable as a partner in government. Since the CDU was in a dominant position, the road to government, of necessity, seemed to run through a CDU–SPD alliance. Neither of the other possibilities – an outright majority for the SPD, or coalition with the Free Democrats – was at that stage a realistic option. Coalition with the CDU was the next logical step. It was an opportunity for the SPD to make the initial entry into government and to demonstrate that the party was *regierungsfähig*, that it could be entrusted with the responsibilities of governing the Federal Republic.

The strategy worked. Firstly, the 1966–9 coalition with the CDU showed that the SPD could work in harmony with other parties. Secondly, the party's performance in government was sufficiently reassuring to win over new sections of the electorate. Its confidence in government and the increase in the party's vote then enabled the SPD to rule independently of the CDU. By 1972, when the SPD became the largest party, it appeared that party reform had been entirely justified.

Yet subsequent developments cast some doubt on the validity of the strategy. The electoral extension came to an abrupt halt after the 1972 election. The fall in support in the *Länder* was confirmed by the outcome of the 1976 election, and the belief, or hope, that the SPD would at some stage be in a position to rule by itself was dispelled. Brandt's own resignation in 1974 also closed a chapter: his style of leadership, a form of 'pragmatic idealism', had somehow embodied the spirit of the Godesberg Programme. His departure, along with the disappointments of the SPD in government and the election reverses, marked the beginning of a new phase for the SPD, a period of re-evaluation for Social Democracy. The SPD had succeeded in the major aim of becoming 'a party of government', but in so doing it was in danger of losing its reputation as a party committed to social reform. The SPD faced competing pressures. The demands of government and the practical restrictions of coalition were matched by others from within the party – among them, that the SPD should rediscover its radical traditions. Those tensions, the Godesberg legacy, continue to beset the SPD.

The Stages of Development
The special power of a catch-all party lies in its ability to accommodate a variety of social interests within its fold. Its initial success assumes that sympathetic changes in society are taking place, weakening existing political loyalties and diminishing the attractions of parties based on particular interests or strong ideology. But once the momentum has been established, the solvent process becomes progressive, especially when the 'logic' of the catch-all party system takes over. The concentration of the vote in the West German party system on the CDU and SPD illustrates this progression in an almost unnerving way.

CDU and SPD Support at Federal Elections, 1949–1976

Election year	CDU–CSU %	SPD %	Aggregate %
1949	31.0	29.2	60.2
1953	45.2	28.8	74.0
1957	50.2	31.8	82.0
1961	45.4	36.2	81.6
1965	47.6	39.3	86.9
1969	46.1	42.7	88.8
1972	44.9	45.8	90.7
1976	48.6	42.6	91.2

The impact of these two parties – their aggregate share growing consistently, even when the fortunes of one or the other have been in temporary decline – has led nearly, but not quite, to a two-party system. The qualification is important, for the continued survival of the Free Democrats has modified the operation of the system in a significant way: the 'strategic presence' of the third party has given a flexibility to the party system which would otherwise be absent. The FDP itself can act as an 'agent of exchange' in the formation of coalitions and the alternation of governments, a role of pronounced importance if the two major parties are of comparable size.

At the present time West Germany has a 'balanced' party system: it has all the essential attributes of a two-party system, but with a different mechanism. Taking the idea of balance as the

The Party System: Five Stages of Development

Stage	Type	Period	Leading Features
I	Nascence	1945–9	The period of party formation; restricted activities and powers; no central government; *Länder*-based parties.
II	Diffusion	1949–53	Low aggregate share of major parties; large number of parties represented; no clear polarisation.
III	Imbalance	1953–66	One party dominant, especially 1957–61. Government and coalition formation largely predetermined. Decline evident from 1961, particularly in coalition.
IV	Transition	1966–9	Intermediate between imbalance and balance. Growing parity between major parties and high aggregate share. Coalition between them marks end of imbalance.
V	Balance	1969–	Increasing aggregate and narrowing gap. New coalition forces ousts previously dominant party. Potential of 'alternation' realised.

central point of reference, we can trace the evolution of the party system through a number of distinctive stages, although in practice the lines of demarcation are not always sharp.

1 The nascent system

How can the party system up to 1949 best be described? The parties were unable to operate freely, there was no German government to act as a focus for their activity, and they were mainly relegated to running the local affairs of the *Länder*. Yet the parties were not helpless; within limits they were able to compete. The system was not an entirely artificial structure imposed from above, and there was a gradual extension of party power and authority. Even though the responsibilities of party leaders were restricted, they acted in the knowledge that they were shortly to become responsible for the future West German state.

With hindsight we can also say that the nascent party system was also the critical formative stage for all subsequent development. Some of the essential characteristics were evident very early on, even in the first round of *Länder* elections held from October 1946 until October 1947. In all there were nine *Länder* elections in this period: between them the CDU and the SPD took over 70 per cent of the total vote. That pattern has been reinforced subsequently but not essentially changed.

What is less easy to determine is the operative force behind the concentration. How far was it a natural development, and how far a consequence of occupation policies? There is a distinction to be made between 'social' and 'institutional' factors, the former reflecting the changes in German society and the latter, in the first instance, the product of occupation policies. Whilst the precise reasons for the electorate behaving as it did in the first elections remain imponderable, the effect of allied intervention was decisive, both in determining the nature of party competition and (through 'licensing' and other discriminatory methods) in deciding who the eligible contestants were to be. In all four zones of occupation the basic grouping of licensed parties was the same, although the exact labels differed. The four original parties, the SPD, the KPD, the CDU and the Free or Liberal Democrats, were admitted because of their generally 'democratic' and 'anti-Fascist' character, whilst others were rejected on these grounds. The most important aim was to discourage the setting up of extreme right-wing parties, but in the Western zones there was also a suspicion of any movement (such as the 'refugees') which could have a disruptive influence or provoke opposition to the creation of a multi-party system, an important consideration for the Americans and British who were naturally hostile to anything but a two-party system. For the purposes of allied control, it was also easier to work through a few large and 'responsible' parties.

Basically, then, a four-party model resulted, but the simplification really went even further: the constituent parties were 'bourgeois' (CDU and FDP) or 'socialist' (SPD and KPD), so that a two-bloc system was the outcome, and it was that format which survived in the opposition of the SPD to the CDU, once the KPD was removed and the FDP became a minor party. The modest place taken by these last two shows that allied goodwill was by itself insufficient, but that does not weaken the case for arguing that there was an overall influence in favour of a clear socialist–bourgeois division.

The allied impact was profound, and it was compressed into a limited period, perhaps not much longer than three years. Other parties were later permitted to function: the Bavarian Party in 1946, the German Party in 1947. By 1948 a more relaxed view was evident as the creation of a West German state became a probability. As a result several parties were formed which had not contested *Land* elections but were in a position to fight the 1949 federal elections, and some – such as the *Deutsche Rechts-Partei* – were hardly to be counted as supporters of a democratic system. Their appearance, however, came too late to affect the composition of existing *Land* assemblies and governments, and by that time, too, the established parties had made their mark in the Economic Council and the constituent Parliamentary Council, setting the framework for a quasi-federal party system.

2 Apparent diffusion

The first impression of the Bundestag election of August 1949 is that the party system showed distinct similarities with the 'normal' German type, a multi-party system which could easily take the direction of fragmentation. That reversion appeared possible, since there was a move away from the consolidation evident in the previous *Land* elections; in particular the combined vote of the CDU and SPD dropped noticeably. The number of parties represented in the first Bundestag (ten) was also much greater than had been the case for any of the individual *Länder*.

However, that first impression is misleading, to the extent that it implies a definite shift in electoral opinion. A growth in the number of parties was to be expected: some had only been able to form in time for the 1949 election; others had gained representation in some *Länder* but not in others and were able to win federal seats because the electoral law was at the outset particularly generous, only requiring that a party should gain 5 per cent of the vote in any one *Land* in order to qualify. Thus it came about that parties which were only of regional importance, such as the Bavarian Party, swelled the total number.

Despite the fall in the CDU and SPD share, their relative position was still exceptionally strong: only the FDP and the KPD secured more than 5 per cent of the federal vote. When the electoral law was tightened in 1953 to make the 5 per cent hurdle

Elections to the Bundestag, 1949–1976

	1949	1953	1957	1961	1965	1969	1972	1976
Electorate (millions)	31.2	33.1	35.4	37.4	38.5	38.7	41.4	42.0
Turnout (per cent)	78.5	86.0	87.8	87.7	86.8	86.7	91.1	90.7
			per cent *Zweitstimmen*/List Vote					
CDU–CSU	31.0	45.2	50.2	45.3	47.6	46.1	44.9	48.6
SPD	29.2	28.8	31.8	36.2	39.3	42.7	45.8	42.6
FDP	11.9	9.5	7.7	12.8	9.5	5.8	8.4	7.9
DP } GDP	4.0	3.2	3.4 }	2.8	—	—	—	—
BHE }	—	5.9	4.6 }					
KPD/DKP, etc.	5.7	2.2	—	1.9	1.3	0.6	0.3	0.4
DRP/NPD	1.8	1.1	1.0	0.8	2.0	4.3	0.6	0.3
Others	16.4	4.1	1.3	0.2	0.3	0.5	0.0	0.2

Notes

In 1949, four other parties were represented in the Bundestag, making ten in all. The four parties were: the Bavarian Party (4.2 per cent), the *Zentrum* (3.1 per cent), WAV (2.9 per cent) and the Danish minority SSW (0.3 per cent). In addition, there were three individual deputies who won constituency seats.

In the 1953 election, the *Zentrum* (0.8 per cent) was also represented by virtue of winning a single constituency seat, whilst the Bavarian Party (1.7 per cent) was not.

Left-wing parties: the KPD for 1949 and 1953; the DFU for 1961 and 1965; the ADF in 1969; the DKP for 1972 and 1976 (in the latter year the splinter KPD is also included as well as the KBW and the GIM).

Right-wing parties: the *Deutsche Rechts-Partei* in 1949; the *Deutsche Reichs-Partei* in 1953, 1957 and 1961; the NPD for 1965 and subsequently.

The DP and the BHE merged for the 1961 election to become the *Gesamt-Deutsche Partei*.

Electoral law qualifications. In 1949, 5 per cent of the list vote in any one *Land*, or one directly contested constituency seat; in 1953, 5 per cent of the federal vote, or one direct seat; from 1957 onwards 5 per cent of the federal vote, or three direct seats. The *Zentrum* was represented in 1949 and 1953 through the direct seat qualification, and the DP in 1953 and 1957.

For details of the 1976 election breakdown according to the *Länder* vote, see p. 131.

apply to a party's *federal* vote, the elimination of some very small parties was inevitable. Their transient presence obscured the real shape of the party system.

That shape was determined by the underlying bipolarity generated by the contest between the CDU and the SPD. The near parity of these two parties – both around the 30 per cent mark – is, however, also open to misinterpretation, if it is concluded that the narrowest of margins decided which of the two should win control over the Federal Republic, that it was a virtual toss-up between Adenauer and Schumacher. Currency is given to that idea by the somewhat dramatic way in which the former was elected chancellor by the bare one vote necessary to gain the necessary absolute majority, but that did not at all mean that almost half the Bundestag would have supported Schumacher. The truth was that the multi-party system already had a definitely lop-sided look: the bulk of the smaller parties were 'bourgeois', and some form of anti-socialist coalition was likely. Adenauer's coalition parties – the CDU–CSU, the German Party and the Free Democrats – represented one possible combination. The government actually formed from those three parties had a relatively small majority (208 votes to the 194 of those outside), but its security was never in doubt. The essential structure of government was settled for years to come: an anti-socialist coalition led by the CDU in which the FDP was an important element. The first president of the republic, Theodor Heuss, was a Free Democrat, and his candidature was supported by the CDU against Schumacher's for the SPD.

3 The period of imbalance
The advance of the CDU in the 1950s was spectacular. In 1953, with 45 per cent of the vote, the CDU had a narrow overall majority in the Bundestag, and in 1957 an absolute majority, both in votes and seats. Those two elections demonstrated the enormous assimilative power of Christian Democracy. The CDU absorbed and concentrated the 'bourgeois' vote at a time when any tendency of the electorate to flirt with right-wing extremism could have had disturbing consequences. That may well be regarded as one of the most important contributions of the Adenauer era: the integration of supporters of the former regime, along with non-Nazis and even active opponents, into one vast party of 'democratic collection'.

The other parties had to contend with this success as best they could. The FDP share of the vote fell from 11.9 per cent in 1949 to 9.5 in 1953, and then to 7.7 per cent in 1957 – uncomfortably close to the 5 per cent barrier. The party also found itself caught by the 'governmental embrace' of the CDU. The FDP split in 1956: the party's four ministers in the coalition, and a number of its deputies, stayed on in support of Adenauer when the FDP itself went into opposition.

These years of ascendancy for the CDU were ones of despair for the SPD. There was comfort in the fact that although the party's share of the vote remained static, a numerical increase occurred – from seven million in 1949 to well over nine million in 1957, rather modifying the view that the CDU carried all before it and that they were 'dead' years for the opposition. A worrying development for the SPD was the fall in party membership, especially since throughout its history it had relied on a high level of voluntary commitment. The decline (as can be seen from the table on page 128) affected the CDU as well: the general fall was symptomatic of a changing mood in the years of economic consolidation.

Demise of the minor parties.   A roll-call of the minor parties reads like a listing of the no-hopers and the also-rans, fleetingly appearing on the federal scene, surviving for a while in the half-light of a few *Länder*, then disappearing without trace. Their decline was almost uniformly the obverse of CDU success, and it may seem sufficient only to concentrate on the positive aspects of the Christian Democratic appeal. But the smaller parties differed considerably amongst themselves: some were ephemeral; others had a long historical tradition; some were purely regional; a few had a potential influence throughout Western Germany. In the end they all went the same way, yet each appeared to have its particular problems in fighting for survival, not just the generalised threat of the catch-all party.

Of all the minor parties, the German Party (DP) had the most favourable chance of securing a slice of the conservative vote, and that in direct competition with the CDU. Its modest showing in 1949, only 4 per cent of the federal vote, obscures the party's regional importance. The DP contested only the four northern *Länder*, and in two of these, Bremen and Lower Saxony, it pushed the CDU into third place. The DP also had strong historical associations with the former Hanoverian Party of Lower Saxony, and in addition to its mainly Protestant and conservative appeal, it sought also to provide a home for explicitly right-wing viewpoints. However, the DP failed to make a convincing entry at the federal level: although it presented lists in all the *Länder* in 1953, it won microscopic support outside its strongholds – in North Rhine-Westphalia only 80,000 votes compared with four million for the CDU. Perhaps the mistake of the German Party was to try to become a federal-wide party, instead of being a 'northern alternative' to the CDU. But for that purpose it had become too closely identified with the CDU in government. Its loyalty in coalition was rewarded by the CDU in 1953: although it then fell below the 5 per cent requirement, the DP won several constituency seats with the help of the CDU. The dependence effect thereafter became pronounced: helped over the hurdle again in 1957, the DP in the Bundestag split in 1960, the party's ministers joining the CDU, and the rump subsequently linking with the BHE to form the *Gesamt-Deutsche Partei*, in an unavailing effort to survive. In one sense, the demise of the German Party was inevitable, but a different strategy – a 'northern course' and one free of the coalition embrace – might have led to a different outcome.

The BHE, *Block der Heimatvertriebenen und Entrechteten*, had the clumsiest of titles ('League of those expelled from their homeland and those deprived of their rights') but the clear aim of representing the millions of expellees and refugees along with those supporters and active members of the Nazi regime who were 'deprived of their rights'. In brief, the BHE was out to garner the votes of all those with a grudge: unlike the CDU, the BHE was *par excellence* the party of non-integration. Not unexpectedly, a party like the BHE was ineligible to receive the reward of an allied licence, and it only contested elections from 1950 onwards, missing the 1949 federal election.

An indication of the BHE's initial attraction can be seen in the results of two *Land* elections: no less than 23.4 per cent of the vote for Schleswig-Holstein in 1950 and 14.9 per cent for Lower Saxony in 1951. The party had enormous potential support, for even without the radical right-wing vote there were some twelve million 'refugees' of one kind or another in Western Germany during the early 1950s. It was not a category which embraced scattered and isolated individuals. The 'expellees' in particular were largely concentrated in the reception *Länder* bordering on Eastern Germany, and the people from the 'lost provinces' had their own vigorous associations, the *Landsmannschaften*, which, although not committed to the BHE, provided a strong political infrastructure.

Yet the BHE, like the German Party, failed to make a successful federal breakthrough. Its vote of 5.9 per cent in 1953 cleared the electoral threshold, but it was a disappointing result and support in both Lower Saxony and Schleswig-Holstein was appreciably lower than a few years previously. The rapid waning of support for the BHE was surprising, for the party's insistence on 'the right of return' to the former homelands was a powerful appeal. But even as early as 1955 the assimilative powers of the West German state, the economic recovery and the CDU were becoming apparent. The attempt of the BHE to tap nationalist sentiment by adding '*Gesamt-deutscher Block*' to its already unwieldy title did not help, for the GB–BHE vote declined further to only 4.6 per cent in 1957 and was thus eliminated by the electoral law.

Like the German Party and the FDP, the BHE also experienced the strains of coalition with the CDU. In 1953 the BHE joined Adenauer's government, but the party was deeply divided over the Saar treaty with France; the result was a split in the party – and what became a familiar story: the party's ministers stayed with Adenauer, whilst the BHE went into opposition. Again, it can be argued, the party might have retained its cohesion had it not fallen into the attractive snare of coalition with the CDU. The belated fusion with the DP also failed in 1961, although that grouping, if it had come into being a decade earlier, might have withstood the CDU in the northern *Länder*.

The re-formed Centre Party presented a different kind of challenge to the CDU, within its home-base of North Rhine-Westphalia and in competition for the Catholic vote. If the CDU's 'religious compromise' had not held, the Centre would have benefited, as it would have done had Adenauer become unpopular within the party, since the Centre was opposed to his leadership. But the challenge from the Centre soon petered out. In 1953 it won only 0.8 per cent of the vote and, reduced to a client status, qualified only by gaining a constituency seat with the help of the CDU.

There was only one other party which threatened to dent the hegemony of Christian Democracy over the 'bourgeois' vote and that was a specifically regional force – the Bavarian Party. The BP was pitched against the sister party of the CDU in Bavaria, the *Christlich-Soziale Union*, itself a concession to the particularist outlook of Bavarian politics. The Bavarian Party had to fight against a CSU which was already well established; in 1946 the CSU won 58 per cent of the vote in the first of all the *Land* elections. Just how much the BP was a threat can be appreciated from the 1949 election – the CSU share slumped to 29.2 per cent in Bavaria, whilst the BP, competing for the first time, won 20.9 per cent, which represented 4.2 per cent of the federal vote.

It is difficult to avoid the impression that the electoral law change implemented for the 1953 election was deliberately aimed at excluding the Bavarian Party: by changing the threshold from a *Land* to a federal basis, the BP was dealt a serious blow. Whilst in 1953 it still had 9.2 per cent of the Bavarian vote, on a federal basis the proportion was only 1.7 per cent. The Bavarian Party then went into a slow decline, surviving in the obscurity of the Bavarian Landtag until 1966, when it was finally extinguished.

The final example of the fate of smaller parties, that of the KPD, was far removed from the influence of Christian Democracy and quite different factors explain its failure. The KPD was one of the early 'privileged' parties, and its voting potential was appreciable: prior to 1933 the KPD had won up to 17 per cent for the Reich as a whole; for the corresponding areas of Western Germany the proportion was rather lower. In the first series of *Länder* elections held from 1946 onwards the KPD appears to have maintained its position, obtaining around 10 per cent in several *Länder*, and in the most important *Land*, North Rhine-Westphalia, no less than 14 per cent in 1947. The slump began in 1949, the KPD only recording 5.7 per cent of the federal vote, and in North Rhine-Westphalia the party's share fell to almost half the 1947 result. That decline was of direct benefit to the SPD and it reflected the association of the KPD with the Soviet Union and the latter's policies in East Germany. By 1953 the KPD was unable to win 5 per cent of the vote in any of the *Länder*, whilst in 1949 it had done so in six. With only 2.2 per cent of the federal vote, the KPD was reduced to the status of a splinter party and had vanished as an electoral force long before 1956, when it was finally banned by the Constitutional Court.

With the demise of the minor parties, the imbalance in favour of the CDU reached its peak. We are left with the impression of inevitability, of the small right-wing parties circling the CDU as satellites, drawn into an ever-tightening orbit. But there were also a number of particular causes for their failure: there was no one overwhelming reason why a multi-party system should not have survived.

4 Transition
The end of CDU dominance was heralded by the loss of its absolute majority in 1961, but there were signs before that of a weakening

hold. They really concerned the position of Adenauer: his singular position of authority within the party was for long accepted, but there was a growing restiveness about the future.[7] Adenauer briefly toyed with the idea of standing as federal president in 1959; had he relinquished the chancellorship then, the problem of succession might have been resolved in good time, even though one may suspect that he would not have allowed a CDU incumbent much independent authority. His decision not to stand after all increased the unease, which became evident in CDU party conferences.

Adenauer's reputation suffered in the course of the crisis of August 1961, the occasion of the erection of the Berlin Wall, for the 'policy of strength' had failed, and the negative judgement of the electorate followed shortly after: the CDU vote dropped for the first time, whilst that of the SPD and the FDP rose. The gap between the two major parties was still large, but no longer totally unbridgeable, and the SPD was reaping the first harvest of the Godesberg Programme. The main point for the CDU was that, having lost its overall majority, a coalition partner – perhaps even a new chancellor – would have to be found. The situation was unprecedented for the CDU: a party coming into coalition would drive some hard bargains.

Two problems faced Adenauer. One was to make sure of his own re-election as chancellor, and the other was to secure a suitable coalition ally. He had to ensure that his own party and the CSU remained compliant, a requirement which could no longer be taken for granted. His position was made precarious by the stand which the FDP took after the election: a coalition with the CDU, but without Adenauer as chancellor. However, once Adenauer had united the CDU–CSU behind his candidature, the FDP found it difficult to refuse agreement, especially as Adenauer had engaged in informal talks with the SPD; a CDU–SPD coalition might threaten the existence of the Free Democrats by changing the electoral system. Nevertheless, the FDP did drive its tough bargain in the form of a coalition treaty, two aspects of which spelt out the end of CDU dominance. One stipulation was that Adenauer should resign before the end of the legislative period; the other was that a coalition committee should consider government proposals before they were brought to the cabinet, thus lessening the danger that FDP ministers could become detached from the party or that the party itself should be outmanoeuvred by the chancellor.

Coalition troubles intensified in 1962 in the course of the *Spiegel-*Affair, when the Free Democrats demanded the resignation of the

CSU defence minister, Franz-Josef Strauss, for his part in the arrest of the journal's editor on a charge of treason after the publication of details concerning NATO strategy.[8] Strauss's high-handed actions, which included bypassing the FDP minister of justice, eventually forced his departure, but not before the government coalition was set in disarray. The FDP only agreed to rejoin if Strauss was dismissed and a specific date was set for Adenauer's retirement.

Erhard was elected to replace Adenauer in October 1963. He proved to be the transitional leader within the era of transition. At the outset his credentials were impeccable. His name, forever associated in the public mind with the 'economic miracle', earned him the reputation of being *die Wahlkampflokomotive*, the CDU's vote-winning 'engine'. The FDP – rid at last of the devious Adenauer – was also happy to work with a chancellor with an economic philosophy identical to its own. The way seemed clear for an indefinite prolongation of the CDU–FDP alliance.

The 1965 election restored CDU fortunes, whilst the FDP lost some ground, but that slight reverse can hardly account fully for the party's subsequent tactics in withdrawing its ministers from Erhard's government, and even the worsening economic position in 1966 was not of itself a sufficient ground. Without FDP support Erhard was helpless, since he would not have been acceptable in a coalition with the SPD. Erhard's difficulties with his own party (brought to a head by losses in the North Rhine-Westphalia election in July 1966) sealed his fate. The luckless chancellor became caught up in a shift that was evidently taking place in the party system; he was the sacrificial victim. But his departure was the result of a serious miscalculation by the Free Democrats, who may have believed that the crisis they had engineered would increase their party's standing.

The Grand Coalition.   No love or thanks came from the CDU for the FDP's part in Erhard's fall. The action merely confirmed the view that the CDU should no longer be held to ransom by the smaller party. The Grand Coalition, for which the SPD had striven since 1961, was surprisingly easily formed, since it suited both parties. The SPD had the chance to prove itself in government, whilst for the CDU it was the most acceptable way of maintaining itself in office. Both parties managed to rationalise the coalition in the same terms: it was desirable, in the national interest, to accept a common responsibility for the grave financial and economic problems facing the country – that at least is how the dent in economic growth was regarded.

The SPD was content to serve under Kiesinger, minister-president of Baden-Württemberg, an urbane figure, who, whilst not quite a political lightweight, proved to be another interim chancellor. The SPD was well positioned, with Brandt serving as vice-chancellor and foreign minister, and there was no question of the two parties co-operating on anything less than equal terms. The FDP stand in 1961 had ushered in the new era. Confidence within the SPD ran high: the electoral benefits of the Godesberg reforms were shown conclusively by the 1965 election; the leadership of Brandt contrasted favourably with the paralysis which had gripped the CDU; and the new coalition was seen as a springboard for the future – not an arrangement which could severely compromise the party. Still, there were doubts and reservations, in the *Länder* and amongst the members of the parliamentary party. They showed their hostility in the election of Kiesinger which followed in December 1966: after allowing for the obviously negative vote of the FDP deputies in the secret ballot, it appears that up to 90 of the SPD Bundestag membership of 202 either voted against the chancellor or abstained.

There were many practical arguments in favour of the CDU–SPD coalition. The voting strength of the two parties, in the Bundesrat as well as the Bundestag, was sufficient to ensure that certain overdue legislation could be agreed and passed, especially where a two-thirds majority was needed to effect a constitutional change. Important reforms were initiated in the economic sphere, particularly the 1967 Law for the Promotion of Economic Stability and Growth, and the Party Law of 1967 showed a consensus between the parties on the question of party regulation and state financing. There were also more controversial matters, in particular the projected reform of the electoral system. Adenauer had attempted to make changes in the 1950s, and that had been one reason why the FDP left the coalition in 1956: 'reform' was a euphemism for making the system less proportional, for eliminating smaller parties, and it aimed at creating a two-party system through some adaptation of the relative-majority principle. With the FDP helpless in opposition, the opportunity for the CDU and SPD to reach an amicable agreement was present, until the SPD realised that the party might well find itself in a permanent minority.

Most controversy surrounded the enactment of the various

Emergency Laws. The Basic Law had been silent on the question of a state of emergency, since this matter had been in the area of powers reserved by the occupation authorities. Failure to secure inter-party agreement on the content of the constitutional amendment required meant that the debate dragged on inconclusively; with the formation of the Grand Coalition, however, the possibility of reaching a compromise was good. The need to have adequate safeguards was admitted by all, but attempts to spell out the precise provisions needed in case of war, civil strife or the breakdown of governmental authority for some other cause immediately evoked the memory of the use made in the Weimar Republic of Article 48, which was symbolic at least of the destruction of the parliamentary democracy and the institution of the 'legal' dictatorship.

Fears that the Emergency Laws would be used to attack the democratic order have proved unfounded, and they have not been used since being enacted in 1968; in fact the West German procedures have more safeguards than is the case for many other countries. But the strength of opposition, both within the Bundestag and without, showed the extent of the general unease. The FDP was joined by a large group of SPD deputies in voting against the legislation, and the trade unions waged their own campaign, fearing that their freedom and the right to strike would be impaired. A further source of opposition, and the most worrying, was that associated with the extra-parliamentary opposition, for the *Ausserparlamentarische* Opposition (APO) could pick on the emergency legislation to make its case against the repressive character of the Federal Republic and the ineptitude of parliamentary democracy.

It became increasingly evident to the coalition parties that there were serious drawbacks to their adopted style of government; any expectations that the Grand Coalition would become a political habit, on a par with the twenty-year 'permanent coalition' practised by the equivalent parties in Austria after 1945, were soon dispelled. For their part, the SPD leaders found increasing opposition in their own party, and this was expressed at the 1968 party conference, where a vote in favour of the coalition was passed only by 173 votes to 129. Beside the general causes for concern, legislation and government policies, there was the depressing fall in the SPD vote in *Länder* elections to consider during 1967, and in Bremen the left-wing German Peace Union (DFU) suddenly appeared to constitute a threat. A combination of the lukewarm response of the electorate to the SPD in coalition with the CDU and the possibility of extremist left-wing parties actually winning representation and outflanking the SPD whilst it governed with the CDU proved sufficient reason for insistence on a change of strategy.

The CDU did not face quite the same pressures, and its showing in *Länder* elections was notably better than that of the SPD. Nonetheless, the difficulties of holding the coalition together were apparent; one hope in 1966 had been that the two parties could develop a successful *Ostpolitik* in common, but as the principal initiatives failed, especially with the occupation of Czechoslovakia by the Soviet Union in 1968, so the differences of viewpoint on how to proceed became marked. But the CDU was also concerned at the threat to its position posed by right-wing extremism, a parallel to the outflanking movement feared by the SPD.

The rise and fall of the NPD.   The extreme right, dormant if not quite dead in the 1950s and early 1960s, flickered to life during the Grand Coalition. There has always been a multitude of right-wing splinter parties in the Federal Republic, but their electoral impact has been negligible. In 1949 the *Deutsche Rechts-Partei*, with 1.2 per cent of the federal vote, won five seats, with support strongest in Lower Saxony, one of the home bases of National Socialism. Its virtual successor, the *Sozialistische Reichs-Partei* (SRP), promised to make a far greater impact, with 11.0 per cent in the 1951 Lower Saxony *Land* election and 7.7 per cent in Bremen. Whether or not the SRP would have met the 5 per cent requirement in 1953 is difficult to say. The party was banned by the Constitutional Court in 1952, and another successor, the *Deutsche Reichs-Partei*, took only 1 per cent of the vote.

That record of impotence was maintained until the mid-1960s, when the NPD took over the running from a motley of right-wing groupings. The party won 2 per cent of the vote in the 1965 Bundestag election, but suddenly sprang into the public eye in 1966, winning seats in the Hesse and Bavarian *Landtage* – in Bavaria actually supplanting the FDP as the third largest party. From then on the NPD gathered strength, and the formation of the Grand Coalition increased its attraction for those who saw the CDU apparently moving to the left and who regarded the NPD as a way of making an oppositional protest. In 1967 the party won seats for the first time in Rhineland-Pfalz, Schleswig-Holstein, Lower Saxony and Bremen; in no case was its vote startling, but, at around 7 per cent in each *Land*, the NPD was set to become a federal force and the first 'new' one in opposition to the established party system. In 1968 the NPD gained its best result, with 9.8 per cent of the vote in Baden-Württemberg. That election was portentous, for the CDU and SPD were in coalition and it was the final *Land* election before the scheduled federal election in 1969. Both major parties lost ground in Baden-Württemberg (the SPD far more than the CDU), but whatever construction was put on the shift in voting support, it seemed a question not of whether the NPD would gain federal representation but of how many seats and whether the FDP would be relegated to fourth place. At all events, the rise of the NPD was the strongest reason for making an end to the Grand Coalition.

Speculations about a radical change in the party system were made idle by the unexpected failure of the NPD to maintain its growth or even live up to its achievements in *Länder* elections. The party's vote of 4.3 per cent in 1969 was insufficient to meet the electoral requirement, and thereafter it rapidly disintegrated. The critical forkway of the party system had been passed, leaving the three other contestants a clear field. It seems evident that the NPD vote was in large measure a form of reaction against the coalition: directly 'normal' party politics was restored and the CDU and SPD were openly competing for power once more, earlier trends reasserted themselves.

Judging by the fate of other smaller parties, the chances of a party making a comeback after it has fallen below the 5 per cent level are fairly slim. The evidence of history, joined with the failure of the NPD since 1969, implies that only new parties or movements are at all likely to threaten the supremacy of the existing parties.

5   The balanced party system

With the gains of the SPD in 1969 – and the losses of the CDU – the conditions for a balanced party system were almost fulfilled: a clear polarisation between two groupings and comparable chances for either to come to power. But the SPD was still a long way from being able to rule on its own account. For the transfer of power to be effected, a link between the SPD and the FDP had to be forged – the exploitation of the possibilities of the 'third side' of the coalition triangle.

In theory at least the two parties could have joined forces at any time after the 1961 election. Once the CDU–CSU lost its absolute majority, and with only three parties remaining, a coalition between the other two was feasible. But it was a majority which existed only on paper. The SPD was enamoured of a coalition with the CDU for obvious reasons: an alliance with the major party would give stable government and, equally important, the reward of 'respectability' for the SPD. Neither would be true in the case of a coalition with the Free Democrats, but even on the question of electing an SPD chancellor (by secret ballot) defections in the FDP were to be expected.

The truth was that well into the 1960s the natural ally of the FDP was the CDU. Despite the party's liberal, non-sectarian traditions and its concern with individual rights, the FDP was conservative in its social outlook, little inclined to engage in experimenting with the SPD. Only a fundamental change in the outlook of the Free Democrats could therefore translate a numerical majority of the two parties into a workable, progressive government.

Signs of change became evident in the period of the CDU–SPD coalition, and they emanated from the *Länder*. In 1966 the SPD almost won an outright majority in North Rhine-Westphalia, a 'test' election which speeded Erhard's decline. Later in the same year, the FDP switched from its coalition with the CDU and formed one with the SPD, a line-up which then ran counter to the Bonn coalition. That transfer, which proved to be exceptionally durable, was of major significance, since it took place in the largest of the *Länder*. The SPD and FDP had already been in coalition before in some smaller *Länder* (Bremen, Hamburg, the Saar) but without wider impact. The movement began to gather momentum. Thus in Baden-Württemberg, historically the home of progressive liberalism, the FDP broke with the CDU-led government, hoping to form a coalition with the SPD. At that time the SPD preferred to join with the CDU in order to cement the federal coalition, but the new stance of the FDP was confirmed in 1968, when both coalition parties lost support whilst the FDP gained.

The reorientation of the FDP in the *Länder* was symptomatic of the pressure to take a new course. At the 1968 party conference Walter Scheel was elected party chairman, representing the progressive wing, and there was also a changing current of opinion in favour of a more conciliatory *Ostpolitik*. The FDP was busily shedding its old image and becoming a party of reform. At the same time the SPD – in the wake of the Godesberg Programme – no longer appeared an impossible partner. There was even less cause for hesitancy once the CDU had taken the plunge. It was only necessary for the Free Democrats to convince the SPD that they were serious in their intentions.

Fairly conclusive evidence was provided by the presidential election held in March 1969. The decision of the FDP to support the SPD's candidate, Gustav Heinemann, in the *Bundesversammlung* was an earnest of good intent, but could the FDP actually deliver its vote? That question was important, since there was no real way of ensuring that the FDP *Länder* delegates to the *Bundesversammlung* – or, for that matter, its Bundestag delegation – would toe the party line in a secret vote. It was a searching test of the party's cohesion, but the FDP delegates held firm through to a third ballot and Heinemann was elected. The way was then open to the parties to form a governing coalition – if a majority could be found.

The result of the October 1969 election was hardly encouraging. Once more the SPD's vote rose, but support for the FDP dropped alarmingly to a mere 5.8 per cent. Yet at that stage the FDP could not afford to look back, neither to being once more in unrewarding opposition nor to acting as a prop for the jaded Christian Democrats.

An SPD–FDP coalition came into being under Brandt, but it had a minimal working majority: 254 seats in the Bundestag against 242 of the CDU–CSU opposition. Even that slender majority was whittled away as members of the FDP's old guard defected and crossed the floor to join the CDU, expressing their distaste with the new coalition and for Brandt's *Ostpolitik;* nor was the SPD itself immune. Nevertheless, the governing parties held together. They had sufficient common ground: Brandt's commitment to 'daring more democracy' aroused enthusiasm and was acceptable to the FDP since it remained at a safe level of generality. There was also the unifying effect of the *Ostpolitik:* not only was the momentum maintained, the *Ostpolitik* was the driving force behind the coalition from 1969 until 1972. The sheer force of the opposition's onslaught against the coalition prompted the SPD and the FDP to close ranks. They realised that disaster would befall them both if the alliance fell apart: a loss of credibility with the electorate would result and the CDU–CSU could be swept back to power for another decade.

In April 1972 the opposition sought to topple Brandt by using the constructive vote of no confidence. The move failed by just two votes, a measure of how far the government's initial majority had been eroded. Subsequently the government failed to carry its budgetary proposals, since the vote ended in a dead heat. A complete stalemate ensued: whilst the opposition was unable to bring down the government, the coalition had no majority for its essential measures.

An early dissolution of the Bundestag was the only remedy. The result of the November 1972 election vindicated the alliance: the coalition parties were returned with a comfortable working majority and for the first time in the Federal Republic the SPD became the largest party. The lingering traces of 'transition', still evident after the 'little' coalition had first come into being, were erased, and the lines in the party system were clearly drawn.

Electoral Connections

If their claims to be *Volksparteien* were to be interpreted literally, it would mean that the CDU and the SPD could count on support which corresponded to a complete cross-section of the electorate and that social variables had no special political relevance. That account would be fanciful: it is as difficult to imagine, say, steel workers in the Ruhr voting massively for the CDU as it is to visualise devout Catholics in deepest Bavaria rallying to the cause of Social Democracy.

Despite the substantial changes which have occurred in German society since the war, many traditional lines of social demarcation have persisted to give both parties fairly solid cores of unwavering support, and by the same token, both parties show corresponding areas of weakness as well. Therefore we should expect to see significant differences between the social composition of party voting, based on such factors as the extent and nature of religious adherence, differences in occupation and economic position, the effects of rural and urban environment and the extent of industrialisation. In addition, there are the demographic variables to be considered, which, even if not forces in their own right, have shown marked differences between the parties in the distribution of the vote according to age and sex. The resulting contrasts in the make-up of the parties' vote can be demonstrated clearly enough, but it is less easy to see how the weight of the various factors may change in the future.

Religious influences

We have to be on guard against treating the CDU as a 'religious' party, but Christian Democracy naturally looks to support from church members for the bedrock of its vote. At first, the mainstay was the Catholic vote, but later the strides made by the CDU in the 1950s – helped by the decline of parties like the BHE and the German Party, with a large Protestant component – gave a better religious balance to the party. The survival of the FDP, with its decided Protestant base, still ensures a Catholic bias in CDU support.

The Religious Composition of the *Länder* and CDU Support

	Population (millions)	Religious composition (%) Protestant	Catholic	CDU–CSU 1976 (%)
Baden-Württemberg	8.7	45.8	47.4	53.3
Bavaria	10.4	25.7	70.0	60.0
Bremen	0.8	82.3	10.1	32.5
Hamburg	1.8	73.6	8.1	35.9
Hesse	5.3	60.5	32.8	44.8
Lower Saxony	7.0	74.6	19.5	45.7
North Rhine-Westphalia	17.0	41.8	52.5	44.5
Rhineland-Palatinate	3.6	40.6	55.7	49.9
Saarland	1.1	24.1	73.8	46.2
Schleswig-Holstein	2.5	86.0	6.0	44.1
West Berlin	2.1	72.1	11.4	44.4*
Federal Republic	60.4	47.0	44.6	48.6

*West Berlin 1979 election.

The connection is important, but not all-determining. If it were, we should expect to find those *Länder* with a high Catholic population to be the ones with a dominant CDU vote – and only those ones. It is true for Bavaria, where some 70 per cent of the electorate is Catholic and the CSU has for years been in an unassailable position, but in the Saarland, where the proportion of Catholics is even higher, the CDU and the SPD obtained almost the same share of the vote in 1976. Some *Länder* are predominantly Protestant, but that does not necessarily mean that the CDU is weak. It is true of the city-states of Bremen and Hamburg, but in Schleswig-Holstein, where almost 90 per cent of the electorate is Protestant, the CDU won 50 per cent of the vote in the 1975 *Land* election.

Nonetheless, the Catholic connection provides the most convincing explanation for the CDU's cohesion and its strong representation in various social categories. Two reservations have to be made, however. In the first place, the fact of church membership need not of itself lead to a political orientation: it is rather the case that religious factors reinforce others – together they result in a disposition to support the CDU. The second reservation is that formal church membership is an unreliable guide (the formal position may be indicated by payments of the church tax, the *Kirchensteuer*) and that the significant distinction is between regular churchgoers and those members who attend irregularly or who have virtually lapsed; those who are regular in observance are much more likely to support the CDU than those who are not, as is evident from the table on page 123.

As one would expect, following the lines of Catholic adherence *and* regular churchgoing, the CDU fares best amongst the self-employed middle class, white-collar workers and pensioners who are also Catholic attenders. Not very surprisingly, the CDU comes off worst amongst ordinary workers who are not churchgoers. The party is also weaker in all industrial areas and the large cities, where we would expect religious ties and observance to be slacker than in smaller townships and rural communities. These variations are on the whole the ones typical of any party which is primarily 'bourgeois' in its orientation. But the CDU does manage to cut across other social affiliations to a degree: the party has a significant support amongst workers who, were it not for their church background, would probably be available for the SPD.

Yet the CDU is in no position to sit back and wait for the harvest of its 'Christian' support to be gathered in automatically. A general decline in religious observance has meant that the party relies on a narrower base than in the past. It also has to take account of the fact that the SPD has finally made its peace with organised religion as a consequence of the Godesberg Programme: there are few grounds – the issue of abortion law reform apart – which would prevent a devout Catholic from voting for the SPD. Most fundamentally, the CDU could lose the benefit of the close social fabric of which church membership is an integral part, an explanation, possibly, of why in the 1960s the CDU appeared to be becoming a more rural-based party.

That view proved to be premature. It was given support by the inroads made by the SPD in 1969 and, particularly, in 1972, but the resurgence of the CDU in 1976 showed that the religious influence was not rapidly declining. A feature of the 1976 election was the appearance of a so-called 'north-south gap', a term used to denote the disparity evident in the CDU–CSU performance: the gains predominated in the southern rather than the northern *Länder*. Strauss, whose CSU had done especially well in Bavaria, was quick to ascribe the difference to the robust anti-socialist campaign in southern Germany (by implication, thanks to his style and leadership). But the 'gap' is better related to the religious composition of the *Länder* involved: the CDU–CSU fared best in general where the Catholic population was greatest. An additional factor governing the swing to the CDU–CSU was the occupational distribution in given areas. In those districts where there was a high proportion both of Catholics and of salaried employees and public officials the SPD's losses to the CDU were largest; conversely, they were smallest in districts with a relatively small Catholic electorate and with a high proportion of blue-collar workers.

Changing social structure

The fundamental challenge facing all parties is the changing structure and growing mobility of West German society. As long as the old social structure, substantially that inherited from the time of the Weimar Republic, remained intact, the stereotypes of class politics were valid and the links of the parties with the various social groups were secure enough. But of all West European societies, Germany was perhaps the most open to the impact of rapid economic and industrial change, a susceptibility which was promoted by the changes wrought by National Socialism and increased by the dislocation of the German defeat.

In particular, the growth of the new middle classes, the more affluent and better educated white-collar workers, including the vastly expanded sector of public service employees, has made the traditional picture of a strictly defined class structure appear sadly anachronistic. Instead of the 'middle classes' having an almost residual status between the 'upper' and 'working' classes, it is rather those two which have had to give way before this large and rather amorphous grouping, the members of which have no roots in any social or political camp, and are firmly committed neither to Christian Democracy nor to Social Democracy. Both parties recognise the challenge – the response is after all inherent in their claim to be *Volksparteien* – but it is equally true that neither can expect to find a secure or exclusive anchorage within the new middle class, despite their claim to represent 'all' the people.

The secular growth of the SPD vote has been impressive – from under seven million in 1949 to over seventeen million at the high point of 1972. It may be treated partly as the consequence of a long-term structural improvement: the SPD was fulfilling its potential in the electorate, building on the 'natural' support which it could expect to find on the basis of traditional assumptions concerning the structure of society. That general scheme may be

leading the party to an electoral dead end. The best hope was to attach Social Democracy to the observable consequences of social change. It could reasonably be argued that what, from one point of view, was a new middle class was, from another, simply a different kind of working class, related to the old one in its background, different in its educational standard, material position and aspirations, but still recognisable. For the SPD to become a *Volkspartei* was an approximate reflex action to that evidence of social change. Yet we should not lose sight of the fact that the former appeal of Social Democracy was not forfeited or discarded overnight, nor perhaps ever completely obliterated. It is still the case that the SPD would be lost if it were unable to count on its traditional vote of the *Arbeiterpartei*, the industrial workers and above all members of trade unions. That connection remains as vital for the SPD as does the religious link for the CDU.

Nevertheless, over several decades the salient feature of SPD development has been the party's adoption by new occupational groups and its decreasing reliance on the vote of the manual worker, even though the latter has increased in absolute terms. Thus in the early 1950s manual workers accounted for some three-quarters of the SPD vote and white-collar employees for less than a fifth. By 1976 the manual worker share had fallen to a half, with the other half coming from the self-employed and the white-collar group. Even though there have been large changes in the composition of the labour force in the post-war years, the alteration in the SPD vote has far exceeded the general movement.

The problem for both parties is to retain proven loyalties at the same time as making a determined bid for a share of the new middle classes. Both the CDU and the SPD operate from secure electoral strongholds and yet hope to attract the middle ground which belongs to neither. Their hopes may not be entirely fulfilled. Throughout Western Europe there is evidence of a growing electoral fickleness, a volatility which takes the form of oscillations between the parties which may become almost mercurial in effect. That position has not been reached in the Federal Republic, and yet the success of the SPD in 1972 may be viewed in the light of this general mood. At the time, the rise in the party's vote was regarded as a continuation of the trend which had been evident for several years. But the sharp reverse in 1976 showed that a section of the electorate had only turned temporarily to the SPD. Whilst the 1972 election apparently allowed the SPD to make a further advance amongst Catholic voters, the swing back to the CDU in

1976 was most marked for this group. It is too early to be sure whether that kind of movement means the reassertion of old patterns or whether, in future elections, oscillations affecting various groups will become apparent.

Demographic variables
Differences in voting behaviour according to age and sex are said largely to represent a form of 'historical encapsulation', that is, they relate to the terms on which successive generations acquired their political loyalties; in particular they refer to the 'social connections' open to voters. In that sense, age and sex differences are mediating variables, but their effect can be important and in the past the CDU has probably benefited from the demographic structure of the West German population.

Traditionally the SPD has always been a male party. In the Weimar Republic the extension of the vote to women under the 1919 constitution was a real electoral handicap for the SPD, to the extent that one of its leaders complained: 'The women's vote has ruined the party!' By that he meant that the SPD would have been in a far better position with an all-male franchise. Other parties, the Centre Party, the German Nationalists and later the National Socialists, were much more successful in mobilising the female vote. The imbalance continued after the war, with the CDU as the main beneficiary. Whilst the SPD relied on its largely male, trade union base, the CDU gained the women's vote via the churches. The result was that the SPD fell far behind the CDU for every age group of female voters, whilst it was ahead for male voters in all groups except the oldest and the youngest.

A part of the 'historic' handicap of the SPD is reflected in the age distribution of the vote; the party did not attract increased support from the older age groups but simply continued at the Weimar level. In addition, in the early post-war years the age structure was weighted towards those groups; and since there was also a preponderance of women, the SPD lost out both ways. However, in the intervening period a process of equalisation has whittled down the CDU advantage. By 1972 the sex differences in party support had almost disappeared, and the SPD for the first time took the lead in its appeal for younger voters, both men and women.

That trend was brought to a sharp halt in 1976; in line with the 'return' of the Catholic vote to the CDU, other patterns were partly reasserted, so that new voters and women again favoured the party. But that movement was rather marginal: now that the basic shift has taken place, the SPD should be able to compete in future elections on roughly equal terms, and the actual outcome will be decided by the particular factors at the time. We should contrast Brandt's idealism and the promise of the *Ostpolitik* in 1972, say, with the difficulties of the coalition in 1976 and Helmut Schmidt's image of hard-headed realism – perhaps young voters found that combination less attractive.

The position of the Free Democrats

The CDU and the SPD are increasingly in competition with one another in the same areas of the electorate. Their vulnerability is evidenced by the possibility of 'direct exchange' between the two parties. But the chance of 'exchange' is increased by the existence of the FDP – a potential threat which has never been realised.

The weakness of the FDP (a characteristic of German liberalism throughout its history) has been that the party has never had a secure base of support, nor, with the strength of competition from the two major parties, has it been able to make the transition to being a *Volkspartei* in miniature. To that long-term problem should be added the difficulties resulting from its change of course in the process of acquiring the attributes of a 'new' party, completed in 1969, and especially noticeable in the changing composition of the party's electorate. In the 1950s and early 1960s the FDP was favoured by the farmers, the self-employed and Protestants; the catastrophic fall in the party's vote in 1969 indicated a decline in support from those groups, which has continued subsequently. Instead, the FDP has moved out of the rural areas towards the cities and has come to rely on the white-collar vote, which now accounts for about two-thirds of its support.

The problems caused by the transition go some way in accounting for the continuing unrealised potential of the FDP: the consequences of the change had first to be digested. Yet there is little indication that in the period after 1969 an era of long-term growth commenced. The party's vote rose gratifyingly in 1972, but sober analysis showed that the increase could be largely explained by the practice of widespread 'ticket-splitting' on the part of SPD supporters, who were anxious that the FDP should not disappear below the 5 per cent barrier. In 1976 that practice was not followed to any great extent. Nor did the fall in the SPD's vote in 1976 mean that the FDP benefited: one hope had been that discontented SPD voters would turn to the FDP (as the lesser evil) rather than to the CDU, but the swing was preponderantly to the CDU.

The failure of the Free Democrats to achieve a breakthrough in their new, progressive guise is somewhat puzzling. In theory, their 'modernity' should be an attraction. The party's appeal, as shown by the social composition of support (urban, white-collar, younger voters) is in line with trends in West German society, yet the party exercises a very diffuse attraction, lacks a distinctive programme and suffers from the absence of a loyal core vote. In consequence, the FDP may be in danger of becoming an electoral staging-post, an agent of exchange between the two large parties, with a high turnover in supporters from one election to another.

These problems are compounded by others. They centre on the FDP's dilemma in relation to government: painfully the FDP has learned that coalition constancy is important if the party is to escape the reputation of being an *Umfallpartei*, too inclined to go back on its commitments to other parties. But in soldiering on loyally with the SPD, the FDP has failed to project a sufficiently independent image to the electorate. There is evidence – seen in the *Länder* elections held during 1978 – that the material for a progressive movement of protest does exist in the Federal Republic, but the FDP has been so far unable to make that cause its own.

Party membership
Traditionally, German parties have been 'membership parties', that is, they have had a fairly high proportion of members to voters, a feature evident in a party of 'democratic integration' such as the SPD, but also conspicuous in the NSDAP, a party of 'total integration'. That tradition was revived in the early post-war years, when all the re-established democratic parties experienced a large influx of members – a sign that the 'instrumental' relationship with politics did not apply to all sections of the population.

Despite some lack of reliability in the figures given – parties are prone to be optimistic or cagey in revealing their true position – the broad movements are clearly discernible. The initial enthusiasm evident before the founding of the Republic was replaced by a waning involvement, partly disguised in the early 1960s by the growth in the size of the electorate, from thirty-one million in 1949 to thirty-eight million in 1965. A remarkable surge occurred in the early 1970s, prompted by enthusiasm for Brandt and the SPD on the one hand, and by the polarising tendencies of the CDU–CSU on the other. But whilst the SPD experienced a cooling-off, notable in the change of chancellor from Brandt to Schmidt and the loss of reform momentum, the CDU succeeded in doubling its membership within a decade.

Estimates of Party Membership, 1947–1977

	1947–8 '000	1950 '000	1955 '000	1960 '000	1965 '000	1970 '000	1975 '000	1977 '000
SPD	880	680	600	650	680	800	965	980
CDU	400	265	230	270	285	300	546	650
CSU	90				100	118	122	140
FDP		80			90	56	74	79

Note
Estimates from various party sources. The figures are more reliable for later years.

The changing total figures of party membership only reveal a part of the alterations that have taken place. This is particularly true for the SPD. On balance the SPD has been able to maintain its reputation as the leading membership party, but its social composition has changed radically. In 1930 some 60 per cent of SPD members belonged in the conventional category of *Arbeiter* (manual workers), and after the war they still formed 50 per cent, yet in the 1970s the proportion had fallen to a quarter. The massive entry which took place in the early 1970s accelerated the change towards the young, well educated, new middle class.

The new element in the party was not any the less radical for its different social background. On the contrary, the arrival of the new members, which caused a drop in average age, was accompanied by increased activism, especially within the *Jung-sozialisten*. That shift destroyed the old image of a typical, rather staid party member, whose highest ambition might be to become the local party treasurer. A disjunction became evident between the basis of the SPD's electoral following and the trend of membership; there was a danger, therefore, of the SPD losing its organic connection with the working class. Just as the change in voting support for the party has taken place faster than that in occupational distribution in the Federal Republic, so the composition of membership has altered more rapidly than the nature of the SPD vote. Increasingly all three parties attract members who belong to one or other branch of the public service; a common end point would be for them all to become parties of salaried officials rather than *Volksparteien*.

The Occupations of Party Members

	SPD (1973)		CDU (1973)	CSU (1975)	FDP (1971)
			% of total membership		
Manual workers	26	(45)	11	15	5
White-collar and civil servants	31	(22)	39	33	53
Independent	5	(14)	28	34	31
Pensioners	13		6	8	
Housewives	10		8	4	
Students and		(19)			11
apprentices	7		5	4	
Other	8		3	2	

Notes
'Independent' includes the professions, self-employed and farming.
For the SPD the figures in brackets are the corresponding percentages for 1952.
For all parties, especially the SPD, the student category has become important since the 1960s; the lowering of the voting age to 18 in 1972 has also had an effect.
Sources: H. W. Schmollinger, 'Abhängig Beschäftigte in Parteien der Bundesrepublik', *Zeitschrift für Parlamentsfragen*, 1974/1. M.-C. Zauzich, *Von der Weltanschauungspartei zur Volkspartei*, Munich, 1976.

The extrapolation may be too extreme, and it may be better to emphasise the democratic support which a high level of party membership supplies. For the SPD the commitment is fairly strong when account is taken of the substantial party dues asked of members, a sliding scale based on personal income. It is also significant that the parties regard a large membership as important, despite the fact that the financing of the parties by the state really lessens their dependence on their members in this respect, since only the size of the vote accruing to a party determines its level of subsidy. Those parties qualify which receive as little as 0.5 per cent of the federal vote. The total amounts involved, calculated at 3.50 DM per vote, are sufficiently large to detract from the importance of contributions made by members. Thus for the 1976 election no less than 147 million DM was allocated for the state financing of the parties.[9]

Effects of the electoral system
The West German electoral system combines the principle of proportionality with the relative-majority system of single-member constituencies as used in Britain. In that sense it is a 'mixed' system, although the mixture is more apparent than real. The seats in the Bundestag are made up half by 'constituency' seats and half from the party lists, 248 each and 496 in all. The *Länder* are each

allocated a number of seats in proportion to the total vote recorded in the *Land*, so that the basis of election is the *Land* rather than the Federal Republic as a whole.

In accordance with the mixed system, each voter has two votes, one for the direct constituency election and a second, the *Zweitstimme*, for the competing party lists presented in the *Länder*. The parties compete with one another both in the constituencies and through their party lists, and they may win seats by either or both methods – hence the apparent mixture. In fact, however, within the *Land* the final allocation of seats to a party *depends entirely on the size of its list vote*. The decisive vote is the *Zweitstimme*, not that in the constituency. Thus the number of seats a party wins outright in the constituencies is *deducted* from its share of the total allocation of seats to the *Land*. That share is determined by the size of the party's list vote and hence is calculated on a purely proportional basis.[10]

On occasion it has happened that a party has managed to win a greater number of constituency seats in a *Land* than the size of its list vote indicates. In that case the party retains the 'excess seats', the so-called *Überhangmandate*; the allocation of seats to the *Land* is duly increased and so ultimately is the size of the Bundestag itself. That is a rather rare occurrence. Usually a party's *Land* representation is made up partly of constituency deputies and partly of those successful on its list. On the other hand, the FDP has to rely entirely on representation from the party list because it has no chance at all of coming ahead of the major parties in the constituencies.

There are no substantial differences involved either way: the deputies in the Bundestag merely have a different origin, and there is nothing to prevent a candidate on the party list from contesting a constituency seat at the same time. The distinction is even less marked if a constituency seat falls vacant during the legislative term: instead of a by-election, the seat is filled by the 'holding' party from further down its party list. The very large size of the constituencies means that they tend to stay the preserve of either the SPD or CDU. If it should happen that, say, the CDU wins a constituency seat from the SPD, then the net result – providing their list votes remain constant – will only be that the CDU will have one more constituency seat and one fewer list seat, whilst the SPD will gain an additional list seat in compensation for the loss of the direct one.

The purpose of introducing the mixed electoral system was to

The 1976 Election: The Distribution of Seats and the Party Vote in the *Länder*

	CDU–CSU % Zweit-stimmen	CDU–CSU Seats Constituency	CDU–CSU Seats List	CDU–CSU Seats Total	SPD % Zweit-stimmen	SPD Seats Constituency	SPD Seats List	SPD Seats Total	FDP % Zweit-stimmen	FDP Seats List	Total *Land* seats
Baden-Württemberg	(53.3)	32	6	38	(36.6)	4	22	26	(9.1)	7	71
Bavaria	(60.0)	40	13	53	(32.8)	4	25	29	(6.2)	6	88
Bremen	(32.5)	—	2	2	(54.0)	3	—	3	(11.8)		5
Hamburg	(35.9)	—	5	5	(52.6)	8	—	8	(10.2)	1	14
Hesse	(44.8)	5	16	21	(45.7)	17	5	22	(8.5)	4	47
Lower Saxony	(45.7)	12	16	28	(45.7)	18	11	29	(7.9)	5	62
North Rhine-Westphalia	(44.5)	28	38	66	(46.9)	45	25	70	(7.8)	12	148
Rhineland-Palatinate	(49.9)	10	6	16	(41.7)	6	7	13	(7.6)	2	31
Saarland	(46.2)	2	2	4	(46.1)	3	1	4	(6.6)	—	8
Schleswig-Holstein	(44.1)	5	5	10	(46.4)	6	4	10	(8.8)	2	22
Federal totals	(48.6)	134	109	243	(42.6)	114	100	214	(7.9)	39	496

Note

Allocation of seats to *Länder* (the final column in table) depends ultimately on the share of the total federal vote each has. The distribution of seats to parties follows the d'Hondt system of proportional representation. Party candidates are nominated exclusively by the *Länder* parties, not federally. The 1967 Party Law controls the process of selection, requiring an elected constituency selection committee (or secret ballot of party members), and – in the case of *Land* party lists – the holding of representative party conventions which determine adoption and the critical 'ordering' of candidates on the lists.

reduce the anonymity associated with pure list systems; the West German compromise can be termed 'personalised' proportional representation. But it is doubtful whether the complex arrangement has been justified: a constituency deputy does not enjoy the same responsibility and prestige as his American or British counterparts. Nor has the introduction of the two-vote system given the electorate very much flexibility of choice in practice.

The overwhelming majority of the electorate gives both its first and second votes to the same party. There is an apparent tactical benefit in vote splitting, which shows some sophistication. In 1972 many SPD voters, in a bid to ensure that the FDP gained representation, gave the SPD candidate their first vote and the FDP list their second, whilst many FDP supporters adopted the reverse procedure. A moment's reflection, however, will show that the ploy was misguided – at least as far as the SPD was concerned. Since it is a party's list vote which counts in deciding the number of seats won, the FDP undoubtedly benefited, but only at the expense of the SPD. It is conceivable that a massive collusion between two parties in one of the smaller *Länder*, especially through the winning of the *Überhangmandate* by one party, could distort the proportional principle to the detriment of a third party, but the possibility of overt manipulation is not a recommendation for an electoral system.

More important breaches of the proportional principle are the threshold requirements: in 1949, 5 per cent of the vote in one *Land*, or one constituency seat; in 1953, 5 per cent of the federal vote; and since 1957 the alternative of three constituency seats. The Bavarian Party, excluded by the 1953 provision, appealed in vain to the Constitutional Court against the double standard involved – a federal threshold but a *Land* allocation of seats. The barrier imposed by the alternative of winning three constituency seats is formidable: the chance of a new, independent party winning any of the large constituencies is extremely remote. The provision is mainly of use to a large party planning to rescue a small one by standing down in its favour in a number of constituencies, the form of client patronage which the CDU employed to keep the German Party in the Bundestag in 1953 and 1957.

Potential for new movements?

Undoubtedly the electoral law does have an effect on the rise of new parties, and it may hasten the decline of others. The latter consequence may have been applicable to the BHE after 1957 (4.6

per cent) and to the NPD after 1969 (4.3 per cent): erstwhile supporters may not wish to risk wasting their votes. Yet it is difficult to believe that the restrictions are sufficiently daunting to hinder the rise of a vigorous new movement or ultimately to prevent the fragmentation of the party system.

It is perhaps more relevant to point to the fact that in 1976 some 99 per cent of the federal vote went to the three established parties with a rate of participation well above 90 per cent. If dissatisfaction with the present parties were to be shown, a challenge would almost certainly first have to come through the *Länder*, where a new party does not face the problems of federal organisation and can exploit local issues. (Even so, the *Länder* also impose their own thresholds on the proportional system, so that minute splinter parties are relatively no better off.) The course taken by the NPD in the late 1960s would represent a typical pattern: a footing in several *Land* assemblies, followed by a determined federal challenge.

The rise of the ecological movement is indicative of the possibilities, and handicaps, facing a new party. The origins of the ecological movement in Germany lay primarily in the widespread protest against the nuclear energy policy and, in particular, against the siting of certain nuclear power stations. *Länder* politics provided a natural focus and forum for the protest. The impetus for the movement did not come from this source alone: a feature of West German society over the past decade has been the greater sense of involvement with local issues which has led to a mushrooming of multifarious *Bürgerinitiativen*, citizens' action groups. Their activity – specific and local – is an indication of a changing relationship with politics and at the same time constitutes a partial rejection of the 'normal' channels provided by party politics.[11]

The ecological movement represents a novel form of politicisation which takes the form of 'the environment versus the economy', and as such it does not fit into the framework of conventional politics. Various groupings coalesced in 1978 to contest local and *Länder* elections with some initial impact: 'Green Lists' were presented in Hamburg (1.0 per cent) and Lower Saxony (3.9 per cent) and a 'Coloured List' (*Bunte Liste*) in Hamburg (3.5 per cent). Their effect was scarcely cataclysmic, but it was sufficient in both *Länder* to rob the FDP of votes and bring about its exclusion from the *Land* assemblies.[12]

It is an open question whether the 'green', 'coloured' or 'alternative' groups are likely to become established in the *Länder*, let alone be able to use them as a springboard for a federal entry. Their advantage is that they can make an appeal to supporters of all other parties, but there is also a diffusion of viewpoint which acts as a disadvantage. As long as the movement is able to avoid being placed somewhere on the left–right continuum, its chances of survival will be enhanced, but the difficulties of attracting a large protest vote at federal elections are considerable.

Attention paid to the ecological movement is admittedly out of proportion to its actual or potential influence. But the example is the only relevant one in default of others. Neither the forces of left- or right-wing extremism nor those of regional loyalties at present appear to offer a serious alternative to the dominant parties.

Notes and References

1. The preceding formulation is broadly that outlined by Otto Kirchheimer in 'The Transformation of Western European Party Systems', in J. LaPalombara and M. Weiner (eds.), *Political Parties and Political Development*, Princeton University Press, 1969. See also, F. S. Burin and K. L. Shell, *Politics, Law and Social Change: Selected Essays on Otto Kirchheimer*, Columbia University Press, 1969.
2. Kirchheimer applied his standpoint to the SPD: 'Germany: The Vanishing Opposition', in R. A. Dahl (ed.), *Political Oppositions in Western Democracies*, Yale University Press, 1968. More generally: 'The Waning of Opposition in Parliamentary Regimes' in Dogan and Rose, op. cit.
3. For the early development of the CDU, see A. J. Heidenheimer, *Adenauer and the CDU: The Rise of the Leader and the Integration of the Party*, The Hague: Martinus Nijhoff, 1960.
4. In May 1979 Kohl stepped down as chancellor candidate in favour of Ernst Albrecht, minister-president of Lower Saxony, a tactical move hastened by Strauss's bid for the CDU–CSU candidature. But in July 1979 Strauss won the vital support of the CDU–CSU Bundestag *Fraktion* with 135 votes to 102 for Albrecht. Since the CSU had only 53 of the 243 CDU–CSU deputies, Strauss won substantial CDU support.
5. In fact, the SPD 'gained' somewhat in potential support by the division of Germany. The equivalent area of 'Western Germany' in the election year of 1928 showed a higher proportion of SPD voters than in the remainder of Germany. On the same measure, the KPD lost more of its voting base. See G. Loewenberg, 'The Development of the German Party System' in Cerny, op. cit., p. 7.
6. The most bitter struggle against the merger with the KPD took place in Berlin. See K.-P. Schulz, *Auftakt zum kalten Krieg: Der Freiheitskampf der SPD in Berlin, 1945–6*, Berlin: Colloquium Verlag, 1965. On the Soviet Occupation, J. P. Nettl, *The Eastern Zone and Soviet Policy in Germany, 1945–50*, Oxford University Press, 1951.
7. The unease and uncertainty concerning the CDU's position after Adenauer's departure is well reflected in R. Altmann, *Das Erbe Adenauers*, Stuttgart: Seewald Verlag, 1960.
8. The 'Spiegel Affair' was only one event in a continuing controversy on the

political and other aspects of Strauss's career. The most provocative treatment in W. Roth (and others), *Schwarzbuch: Franz Josef Strauss*, Cologne: Kiepenheuer und Witsch, 1972.

9. For a brief account of the legal position concerning party financing, see K. Sontheimer, 'The Funding of Political Parties in West Germany', *Political Quarterly*, September 1974. See also, W. Hoffmann, *Die Finanzen der Parteien*, Munich, 1973.

10. For more detailed accounts of the electoral system see T. Burkett, *Parties and Elections in West Germany*, C. Hurst, 1975; U. Kitzinger, *German Electoral Politics*, Oxford University Press, 1960; S. E. Finer (ed.), *Adversary Politics and Electoral Reform*, Anthony Wigram, 1975; D. P. Conradt, 'Electoral Law Politics in West Germany', *Political Studies*, September 1970.

11. An excellent discussion of the role of the *Bürgerinitiativen* as a challenge to the party and parliamentary system is provided by B. Guggenberger and U. Kempf (eds.), *Bürgerinitiativen und repräsentatives System*, Opladen: Westdeutscher Verlag, 1978. (Bibliography.)

12. For an assessment, see G. Pridham, 'Ecologists in Politics: The West German Case', *Parliamentary Affairs*, Autumn 1978.

Further Reading

K. von Beyme and M. Kaase (eds.), *Elections and Parties: Socio-Political Change in the West German Federal Election of 1976*, Sage Publications, 1979.

T. Burkett, *Parties and Elections in West Germany*, C. Hurst, 1975.

K. H. Cerny (ed.), *Germany at the Polls: The Bundestag Election of 1976*, Washington: American Enterprise Institute, 1978.

D. Chalmers, *The Social Democratic Party of Germany*, Yale University Press, 1964.

S. L. Fisher, *The Minor Parties of the Federal Republic of Germany*, The Hague: Martinus Nijhoff, 1974.

O. Flechtheim (ed.), *Die Parteien in der Bundesrepublik Deutschland*, Hamburg: Hoffmann und Campe, 1973.

W. Graf, *The German Left since 1945*, Cambridge: Oleander Press, 1976.

H. Grebing, *History of the German Labour Movement*, Oswald Woolf, 1969.

M. Greiffenhagen (ed.), *Demokratisierung in Staat und Gesellschaft*, Munich: Piper, 1973.

R. Irving and W. Paterson, 'The West German General Election of 1976', *Parliamentary Affairs*, Spring 1977.

W. Kaltefleiter, *Vorspiel zum Wechsel. Eine Analyse der Bundestagswahl 1976*, Berlin: Duncker und Humblot, 1977.

H. Kaack, *Geschichte und Struktur des deutschen Parteiensystems*, Opladen: Westdeutscher Verlag, 1971.

W. Paterson, 'The German Social Democratic Party' in W. Paterson and A. H. Thomas (eds.), *Social Democratic Parties in Western Europe*, Croom Helm, 1977.

G. Pridham, *Christian Democracy in Western Germany*, Croom Helm, 1977.

H. K. Schellenger, *The SPD in the Bonn Republic*, The Hague: Martinus Nijhoff, 1968.

D. Staritz (ed.), *Das Parteiensystem der Bundesrepublik*, Opladen: Leske und Budrich, 1976.

4 Coalition and Opposition

The Rules of Coalition

A governing imperative

The fragmentation of the party system in the Weimar Republic made it difficult to maintain lasting coalitions. No sooner was one formed than one or other of the partners would find a pretext for leaving. Coalitions were temporary marriages of convenience and governments were always expendable. The parties were intent on preserving their own interests and position, and those could be just as well served in opposition. They were free to determine the form their opposition took in their own way, showing either hostility to the government of the day or antagonism to the whole republican system.

In contrast, the parties in the Federal Republic share a strong governing orientation. The CDU was in office continuously for twenty years from 1949, the SPD for well over a decade since 1966, whilst the FDP's total period of participation exceeds even that of the CDU. Only once has the Bundestag been dissolved before the completion of a four-year term, and the cause was the 'hung' parliament of 1972, not government instability. The long service of Adenauer as chancellor doubtless makes the average term of the head of government – around six years – a little misleading but it is still an impressive index of government stability. Also to be taken into account is the high degree of continuity from one government to another: all the changes have been 'partial', in the sense that a new coalition has always had one of the parties from the previous government. Bonn is not only unlike Weimar, it is also quite unlike the vast majority of other West European states.[1]

The inclination of the parties towards government is typical of those which lack a strong ideological base. Without such a base, there is no strong objection to sharing a coalition with other parties and it is difficult to find good reasons for leaving. If they are in opposition, parties are unable to propound radical alternatives and instead have to wait for the government to make mistakes, whilst trying to show that they could manage things marginally better. That is a weak position, so that each party has constantly to aim at entering government, to try to impose its own coalition formula and avoid antagonising potential allies. That picture applies to many party systems, but not to the extent true of the Federal Republic for the past twenty or so years.

Perhaps the experience of the FDP is a partial exception, for if the party has a proclivity for government, it has also been tempted on occasion to leave coalitions of its own accord. Yet the results of making a stand – always against the CDU – have never been encouraging. Withdrawal in 1956 led to a split in the party and to a fall in its vote the following year. Standing up to Adenauer in 1962, forcing his retirement and the resignation of Strauss, brought no benefit in the 1965 election. The desertion of Erhard's government in 1966 led directly to the formation of the Grand Coalition, and the FDP had to serve out a spell in lonely opposition. It was a poor reward for the party to receive a million fewer votes in 1969 than it had in 1965. The problems of the FDP are peculiar to all small 'third' parties, but of all the strategies the FDP can follow, the march into opposition seems the least desirable: survival depends on participation in government.

The SPD took some time to adjust to the governing imperative, content at the outset to be the forceful, democratic opposition. But it also found opposition unfruitful, and from the late 1950s dedicated itself to the strategy of *Annäherung* to the CDU: coalition without Adenauer if possible but with him as chancellor if necessary. Once the prize had been awarded, the SPD showed equal dedication to the cause of remaining in office, despite the fact that the party's chances of furthering 'democratic socialism' with either the CDU or the FDP were non-existent. The question of whether the SPD should regenerate itself in opposition and oppose the policies of the other parties with its own is not treated as a matter for serious discussion – nor can it be if the party has no ideological base.

There are similarities in the outlook of the CDU and the SPD, but their experience has been fundamentally different through their reversed sequence of opposition and government. Whilst the SPD had to come to terms with government, the CDU was that government for an extraordinarily long period – it had to come to terms with opposition. Moreover, the SPD's opposition took place when the party itself was changing, but the CDU started in opposition after the parties had reached a common position; the strategy of *Annäherung* was simply not applicable in the new type of party system.

The perspectives of the three parties therefore differ considerably, but they all point towards the same objective. Once a government has been formed, there is a strong presumption that it will continue in being until the balance of party strength alters decisively. This rule of coalition owes its force to the outlook of the parties, but it is reinforced by what we can term the 'elective function' of the Bundestag.

Chancellors and Coalitions in the Federal Republic

September 1949	Adenauer I	CDU–CSU, FDP, DP
October 1953	Adenauer II	CDU–CSU, FDP/FVP[1], DP, BHE[2]
October 1957	Adenauer III	CDU–CSU, DP[3]
November 1961	Adenauer IV	CDU–CSU, FDP[4]
October 1963	Erhard I	CDU–CSU, FDP
October 1965	Erhard II	CDU–CSU, FDP[5]
December 1966	Kiesinger	CDU–CSU, SPD
October 1969	Brandt I	SPD, FDP
December 1972	Brandt II	SPD, FDP
May 1974	Schmidt I	SPD, FDP
December 1976	Schmidt II	SPD, FDP

Notes
1. The FDP split in February 1956: a splinter group, later the FVP, stayed in the coalition, whilst the FDP went into opposition.
2. The BHE left the coalition in October 1955, the party's ministers remaining in government.
3. The DP split in July 1960; the major part of Bundestag party joined the CDU.
4. Temporary withdrawal of the FDP from coalition in November 1962.
5. FDP left the coalition in October 1966.

The changing elective function

Basic to a parliamentary system is the power of the elected assembly to make and break governments. In the Federal Republic the system of electing the chancellor through the Bundestag and the means of securing his replacement ensure the assembly's inalienable power. But the static constitutional position has had to be adjusted to the changing political reality. The elective function gives the parties the freedom to decide amongst themselves on the life and composition of governments, but that ideal interpretation has to be modified in practice by the operation of the party system.[2]

In a flourishing multi-party system the outcome of an election can rarely be predicted in detail beforehand. Parties, and particularly their leaders, have to have plenty of room for manoeuvre. Once the election is over, the compromises necessary for coalition-building begin and an apparently unlikely governing combination may result. That situation certainly applied in the Weimar Republic, and seemingly in 1949, although most of the action took place within the CDU. As the CDU later moved to a position of dominance, the flexibility of the parties was lost, since it was mainly a question of which party or parties the CDU would favour. However, the freedom of action of those coalition partners was unaffected. The BHE in 1955, the FDP in 1956 and the German Party in 1960 all demonstrated that they were not 'tied' to coalition. Their departure, however, did not affect the stability of the government. The later withdrawals by the FDP in 1962 and 1966 had much more drastic consequences in robbing the government of its majority.

Parties, in fact, retained their freedom. They could do so with the justification that the government's policies were wrong or harmful to their interests, and no binding commitments were broken by a decision to leave the government. The flexibility was almost completely restored after the election of 1961, when the CDU–CSU lost its absolute majority. Adenauer deliberately floated the idea of a coalition with the SPD in order to put pressure on the Free Democrats, and eventually the FDP came round, even though the FDP had made an election pledge that the party would not serve under Adenauer.

A somewhat similar mood of uncertainty shrouded the election of 1965. During the campaign no authoritative view emerged from the parties on what kind of coalition would, or should, transpire. Chancellor Erhard favoured a continuation of the alliance with the FDP, but his view was only one: there were important voices in his party openly advocating the experiment of a coalition with the SPD. President Lübke's intervention during the campaign illustrates just how little electoral opinion was a factor in determining the coalition: he asked that the parties should preserve 'maximum

flexibility' on the question of the composition of the new government. The tradition was continued in the events leading to the
formation of the Grand Coalition. Even though the switch took
place in the middle of the legislative term, and the change of
course was fairly momentous, none of the party leaders concerned
in the negotiations thought that anything untoward was involved.
The electorate was only concerned with electing parties, not
governments.

A marked change occurred as the move to a balanced system
took place, or rather, the change made the balance apparent.
Even before the 1969 campaign began, Brandt and Scheel had
arrived at an understanding that their parties would join in coalition
if a majority was forthcoming. Their agreement was common
knowledge, and it followed naturally from the successful alliance
to secure the election of President Heinemann. Anyone voting for
either the SPD or the FDP could be reasonably sure of what kind
of government he wanted and what kind of government would
result. But even at that stage the agreement was an understanding,
not an explicit undertaking to the electorate.

Later, in 1972, the attempt by the CDU to unseat Brandt in
mid-term and replace him by its own nominee, Rainer Barzel, was
an echo of the independent elective function of the Bundestag.
But it was indicative of changing popular attitudes that the action
by the CDU – whatever its political and constitutional justification
– sparked off widespread public protest: the verdict on the government, it was implied, belonged to the electorate, not the parliamentary opposition. The 1972 election had not just been a choice
of party, but a choice of government.

That interpretation also creates problems. The West German
system does not easily allow a reference back to the electorate.
In contrast, say, with the British practice, by which the prime
minister can go to the country when he wants by having a free
hand to call an election, the German chancellor has little power in
the matter. He has to sit it out. According to Article 68, a
chancellor is only able to request the president for a dissolution if
the government has first failed to win its own motion of confidence
in the Bundestag. Even then, the president need not accede if he
thinks there is a chance of a successor to the chancellor being
found, and it is still open for the Bundestag to elect a new
chancellor before the dissolution takes effect. In 1972 a stratagem
had to be devised to secure a dissolution: the government ensured
its defeat on its own motion of confidence. The opposition duly

voted against the government, the coalition parties in favour, whilst the government's ministers abstained.

Apparently, as this roundabout method illustrates, the Basic Law is geared to maintaining the elective function within the Bundestag. But in another way the constitution can be seen actually to reinforce the electoral position according to the new rules of coalition. What, then, are these new rules? In the first place, they require the parties to make their coalition intentions explicit before an election is held: the expressed intentions therefore become an integral part of the election campaign. Secondly, they require those intentions to be treated as binding commitments, not only at the stage of the initial formation of the government but for the whole legislative term. It follows also that the parties will conclude an informal (or even a formal) coalition pact establishing the guidelines of government policy.

These rules fit with the constitutional expectation that a chancellor is elected for the whole life of a Bundestag, so that the combined effect of the change in the party system and the emphasis of the Basic Law strengthens the connection of the electorate with the government and weakens the independent elective power of the parties. The institution of the 'chancellor candidate' supplies an additional direct link.

How unambiguously the new rules have been applied is evident from the relatively short experience of the balanced system. Prior to both the 1972 and the 1976 elections the SPD and FDP pledged themselves to continuing the coalition behind the SPD chancellor (Brandt in 1972 and Schmidt in 1976). Nor was the CDU–CSU at all able to pursue a policy of infiltration on either occasion. Of equal importance is the fact that the coalition has been highly stable, with no hint that it might break up between elections. The explanation may be partly political: the FDP feels a compatibility with the SPD, while its relationship with the CDU is uneasy. Yet it is also true that the conditions facing the FDP have altered: the rules have modified party behaviour.

The consequences for opposition

It is too early to judge how the parties may be affected by these changes when they are in opposition, and it is at least conceivable that the rules could be broken: a particular government crisis may lead to one or other of the parties in the coalition walking out, in desperation or high dudgeon. But until that event occurs, the party or parties in opposition have to evolve a suitable strategy.

The forms and techniques of opposition are varied, although some do not apply in the circumstances of the Federal Republic. The question of 'opposition in principle' scarcely arises, since strong ideological parties are absent, as are the 'anti-system' ones. Of course, they would in fact be well suited to a form of opposition against a cohesive governing bloc, since their strategy is based on long-term assessments of political development.

More relevant in the present situation is the experience of the CDU–CSU, which has taken the full brunt of coalition stability. In a sense the CDU since 1969 has been in an unprecedented situation – it has been the first party to face the problems of opposition in the changed form of the party system. Not surprisingly, the initial reaction of the CDU implied that the party was unaware that there were any problems at all – beyond that of getting the government out. The CDU felt that it had been unjustly deprived of its governing position in 1969 by a combination which lacked credibility and proper authority. Righteous indignation – the party's claim that 'we was robbed' – made it difficult for the leadership to consider a long-term strategy. Since the CDU–CSU was still by far the largest party and the coalition majority was slight, the best tactic was to harry the alliance until it broke up. The *Ostpolitik* was an excellent issue for the purpose.

The failure to bring down the government, followed quickly by the election reverse of 1972, brought full realisation of the party's difficulties. The election result itself, in conjunction with that of 1969, could even be read as an indication of a secular decline in the fortunes of Christian Democracy. The knowledge that the SPD–FDP coalition might continue indefinitely deepened the gloom; it implied that the CDU–CSU would have to aim at winning an absolute majority by itself, a feat which only Adenauer at the peak of his power had achieved. To add to the problems, there was the leadership issue which had bedevilled the party for so long.

Yet the CDU did appear to adjust to its position. Helmut Kohl emerged as party chairman in 1973 and chancellor candidate for the 1976 election. With him the party almost won an absolute majority. But the hard fact was that Kohl did not win: the CDU remained in opposition. Weakened by an indifferent CDU showing in *Länder* elections and CSU hostility, Kohl was unable to consolidate his position as 'alternative chancellor' (until eventually replaced by Franz-Josef Strauss in July 1979) – unlike Brandt who, twice unsuccessful, (1961 and 1965) still retained the allegiance of the SPD.

The most favourable development was the party's performance at the *Länder* elections in the 1970s, even controlling an absolute majority in five *Länder* assemblies.[3] That performance accords with a pattern: the CDU–CSU has almost consistently won a higher share of the vote in *Land* elections than it has at preceding and succeeding federal elections. The variation is to be expected, since federal elections allow the 'chancellor effect' full play and the federal issues then predominate. But the extent of the CDU–CSU

The Development of the Party Vote in the *Länder* during the 1970s

Bundestag (B) and Land (L) elections	CDU	SPD % votes cast	FDP	Bundestag (B) and Land (L) elections	CDU	SPD % votes cast	FDP
Baden-Württemberg				**Bavaria (CSU)**			
L '72	52.9	37.6	8.9	B '72	55.1	37.8	6.1
B '72	49.8	38.8	10.2	L '74	62.1	30.2	5.2
L '76	56.7	33.3	7.8	B '76	60.0	32.8	6.2
B '76	53.3	36.6	9.1	L '78	59.1	31.4	6.2
Bremen				**Hamburg**			
B '72	29.6	58.1	11.1	B '72	33.3	54.4	11.2
L '75	33.8	48.7	13.0	L '74	40.6	44.9	10.9
B '76	32.5	54.0	11.8	B '76	35.9	52.6	10.2
L '79				L '78	37.6	51.5	4.8[1]
Hesse				**Lower Saxony**			
B '72	40.3	48.5	10.2	B '72	42.7	48.1	8.5
L '74	47.3	43.2	7.4	L '74	48.8	43.1	7.0
B '76	44.8	45.7	8.5	B '76	45.7	45.7	7.9
L '78	46.0	44.3	6.6	L '78	48.7	42.2	4.2[1]
North Rhine-Westphalia				**Rhineland-Palatinate**			
B '72	41.0	50.4	7.8	B '72	45.9	44.9	8.1
L '75	47.1	45.1	6.7	L '75	53.9	38.5	5.6
B '76	44.5	46.9	7.8	B '76	49.9	41.7	7.6
L '80				L '79	50.1	42.3	6.4
Saarland				**Schleswig-Holstein**			
B '72	43.4	47.9	7.1	B '72	42.0	48.6	8.6
L '75	49.1	41.8	7.4	L '75	50.4	40.1	7.1
B '76	46.2	46.1	6.6	B '76	44.1	46.4	8.8
L '80				L '79	48.3	41.7	5.8
Berlin[2]							
L '71	38.2	50.4	8.5				
L '75	44.0	42.7	7.2				
L '79	44.4	42.6	8.1				

Notes
1. Not represented in the *Land* assembly.
2. Berlin does not participate in the federal elections, but sends 22 representatives, roughly in proportion to the strength of the parties – at present 11 CDU, 10 SPD, 1 FDP.

advance has allowed the party to gain a formidable supremacy in the Bundesrat and therefore to acquire an alternative site to the Bundestag for opposition – and one which is possibly more potent.

Prospects for the Parties

A future for the Free Democrats?

The essential contribution towards the balanced system was the part of the critical 'hinge' played by the FDP in bringing about a change of power. The FDP can be made to appear as the key regulator of the party system: its decisions determine how the party system will operate. It is true that both the CDU and the SPD have to take account of the possibility of the FDP changing sides, but the power of the FDP can easily be overrated. One false move, a suspicion of wilful change, and an electoral penalty could follow, since a large majority of the party's supporters still favour the 'social–liberal' alliance.

The question of whether the FDP will survive has often been posed. The party has frequently been close to the 5 per cent barrier and threatened by proposals to change the electoral system from one of proportional representation, and on two occasions, in 1956 and 1972, there have been serious splits in the parliamentary party. Yet the fact that the FDP has not succumbed in the past thirty years leads to the belief that it will escape extinction. The FDP enjoys a federal prestige: four senior cabinet posts have been held by the party since 1969 – foreign affairs, economics, interior and agriculture – and the party's leader, Hans-Dietrich Genscher, is vice-chancellor in the government as well as foreign minister. His predecessor, Walter Scheel, was elected to the presidency in 1974 and whilst that position required his withdrawal from party politics, the advantage to the FDP of prestige should have followed.[4] Finally, there is the practical parity of the FDP in coalition with the SPD: in deciding major issues of policy the party's assent has to be obtained.

Why the party has been unable to capitalise on its prestige and influence, which are quite out of proportion to the size of the FDP, is unclear. The change of course in 1969 meant that the party had to build up a new structure of electoral support, which in part explains its slow growth subsequently. That interpretation, however, is less convincing when account is taken of the FDP's dismal performance in the *Länder* elections which took place after 1976:

the 1978 elections in Hamburg and Lower Saxony, with the FDP recording only 4.8 and 4.2 per cent respectively, showed conclusively that the FDP had failed to project its new image.

That image was perhaps not clear even in the mind of the FDP. The idea behind the coalition with the SPD was that the party should act as a liberal corrective to Social Democracy. But how has the strategy operated in practice? For the correction to work, it would first be necessary for the SPD to undertake a series of radical measures which the FDP would then proceed to block or tone down, as a last resort threatening to break the coalition. Yet the SPD has perhaps been even more concerned than the FDP to avoid a left-wing course: the presence of the FDP in fact presented the SPD leadership with a good argument for not introducing radical proposals. The liberal corrective applied fully on only one occasion: in the passage of the new (1976) law on industrial co-determination the FDP insisted that higher management should be separately represented on the supervisory boards of firms, in opposition to the SPD's attempt to have a common representation of all employees, a formula which would have given the trade unions a decisive voice. The FDP dug its heels in and the force of the corrective was demonstrated with public effect, but most other differences have been resolved amicably and usually in the seclusion of the coalition committee.

Scheel and Brandt were united on the *Ostpolitik*, and after they left the government in 1974 the partnership between Schmidt and Genscher has been almost as harmonious. In fact, the transfer from Brandt to Schmidt – from idealism to realism – gave the FDP even less chance to apply a brake. Gradually the party lost its independent profile in government.

One source of support the FDP has lost through its association with government has been that of liberal protest. The rise of the ecological movement is a case in point: the FDP lost votes directly to the Green Lists in *Länder* elections – inevitably so, since the party is absolutely identified with the government's nuclear energy programme.[5] A further loss of liberal protest is evident in the whole area of personal freedom and restrictive law in the liberal state, in the controversies surrounding such questions as the *Radikalenerlass* and anti-terrorist legislation. Far from being able to adopt a critical standpoint, the Free Democrats – especially through their control of the interior ministry – became identified with the extension of executive power.

A possible strategy for the FDP is indicated by the move to

secure an *Auflockerung* of the party system, a 'loosening' which would mark at least a partial step towards a policy of 'free alliance' and avoid the impression that the party is becoming a satellite of the SPD. A peculiar stalemate in the Lower Saxony assembly led to the formation of a CDU–FDP coalition as the only way of providing a governing majority. The SPD did not object: the presence of the FDP in the Lower Saxony government would partially sterilise the *Land*'s vote in the Bundesrat, preventing the CDU from using it to oppose federal government legislation. A similar 'cross-cutting' coalition was formed for the Saarland in 1977 and was again caused by the awkward balance of the parties. These examples show how the process of *Auflockerung* might proceed, although in Lower Saxony the move did not help the FDP at all in 1978. Possibly the signal from the *Länder* will have the same effect for the FDP's federal direction as did the change in North Rhine-Westphalia in 1966. But the FDP does not have the flexibility which it enjoyed in earlier years: the party will have to indicate firmly where it stands for a future federal election.[6]

The SPD: a party of reform?

The years after 1972 have been critical ones for the SPD. Although the adoption of the Godesberg Programme was the historic turning point in the post-war development of the party, it was not until the SPD was securely in power that the extent of its problems became apparent. Both the coalition with the CDU and the first one with the FDP were essentially experimental phases and neither could demonstrate the full potential of the party in government. After the 1972 election the SPD enjoyed the promise of stable power. It was the largest party, had a proven and popular leader, a firm alliance with the FDP and a comfortable majority in the Bundestag which was secure at least until 1976 and possibly until the end of the decade.

Yet the hope that the SPD would bring about substantial changes was not fulfilled. On the contrary, the party stumbled from one crisis to another. The 'finest hour' of the 1972 election was followed by a run of defeats in the *Länder;* the accolades heaped on Brandt for his *Ostpolitik* were followed by a growing disillusion with its outcome. Brandt's own resignation somehow reflected that disenchantment, but his departure also epitomised the loss of direction suffered by the SPD. The initial euphoria of growing electoral success and governmental power gave way to a lack of self-confidence and to dissension within the party. The replacement of Brandt by Schmidt exposed the problems more clearly, for up to a point Brandt had managed to conceal the difficulties by supplying the rhetoric of social and political change without its content. Schmidt's severely practical style, in contrast, weakened the illusions and the fragile consensus. Schmidt proved to be a strong national leader in the crises which occurred during his chancellorship.[7] The West German economy proved more resilient than most in meeting the twin perils of inflation and recession, and his government also had to meet the full onslaught of terrorist attacks which reached a peak in 1977. The surmounting of these crises, however, helped to show the SPD as a successful party of government without re-establishing its reforming reputation.

The feeling that the party had somehow been blown off course by accidental crises was not completely unjustified, but their occurrence only served to raise the basic questions relating to reform rather earlier than might otherwise have been the case. Thus the comforting assumption that economic growth would continue unhindered staved off for a time the question of how burdens would be equitably shouldered, but the onset of a long-term problem of unemployment forced basic issues once more into prominence.

A simplified version of the choice facing the SPD is based on the relationship the party has with government. One view, the predominant one, equates the presence of the SPD in government with reform, whilst the other – representing a number of viewpoints – by no means makes this connection. The idea of the *Volkspartei* is tantamount to an equation: in claiming to speak for all the people, the SPD in government can act for them as well. There follows an emphasis on the SPD's 'national' identification, as in the 1976 election campaign: '*Modell Deutschland*' stressed the achievements of the Federal Republic and the SPD's part in the success story. Also evident is the popular identification sought with the state – 'our state' – with the SPD providing the important link through government. In this sense the SPD is committed to being a *Staatspartei*.

Critics within the party take a less optimistic view and claim precisely that this identification is objectionable, since it implies that the SPD will continue to underwrite the existing state system in all its essentials and that therefore the chances of securing fundamental reform are negligible – with or without the presence of a restraining coalition partner.[8] Indeed, the obligations can lead to an SPD government itself taking repressive action. That line of attack has been present in the debate over the employment of radicals in the public service and came to a head in the wake of the political assassinations which took place in 1977. The SPD regarded the anti-terrorist legislation which it then introduced as essential to the preservation of the *Rechtsstaat*, Chancellor Schmidt argued that he would go 'to the limits of the *Rechtsstaat*' in combating terrorism.

The formula of 'responsibility for our state' puts an overriding claim on the loyalty of party members and the parliamentary party towards an SPD government. In the voting on the anti-terrorist legislation a small number of SPD deputies opposed: at the subsequent Hamburg Conference of the party held in 1976 they were accused of treachery to the government and of acting in defiance of the wishes of the voters.

This line of division within the SPD is approximately the one which also separates the moderates from the party's left wing. Although the adoption of the Godesberg Programme might seem to have settled the issue of whether the SPD was a *Volkspartei* or a *Klassenpartei* for good, in practice the debate is not closed. There are restrictions: it is difficult for left-wing critics to evolve a consistent line of argument without running the risk of adopting an unacceptable Marxist stance, too close to that of the DKP, or of reintroducing class politics. Argument on these lines – to hold, say, that Christian Democracy represents the 'class enemy', or to advocate a popular front policy – invites penalty.

Nonetheless, the Godesberg Programme is open to various interpretations, since it leaves the door open for an unspecified form of 'democratic socialism' quite compatible with a policy of state intervention in the economy and a radical redistribution of wealth. The need for the party to 'fill out' the Godesberg Programme resulted in the adoption of a middle-range plan to take it until the 1980s, the *Orientierungsrahmen '85*, which in a revised form was accepted in 1975. The first version was rejected because of its too-ready identification with economic growth and a 'technocratic' acceptance of the existing structure of society and the economic system. The revised document emphasised the distinction between 'democratic socialism' and 'political liberalism'. The difference is shown in the attention given to the role of the state in the direction of the economy, the planned redistribution of wealth, the democratisation of society. If not quite a return to old-style militancy, *Orientierungsrahmen '85* reintroduced the idea of definite objectives, and brought back 'strategy', 'struggle' and 'goals' to the party's vocabulary.[9]

The new plan can be regarded as a rather anodyne treatment, sufficient to keep the less radical critics quiet without a revival of socialist dogmatism. It was also a compromise between the moderates, who wished to preserve the flexibility the party had gained, and the activists, who had hoped to restore 'theory' and return to fundamentals. But the point is that *Orientierungsrahmen '85* implied the possibility of a revival of 'ideology', even though it did not take place in the 1970s.

What kind of reform party the SPD will eventually become depends on various factors: the nature of the party leadership and its relationship with the membership base, the balance of power which emerges between the competing party factions, the changing composition of party membership. These factors can all be related to another variable: whether or not the SPD remains in government in the 1980s. We can look at each of these aspects in turn.

A remarkable feature of the SPD is the extent to which certain figures dominate the party leadership. Brandt's unifying role, spanning almost two decades, has easily been the most important. Since he was first adopted as chancellor candidate in 1960, Brandt has been identified with the spirit of Godesberg and has provided the important element of continuity. His election as party chairman in 1964 – a post he continued to hold after relinquishing the chancellorship in 1974 – confirmed the ascendancy of the reformist wing. Almost as important for the cohesion of the party (and similarly identified with the Godesberg Programme) is Herbert Wehner who, as leader of the SPD's parliamentary party, wields a dominating power over the SPD *Fraktion* in the Bundestag. Wehner has earned the title of the party's master strategist, combining personal aloofness with considerable flair for the hurly-burly of party in-fighting. Finally, Chancellor Schmidt supplies firm executive leadership in government. His background – he was a member of the *Land* government of Hamburg, spent time in parliamentary service, and was subsequently minister of defence and finance minister – enabled him to consolidate his position rapidly after taking office in 1974. His reputation generally as a strong chancellor came to equal Adenauer's, though the esteem in which he was held did not rub off very much on the party at elections. As long as the SPD remains in power there is no likelihood of Schmidt's authority being challenged.

These three leading figures, Brandt, Wehner and Schmidt, constitute the core of the *Parteivorstand*, the party presidium, elected and re-elected by the congress of the party with over-whelming majorities. Brandt's personal popularity in the party, Wehner's grasp of parliamentary strategy, and Schmidt's control of government, give a strong central direction to the party and that is backed by the control issuing from the party's bureaucracy, the *Apparat*. There is no room for an alternative leadership to emerge from within the senior ranks of the SPD, nor does the structure of the party encourage party leaders in the *Länder* to carve out positions of independent power for themselves.

The homogeneity of the leadership positions in the SPD is one of the important factors contributing to stability within the party. The triumvirate of Brandt, Wehner and Schmidt accords with this ideological homogeneity – they are each exercising a functional authority, not occupying positions of rival power.

It is with this picture of a unified leadership in mind that the question of factions inside the SPD can be assessed, for it is evident that the ones which are opposed to the party's policies have very little real power: differences run *horizontally* across the SPD – and usually at the periphery – rather than vertically from top to bottom. The main peripheral element is the party's youth wing, the *Jungsozialisten*, membership of which is open to all members of the SPD up to the age of thirty-five. In practice, only a small proportion of SPD members join and participate in '*Juso*' activity, and that results in a body with an overwhelmingly left-wing complexion, combining a host of struggling factions, united only by a love of theory and a scorn for the lack of ideological analysis within the party as a whole. Their criticism of the leadership is that is has become divorced from the mass base of the membership, that it has accepted capitalism, and especially monopoly capitalism, that it has failed to raise the political consciousness of the working class.

The *Jungsozialisten* represent the most clearly delineated factional grouping within the SPD and their influence is felt most strongly at local and *Land* level, and most frequently in the larger cities, such as Frankfurt and Munich. Possibly the major effect of '*Juso*' radicalism and activism has been to give the party a divided (*zerstritten*) image in the eyes of the electorate – with the most harmful effects precisely at local and *Land* level where their influence has been greatest.[10]

A second potential source of opposition to the leadership is within the Bundestag *Fraktion* of the SPD. There are no hard-and-fast lines of division, however, within the parliamentary party, which is dominated by a loyalist faction, the strangely named *'Kanalarbeiter'*, whose allegiance to the SPD government is profound. The number of left-wing deputies cannot be precisely calculated (perhaps a fifth of the total membership of over 200), but in reality many of those who might so describe themselves would be located amongst the moderates of, say, the Labour Party in the House of Commons. Party loyalty and discipline also make strong demands – despite the opposition from the party's left wing, only four members of the SPD *Fraktion* voted against the anti-terrorist legislation in the end. There is also a socialisation process at work: left-inclined deputies belong to the university-trained elite, the base of the *Jungsozialisten*, but in entering the Bundestag they have to come to terms with the much more realistic approach of the majority of ordinary members who have strong links with the trade unions and who make up the *'Kanalarbeiter'*

We have already seen that the composition of SPD party membership has altered drastically in the past decade or so, becoming younger, better educated, more middle class, so that the SPD is now more a 'public service' party than an *Arbeiterpartei* in the traditional sense. But it is also true that the average SPD member is quite representative of the electorate as a whole, especially in terms of indices such as savings, net income and home ownership. It does not seem for these reasons that the party leadership is likely to lose touch with the grass roots of the membership, although the new and growing category of students in the occupational structure of members indicates that a new generation will not allow the ideological debate in the party to die away.

As long as the triumvirate holds power in the party, no pronounced shift in the interpretation given to the Godesberg Programme is likely. But the eventual replacement of Brandt and Wehner, the retirement of the old guard, would lead to substantial changes. The same is true if the SPD were once more to find itself in opposition; the immunity of Helmut Schmidt, no longer able to deliver his 'chancellor bonus' to the party at elections, would disappear. It is sometimes argued that the SPD faces greatest internal dissension when in office, but the demand for the party to put forward a 'real' alternative to Christian Democracy whilst it is in opposition could also lead to a radical reinterpretation of Social Democracy.

The CDU versus the CSU?

Once the battles over the *Ostpolitik* had receded, the CDU–CSU opposition had to concentrate on domestic matters, the bread-and-butter issues of the economy, made pressing with the onset of the oil crisis in October 1973 and leading to the problems of recession, unemployment and inflation. The issue of law and order also became urgent – a socialist government was unable to deal firmly with the extreme left or to cope with the violence of urban terrorism. These emphases were reinforced by long-standing prejudices against the SPD, which were most pointedly formulated in the election slogan 'Freedom or Socialism'. Despite the gains made by the CDU–CSU in *Länder* elections during 1974 and 1975, the party was relegated to opposition for the third time running in 1976.

In the aftermath of the election an open breach occurred between the CDU and the CSU, threatening the existence of Christian Democracy as a cohesive movement. There was even immediate speculation that the whole party system was about to revert to its Weimar pattern. Had the break become absolute, the fragmentation of the CDU–CSU could have had wider consequences. In retrospect, the episode was less momentous than it appeared at the time, but the crisis in the party illustrates the power structure of the CDU–CSU relationship and the nature of the CSU in Bavaria, and, perhaps most important, it had implications for the future of the West German party system.

The Christian-Social Union is a peculiar offshoot of German Christian Democracy. Unlike the CDU and its *Länder* parties, the CSU has managed to anchor itself in a particularist tradition. The CSU is as much the Bavarian 'state party' as it is an expression of Christian Democracy. Such an apparently powerful combination did not occur automatically. Initially there was strong competition from the Bavarian Party which, as a primarily Catholic and rural movement, had claims to precedence. The CSU had to overcome the Bavarian Party and unite the Catholic vote as well as make an appeal to the minority of Protestants in the electorate. But by far the most difficult task for the CSU was to strike an acceptable balance between Bavarian traditionalism and the federal orientation of Christian Democracy.[11]

The ability of the CSU to straddle both realms is the key to an understanding of the party's success. The Bavarian aspect should not be underestimated: it is a consciousness which rests on a distinctive cultural tradition – the bonds of dialect, the monarchical associations of the historic Bavarian state, and the peculiarly important place of the Roman Catholic Church. There are elements of a backward-looking nostalgia in Bavarian politics, but the CSU combines them with a practical modernity: the party maintains its federal presence with its own views on domestic and foreign policy, and the CSU has little to learn from the CDU about the benefits of party organisation, the retention of a high party membership, or the projection of its special image. A measure of the CSU's success was the *Land* election of 1974, when it won 62.1 per cent of the vote, a result unsurpassed by any other party in any other *Land*.

Unlike the *Länder* parties of the CDU, the CSU is quite independent, subject to three qualifications. In the first place, the CDU and CSU form a common parliamentary group, a CDU–CSU *Fraktion* in the Bundestag. This *Fraktionsgemeinschaft* commits the two parties to the common discipline of the *Fraktion* once policy has been agreed. A second requirement is for the CDU and CSU to adopt a joint chancellor candidate (in practice this has meant that the CSU has been obliged to accept the person favoured by the CDU). Finally, the CSU has to respect a territorial limitation: the CSU may not organise and compete outside Bavaria, while a similar limitation applies to the CDU within Bavaria. These restrictions do not affect the CSU in its home territory, and the party obviously benefits from its flexible association with the CDU, but the fact remains that, considered federally, the CSU is only one segment of a much larger party.

It is, or was, a fairly amicable arrangement. But two other considerations have to be taken into account which illustrate that the co-existence of the CSU and CDU is a complex matter. One is an ideological distinction: the CSU stands well to the right of the CDU as a whole. Partly the CSU is simply a more conservative party, but it is also more 'fundamentalist', often stridently anti-socialist, paradoxically more nationalist, and wedded to traditional values of state and society. Voting for the CSU in Bavaria has a rather different connotation from voting CDU elsewhere. Thus the CSU does more than just stand for Bavarian interests: the party also puts forward political ideas which find support amongst CDU voters, albeit a minority.

The second complicating factor – some would say the decisive one in determining the role of the CSU – is its leader, Franz-Josef Strauss. Under his leadership the CSU has risen to its dominant position in Bavaria. His undisputed control of the party and its autonomous position have given him a secure place in federal politics. On many counts Strauss is the most able and experienced of the CDU–CSU hierarchy, certainly one of the few with political flair and presence. Yet the sources of his support were also disabilities: neither his Bavarian image nor his representation of CSU values were recommendations to the CDU – the party did not wish to risk adopting him as chancellor candidate. Strauss played a negative role: unable to win control of the CDU–CSU himself, he used his influence to undermine the authority of CDU rivals. His machinations were eventually successful in 1979 when he replaced Kohl as chancellor candidate and virtual leader of the CDU–CSU.

Helmut Kohl won the CDU–CSU candidature for the chancellorship for the 1976 election, despite the opposition of Strauss and the CSU. The CSU had no alternative but to rally round the new leader – at least until the election was over. Kohl had every reason for satisfaction in having made a forceful impact, but the actual outcome was sobering: the return to power was as elusive as ever.

It was in this atmosphere of 'the morning after' that the CSU struck. At a meeting held at Wildbad-Kreuth in November 1976 the CSU parliamentary delegation voted by a large majority to end the *Fraktionsgemeinschaft* with the CDU, an agreement which had been in force since 1950.[12] At once the CSU was at pains to play down the significance of the decision, pleading that the main effect would be to give an independent CSU a higher status in the Bundestag: its own representation on committees, a share of plenary debating time, access to official financial support. Far from weakening the opposition, the effect of the two parties working in partnership would amplify the voice of Christian Democracy. The CSU was quick to deny any intention of challenging the CDU and certainly disclaimed any thought of taking the party beyond its Bavarian frontiers.

Despite these protestations of good faith, the coup was generally seen as a deliberate challenge to the authority of the CDU and, more particularly, aimed at Helmut Kohl. Strauss had made no secret of his belief that the CDU leader lacked the proper qualities for a chancellor. Even though the CDU as a whole had improved its position at the election, the CSU had done much better. Had the Bavarian result of 60 per cent been approached federally, the CDU–CSU would have been triumphant. The result, in fact, marked a clear north–south difference; some of the northern *Länder* showed only a minimal improvement over 1972. The implications were apparent: if Strauss had been chancellor candidate, then the campaign would have been more forceful and the result different.

Kohl, for his own survival, had to pick up the gauntlet. He realised that if the CSU move went through unchallenged, his own position would become untenable. Moreover, once the CDU conceded full independence to the CSU, there would be little to prevent an escalation, nothing to prevent Strauss taking the CSU into the federal arena. Kohl therefore went the whole way and demanded that the CSU renounce the Kreuth decision completely. He justified his stand on the ground that the Kreuth proceedings were not representative of the CSU as a whole, since they were determined only by the parliamentary caucus. He also argued that a large part of the vote accruing to the CSU had been directly in support of the chancellor candidate – Kohl, not Strauss. Finally the ultimatum was made: if the decision were not rescinded, the CDU would go over the head of the CSU and appeal directly to the Bavarian electorate by establishing its own organisation in the *Land*.

Strauss had not bargained for this strong reaction. He was also weakened by the clandestine nature of the Kreuth revolt: the CSU in Bavaria was taken by surprise, since neither the membership nor the local party officials had been consulted beforehand, and many were appalled at the prospect of an open contest between the two parties. If it did come to a showdown, it was evident that whole sections of the CSU might desert to the CDU. That applied especially in areas such as Franconia and Swabia, provinces which had only been absorbed into Bavaria in the nineteenth century and did not share the traditions of 'old Bavaria'. The prospect of a counter-revolt within his own party had perhaps not occurred to Strauss.

He realised that competition with the CDU inside Bavaria would spell the end of CSU dominance. The logical response of setting up the CSU as a federal-wide fourth party was, of course, attractive. But the move, if it came, should be at the end of a process, not the immediate reaction to the confrontation. There was a danger that the fourth party would end up as no more than a splinter group. These doubts prompted caution on Strauss's part, and perhaps all along he had hoped that a real break would not be necessary, that the effect of Kreuth would be just sufficient to lead to Kohl's downfall and enable him to assume the federal leadership of the CDU–CSU sometime in the future – as did happen.

At that stage both sides were anxious to avoid a war of attrition, especially since the SPD and the FDP might be the ones to benefit if Christian Democracy lost its credibility. Peace was restored in December 1976. The *Fraktionsgemeinschaft* was reinstated and, despite the concessions made to the susceptibilities of the CSU (increased freedom of action for the CSU parliamentary group), the immediate victory belonged to Kohl. It is unlikely that the CSU would relish another trial of strength with the CDU in the near future. But the outcome failed to give Kohl uncontested primacy. He had a firm enemy in Strauss who saw his best chance of settling the struggle in the framework of the CDU–CSU alliance. In that strategy he was spectacularly successful. As Kohl's prestige waned – especially in contrast with Schmidt's standing – the CDU believed that a gamble on Strauss was preferable to inevitable defeat with Kohl.

The power struggle within the CDU–CSU is important. But also significant is the kind of assumption Strauss had made about West German politics and his version of a resultant party system. This aspect we can examine later as one of the perspectives of the developing party system.

Perspectives on the Party System

A 'split' system
There is an inherent tension in the combination of the principle of federalism with parliamentary government: one relies on the dispersal of power, whilst the other encourages its concentration. In Western Germany that tension is not shown through conflict between the federation and the states but as a quality of the party system. The operation of federalism in fact may have encouraged the drive towards integration and the growth of a West German national consciousness. But the federal institutions have also brought about a disjunction in the party system which is made evident in the present relationship of the Bundestag and Bundesrat.

According to the theory of the Basic Law, the federal structure can be seen as an attempt to provide protection against undesirable centralising influences and to supply a cohesive administrative framework by associating the *Länder* with the work of the federal government. Both aims are evident in the fashioning of the composition and powers of the Bundesrat: the representation of individual *Länder* governments and their administrative as well as legislative competence on a federal level.

We can suppose that the view behind the Basic Law was of a number of governing entities concerned to safeguard the interests of the *Länder*. When those interests conflicted with the aims of the federal government, it would be because the *Länder* saw a threat to their collective position or else reacted to some regional or special concern. Whatever the form of the conflict, the assumption appears to have been that the interests of the *Länder* as such would be the paramount factor.

That conclusion was not undermined by the realisation that *Länder* governments would also be party governments. From the viewpoint of the early post-war period, there was no reason to believe that any *particular* pattern of government in the *Länder* would emerge. Coalition government would be the rule and the coalitions would vary from one *Land* to another – especially with the addition of purely regional parties. A *Land* coalition would principally be concerned with representing the interests of the *Land* at the federal level and, by providing that the votes of a *Land* delegation had to be cast *en bloc*, party differences would be subsumed in a common standpoint for the *Land*.

These expectations were reinforced by the way in which federalism had previously worked in Germany, by the administrative ethos typical of the Bundesrat in the Empire and the Reichsrat in the Weimar Republic, and since at the time the Basic Law was drafted the *Länder* were the sole organs of responsible government, it was fair to assume that they would take a similar role, through the Bundesrat, in the new republic.

The development of the party system has to be seen against the background of assumptions and expectations concerning federalism in the Basic Law. In the event a multi-party system did not prevail, with the result that the concentration of power in two major parties transformed the constitutional position. Once the CDU and the SPD became dominant on the federal stage there was an inevitable 'nationalisation' process at work in the *Länder*, for they could not be immune to the federal pressures.[13] Put another way, the CDU and the SPD had to follow the logic of their federal contest and seek to impose a similar pattern on the *Länder*. Since control over a *Land* government is immediately reflected in the distribution of seats in the Bundesrat, a straight line connects an election in even the smallest of the *Länder* with the balance of power at the federal level.

A prevailing pattern for the long term was thus set: *Länder* alignments and coalitions as miniature versions of the federal line-up. Even those CDU–SPD *Länder* coalitions established before 1949 were soon replaced to suit the composition of the first federal government. But the complete pattern did not emerge at once. Minor parties survived in the *Landtage* after they had disappeared from the federal stage, or, as was the case with the NPD, without ever having made a federal breakthrough. Until the 1960s the *Land* arrangements were still fairly flexible, and the FDP in particular, keen on asserting its potential as a third force, was willing to engage in cross-cutting coalitions, helping the Bundesrat to maintain a diffused political character.

The full effect of the changes was also masked by the dominant position of the CDU. Even though the SPD consistently fared better in the *Länder* elections than it did federally, there was no strong tension between the Bundesrat and the Bundestag, since the CDU's majority was normally sufficient in both houses. The masking effect was further maintained for the period of the Grand Coalition, and CDU–SPD alliances were formed in some *Länder*. Only with the break-up of the coalition did a gap become evident between political practice and the supposed constitutional norms affecting the Bundesrat.[14]

With the formation of the SPD–FDP coalition in 1969, the appearance of rival majorities in the Bundestag and Bundesrat introduced a new factor into the working of parliamentary government. The intense polarisation between government and opposition immediately focused attention on the Bundesrat, where the CDU–CSU had a slender majority, and by 1970 – for the first time – the *Länder* pattern exactly reflected the federal one: there were no 'deviant' coalitions.

The disparity became more marked when the SPD–FDP coalition won the 1972 election and was even greater in the subsequent *Länder* elections. By 1978 the CDU had so strengthened its position in the Bundesrat that it was within sight of having a 'magic' two-thirds majority (twenty-eight votes out of forty-one). Such an impregnable majority would put a stranglehold on all federal government legislation with the force of an absolute veto.

Since 1969 the party system has developed this 'split' character which resulted from the move away from the constitutional assumptions and towards a 'party federalism'. The 'split' system depends on two sources of legitimacy, and each part is responsible to a different constituency. If the Bundesrat were a directly-elected senate, such a division could still occur (as can be the case for the two houses of the United States Congress), but the effect would be

The Composition of the Bundesrat, 1964, 1970 and 1979

	Votes	+ or −	1964 Government	1970 Government	1979 Government	1970 Government	1970 Opposition	1979 Government	1979 Opposition
Baden-Württemberg	5	0	CDU/FDP	CDU	CDU	—	5	—	5
Bavaria	5	−2	CSU/BP	CSU	CSU	—	5	—	5
Bremen	3	+2	SPD/FDP	SPD/FDP	SPD/FDP	3	—	3	—
Hamburg	3	+2	SPD/FDP	SPD/FDP	SPD	3	—	3	—
Hesse	4	0	SPD/GDP	SPD/FDP	SPD/FDP	4	—	4	—
Lower Saxony	5	0	SPD/FDP	SPD/FDP	CDU	5	—	—	5
North Rhine-Westphalia	5	−7	CDU/FDP	SPD/FDP	SPD/FDP	5	—	5	—
Rhineland-Palatinate	4	+1	CDU/FDP	CDU	CDU	—	4	—	4
Saarland	3	+2	SPD/FDP	CDU	CDU/FDP	—	3	(3)*	—
Schleswig-Holstein	4	+2	CDU/FDP	CDU	CDU	—	4	—	4
	41					20	21	15 (3)	23

*Cross-coalition

Notes

Composition of the Bundesrat Article 51 of the Basic Law provides that all *Länder* have at least three votes in the Bundesrat; those with more than two million people to have four votes and those with more than six million to have five. The smaller *Länder* are therefore over-represented, as will be seen from column 2. At present the distortion works in favour of the CDU–CSU.

Government and opposition The composition of the Bundesrat in earlier years did not lend itself to this ordering, as is evident from the position in 1964. It operated completely in 1970, when the CDU–CSU had a 21 to 20 majority.

Cross-cutting coalitions Apart from a short period from 1977-8, when there was a CDU–FDP coalition in Lower Saxony, the only exceptional coalition is in the Saarland. Even in that case the direction of the Bundesrat vote is determined by the majority party. However, on those issues which affect the federal coalition the FDP has a practical veto.

West Berlin The four votes of West Berlin, ruled by the SPD–FDP coalition, only count in committee but are of importance in the *Vermittlungsausschuss*.

Vermittlungsausschuss Each *Land*, including West Berlin, has a single vote on the conciliation committee formed jointly with the Bundestag – eleven votes in all, together with eleven from the Bundestag, in accordance with party strength. As a result of the 1978 *Land* elections, the CDU–CSU controlled a majority on the committee.

less pronounced. Thus the American system does not operate in practice through sharp party lines, nor does the lower house bear the responsibility of parliamentary government. In the Federal Republic both factors are present and both make the possibility of a direct confrontation that much greater.

Only a radical change in the number of parties represented would alter the present pattern. The more likely development is for the CDU–CSU to win control of the federal government. But that would hardly remove the underlying tensions. It is also conceivable that the SPD, at some time in the future, might win a Bundesrat majority and yet be in federal opposition. Either way, the constitution itself prevents any fundamental change and preserves the dualistic character of the party system. The way the party system has evolved makes some aspects of the federal structure functionally redundant, although institutionally irremovable.

Two models for the 1980s
Even though, in terms of its institutional arrangements, the West German party system appears to have a 'split' character, that description need not prejudice how the system operates in practice. In present circumstances (a CDU majority in the Bundesrat facing the federal coalition of the SPD and FDP in the Bundestag), the inherent constitutional tension is joined by a political confrontation, but – quite apart from the possibility of either or both majorities changing – the 'split' system is compatible with two quite contrasting renderings.

One view is based on the sharpness of the lines of party conflict drawn since 1969: the almost exact reproduction of the federal alignment in the *Länder*, the polarisation between the forces of government and opposition, and the use made by the CDU–CSU of its Bundesrat majority. The picture is one of hardening cleavage, and, provided that the balance of political forces remains the same, the future of West German politics will be dictated by this polarisation. But another view does not follow this line of reasoning. Assuming that the party political complexion of Bundesrat and Bundestag continues to be at variance, does this necessarily imply a polarised political system?

A possibility is that a modified constitutional solution will prevail: the Basic Law's assumption that a reconciliation between the federation and the *Länder* should be feasible can be translated into party terms. The conditions for such a reconciliation can be seen in the calculations of the parties. For the CDU–CSU to use its stranglehold on the legislation of the federal government could be counter-productive and might merely result in the party gaining a negative political image; it could be seen as bent on wrecking the parliamentary system of government. It would be small comfort for the CDU–CSU permanently to have the power of veto at the cost of permanently being in opposition. For the SPD in federal government the course of inviting confrontation scarcely has a value. Even though the party (or the governing coalition) has its legislative priorities, the desirable strategy is to work for a compromise with the CDU–CSU rather than to make no progress at all. On that reckoning, the *Vermittlungsausschuss* of the Bundesrat and Bundestag could become the symbolic venue for disguised all-party government – a hard-fought consensus, not an irreconcilable polarisation.

Material for both views is available. It is a matter of record that the vast majority of government bills – well over 90 per cent of the total – are not opposed by the opposition in their final form. On the other hand, its resistance to certain aspects of government legislation in key issues has provided the substance of political debate. The question is not really resolvable in those terms at all: the forces affecting the behaviour of the parties within parliament have to be traced back to those operating outside. Ultimately, the question of whether the party system is likely to become more or less polarised has to be answered with the help of a wide range of indicators, electoral considerations as well as the significance of specific issues.

The evolution of the party system towards its balanced form, and the consolidation of that balance, do not of themselves give a firm guide one way or the other. A balanced party system is compatible with a high or a low degree of polarisation: the two groupings may stand in sharp antithesis to one another or may exhibit minimal differences. In a sense, therefore, the future of West German politics does not depend on what happens to the *number* of the parties: a fragmentation – so often dreaded – could in practice foster a spirit of compromise, whilst the present framework could just as well inhibit it. Nor, on the other hand, would the survival or extinction of the FDP necessarily be symptomatic of either lesser or greater polarisation.

A Volkspartei plateau

It is impossible to skirt the evidence of the *Volkspartei*, still less that of the catch-all party system. The principle behind the formation of the *Volkspartei* – and the most important reason for its continuing success – is that political differences between major social groupings can be reconciled. The argument proceeds *a fortiori* when two such parties compete and dominate the political stage.

It is worth summarising the main attributes of the CDU and the SPD in this light. Neither party has as yet shown a tendency towards ideological rejuvenation, the outcome of the Kreuth revolt for the CDU–CSU and the dominant spirit of Godesberg for the SPD. Unless sharp differences over particular policies can be related to a distinctive ideological outlook, the possibility of the contestants being able to maintain an intense *and* prolonged polarisation is not present.

A second quality of the *Volkspartei* is associated with the social composition of support. It is certainly not the case that either party is able to maintain the support of a complete cross-section of the electorate, and the skews for both are still pronounced in some directions. Nevertheless, the process of equalisation has been fairly unimpeded and an absolute uniformity is not requisite: the important point is that the CDU and SPD have to compete with one another across an increasingly large margin in the electorate, and to do so successfully, the policies they advance should not be diametrically opposed. Moreover, the social changes themselves, whether they are counted in terms of social structure or of social affiliation, point towards a widening area of equal competition.

Finally, we have to take into account the overall characteristics of the party system, the 'increasing aggregate and narrowing gap' between the CDU and SPD. There is no hard evidence that a marked reversal is occurring to other types of party formation; rather more that the FDP is caught between the two wheels. It is difficult to visualise that either or both of the major parties will experience a dramatic change of fortune over the coming decade. The favoured model for the 1980s is therefore one which sees the development of the party system as having reached a broad plateau, a stage of positive entropy, affecting the electorate and setting the parameters of coalition and opposition.

The polarised alternative

There are similarities between the inertia of the *Volkspartei* system and the earlier dominance of the old-type parties based on fixed ideology and special interest. The conditions under which the parties were established in the nineteenth century led to a long period of consolidation: party systems were extremely resistant to change. Yet in the end even the most intransigent parties were forced to adopt a different stance; the phenomenon of Euro-communism was the last in a long line of adaptations. Despite the unpromising outlook, it is just as well to consider the possibility of a change of direction taking place in the present system.

How can the alternative model best be applied to Germany? The least promising of all lines is that which relies on the sudden appearance of radical forces given expression by new political parties located on the extremities of right and left. If it were the case that such parties as the DKP and the NPD were only held in check by the restrictions of the electoral law, then the case might be different. But their failure over a long period to approach even 1 per cent of the total vote in federal or *Land* elections makes a spectacular resurgence unlikely.

But even if, for the sake of argument, a limited recovery were to take place, the consequence need not be a more polarised *party system*, since the reaction of the other parties has to be allowed for: they would be more inclined to guard against the outflanking movements than to enter into a co-operative relationship with them and thereby polarise the system as a whole. The question of whether a polarising effect could occur has yet to be put to the test.

The nearest approach to the conditions in which such polarisation could occur was in 1966. If the NPD had obtained marginally more votes, the party would have had around twenty-five to thirty seats in the Bundestag, possibly just sufficient to give the CDU–CSU a majority for a rightist coalition. What might have happened is speculation, since the CDU did not in principle exclude any option beforehand. The temptation to try a CDU–NPD combination would have been present, but at considerable risk to the internal cohesion of the party, and to make the NPD a present of governmental respectability at the first time of asking would have perhaps entailed the permanent acceptance of a right-wing competitor. The probability is that the CDU would have sought to avoid an alliance with the NPD; its alternatives would have been either to revive the coalition with the SPD or to call upon the Free Democrats. Neither wanted a coalition with the CDU and both wanted to try out the SPD–FDP link, but with that option closed, either party would have been available.

Although these conditions would not necessarily obtain in the future, the drift of the argument is convincing enough: radical parties would not bring about a polarisation in the party system as an automatic consequence and the first result could be an actual decrease in polarisation. That at least would be the short-run picture; all types of development are possible in the longer term. Since we are primarily concerned with the 1980s, the more hypothetical twists and turns have to be left out of account.

If we leave aside the chances of a fragmenting polarisation, the remaining possibility is of a polarisation developing within the existing party system, and with nothing of the essential structure altered. Although the idea of polarised *Volksparteien* has a rather strange ring, it is not quite to be dismissed out of hand. The best illustration, in fact, can be taken from some aspects of CSU thinking at the time of the party's open dispute with the CDU. Indeed, the view of the West German party system *à la* Strauss stands as one viable course for the CDU and CSU.

The validity of Strauss's basic conception is not affected by the patched-up peace between the CDU and CSU, though the restoration of the *Fraktionsgemeinschaft* obviously makes it less applicable as a strategy. Basic to the argument put forward by Strauss was that the party system had taken on a permanent two-bloc formation: the alliance between the SPD and FDP had gone beyond a decision to continue their coalition for a further period to a point where the FDP had become indissolubly wedded to the larger party. That left Christian Democracy with no alternative to seeking power by itself, but to do so presented a considerable problem in organising the requisite vote under one party label. If, however, the CDU and CSU were to operate as two distinctive parties throughout the Federal Republic, their combined catchment could produce a majority. Whilst the CDU would still attract its mainstream support, the CSU would be free to supply its own brand of conservative-national politics. Secure in their partnership, the CDU and CSU would present the other side of the two-bloc system.

Various comments are provoked by this appreciation of the developing party system. One is to query whether there really are electoral reservoirs waiting to be exploited by an explicitly conservative party – or whatever label may be thought appropriate for a federal CSU. The evidence here is not absolutely conclusive either way. On one count there are few reserves available, if the experience of the *Aktionsgemeinschaft Vierte Partei* (AVP) is any guide. This fourth-party exercise – widely interpreted as a kite-flying expedition on behalf of Strauss – failed dismally in 1976, as had other similar moves under different labels in previous *Land* elections. However, that does not quite close the matter, since public opinion polls published after the 1976 election indicated that the combined support for the CDU and CSU fighting separately might just about have won an absolute majority of votes.

The difference in evaluation can be quite easily explained: a *bona fide* fourth party in the shape of the CSU under the leadership of Strauss would have a decided electoral impact, even drawing some support from SPD and FDP voters. Furthermore, the CSU would still have a Bavarian base: the CSU won 10.6 per cent of the *federal* vote in the 1976 election – a much better performance than the FDP overall – and even if the party had to forfeit a sizeable share of its Bavarian following to the CDU, the party would still clear the 5 per cent clause without difficulty.

On these grounds it is reasonable to suppose that the model proposed by Strauss could work in the immediate sense of providing an alternative bloc to the SPD–FDP formation, even though it might not succeed in gaining an overall majority in the first instance. But the implications for the West German party system are less fathomable. What, after all, would be the exact contribution to be made by the CSU? Strauss has frequently indicated that his preferred political style is polarisation for the sake of polarisation, with few holds barred. That emphasis, made plain in his secret *Sonthofener Rede* to CSU leaders in 1974, was deliberately aimed to raise the political temperature in the Federal Republic: an injection of emotional irrationality which, if translated into the two-bloc thesis, could lead to a rather negative 'rediscovery' of ideology.[15]

Thus far from being just a 'conservative corrective' to the CDU, the potential of the CSU could be viewed as a lever on the whole party system. Necessarily, the CDU would be taken some way along the same path, and just as surely the SPD and FDP would be taken along a divergent one. That scenario, if at all convincing, raises an important question, namely, how far it is possible for the superstructure of political leadership to determine the course of political argument, despite the fact that all the social indications of party politics in Western Germany point to an amelioration rather than an escalation?

Notes and References

1. The concept of 'stability' is not entirely unambiguous. See D. Sanders and V. Herman, 'The Stability and Survival of Governments in Western Democracies', *Acta Politica*, 1977/3. However, even on their 'survival' index,

West German governments must rate highly quite apart from the more deficient measures of longevity, ministerial turnover, etc.

2. The nature of 'elective functions' of legislatures is examined more generally in G. Smith, *Politics in Western Europe*, Heinemann, 1979.

3. The reverse situation applied in the 1950s when the CDU was dominant. Then the SPD fared relatively well at Länder elections. See U. Kitzinger, *German Electoral Politics*, op. cit. The 'chancellor effect' may go some way explaining the comparative weakness of a federal governing party shown in *Land* elections.

4. Walter Scheel's election in 1974 depended on the SPD–FDP majority in the *Bundesversammlung*. But as a result of subsequent *Länder* elections and the 1976 federal election, the CDU–CSU had a majority preventing Scheel from taking a second presidential term. Karl Carstens, the CDU–CSU candidate, was elected in May 1979.

5. After the defeats in early 1978, the FDP recovered its position somewhat in subsequent *Länder* elections (see table p. 143) but there was no question of the party being well clear of the electoral threshold in any of the *Länder*.

6. Very little of substance has appeared in English on the Free Democrats. The most recent inclusive account is H. Kaack, 'The FDP in the German Party System' in Cerny, op. cit. See also the same author in R. Löwenthal and H.-P. Schwarz (eds.), *Die Zweite Republik, 25 Jahre BRD–Eine Bilanz*, Stuttgart: Seewald, 1974.

7. The argument on the effect on the SPD of the change from Brandt to Schmidt in 1974 is not quite clear cut. Brandt's 'democratic' style encouraged both factionalism *and* enthusiasm, whilst Schmidt's 'no-nonsense' approach enforced a greater unity *and* probably less commitment. There was an electoral benefit as shown by the 1976 election result compared with the preceding *Länder* losses. See W. Paterson, 'The SPD after Brandt's Fall', *Government and Opposition*, Spring 1975.

8. For a critical assessment of the SPD since Bad Godesberg, see W.-D. Narr (and others), *SPD – Staatspartei oder Reformpartei?* Munich: Piper, 1976. Also: C. Fenner, *Demokratischer Sozialismus und Sozialdemokratie: Realität und Rhetorik der Sozialismus–Diskussion in Deutschland*, Frankfurt: Campus Verlag, 1977.

9. Thus Wilhelm Hennis in *Organisierter Sozialismus*, Stuttgart: Ernst Klett, 1977, sees a definite retreat from the liberal principles of the Godesberg Programme in the formulations of *Orientierungsrahmen '85*.

10. A brief account of the 'Jusos' and their ideological positions is given by W. Krause (and others) in *Zwischen Anpassung und sozialistischer Politik: Zur Geschichte der Jungsozialisten seit 1945*, Berlin: Demokratische Verlags-Kooperative, 1976.

11. The basic work on the CSU is A. Mintzel, *Die CSU: Anatomie einer konservativen Partei*, Opladen: Westdeutscher Verlag, 1975. In English, a recent evaluation is by C. Carl-Sime, 'Bavaria, the CSU and the West German Party System', *West European Politics*, January 1979.

12. The 'Kreuth' revolt of the CSU is documented and assessed in A. Mintzel, 'Der Fraktionszusammenschluss nach Kreuth', in *Zeitschrift für Parlamentsfragen*, 8/1977.

13. See G. Pridham, 'A "Nationalization" Process: Federal Politics and State Elections in West Germany', *Parliamentary Affairs*, Spring 1973.

14. The tensions of the 'split' party system are shown by G. Lehmbruch, 'Party and Federation in Germany: A Developmental Dilemma', *Government and Opposition*, Spring 1978.

15. It would be unfair to make Strauss solely responsible for the outlook of the CSU. The party has its own right-wing credentials. See S. Schmidt (ed.), *Schwarze Politik aus Bayern: Ein Lesebuch zur CSU*, Darmstadt: Luchter-

hand, 1974. See also, C. Amery and J. Kölsch, *Bayern–ein Rechtsstaat?*
Reinbeck: Rowohlt, 1974.

Further Reading

W. Besson, *'Regierung und Opposition in der deutschen Politik'*, *Politische Vierteljahresschrift*, September 1962.
K. D. Bracher, *The German Dilemma*, Weidenfeld and Nicolson, 1974.
J. Dittberner and R. Ebbighausen (eds.), *Parteiensystem in der Legitimationskrise*, Opladen: Westdeutscher Verlag, 1973.
A. Grosser, *Germany in Our Time: A Political History of the Post-War Years*, Penguin Books, 1974.
G. Lehmbruch, *Parteienwettbewerb im Bundesstaat*, Stuttgart: Kohlhammer, 1976.
G. Lehmbruch, 'The Ambiguous Coalition in West Germany', in M. Dogan and R. Rose (eds.), *European Politics*, Macmillan, 1971.
R. Löwenthal and H. P. Schwarz (eds.), *Die Zweite Republik – 25 Jahre Bundesrepublik: Eine Bilanz*, Stuttgart: Seewald, 1974.
W. D. Narr (ed.), *Auf dem Weg zum Einparteienstaat*, Opladen: Westdeutscher Verlag, 1977.
H. Oberreuther (ed.), *Parlamentarische Opposition: Ein internationaler Vergleich*, Hamburg: Hoffmann und Campe, 1975.
G. Pridham, 'The CDU–CSU Opposition in West Germany, 1969–1972', *Parliamentary Affairs*, Spring 1973.
P. Pulzer, 'Responsible Party Government and Stable Coalition: The Case of the Federal Republic', *Political Studies*, June 1978.
P. Pulzer, 'The German Party System in the Sixties', *Political Studies*, March 1971.
H.-G. Schumann (ed.), *Die Rolle der Opposition in der Bundesrepublik Deutschland*, Darmstadt: Wissenschaftliche Buchgesellschaft, 1976.
G. Smith, 'West Germany and the Politics of Centrality', *Government and Opposition*, Autumn 1976.
H.-G. Veen, *Opposition im Bundestag*, Bonn: Eichholz Verlag, 1976.

5 The Constraints on Politics

Cycles of the National Issue

The German Question, or at least its legacy, has dominated much of the political history of the Federal Republic. The division of Germany in 1945, the loss of the eastern territories, the establishment of two rival states on the territory of the former Reich, their absorption into the opposing power blocs of East and West – these are all related to the original German Question. Its formulation in the nineteenth century was centred on the quest for German unity and on the terms on which unification could be achieved.

Yet the form of its realisation in 1871 did not end the matter, but rather changed the question: the new Reich posed problems concerned with Germany's place in Europe and with the nature of her 'self-identity': of external and internal coexistence. With these two ingredients, German history in the first part of the twentieth century can be portrayed in terms of an unstable dynamic which reached a climax (internally as well as externally) in the National Socialist dictatorship.

After 1945 that dynamic was dispersed. A kind of exhausted equilibrium supervened: at least temporarily, 'Germany' disappeared from the European map, and the remnants were patched into the framework of the two hostile alliances, almost a guarantee that the disappearance would be made permanent. From this point of view we are concerned with the legacy of the German Question, not with the question itself, not anyway with the forms in which it had thus far been presented.

What, then, is that legacy? In the first place, it took shape as a simple and natural reaction: Germany was divided; her unity must be restored. The German Question was an imperative of reunification, an absolute demand and a touchstone against which all particular policies had to be judged (as much the policies advanced by the parties and the government of the Federal Republic as those followed by the Western allies). The fact that the hopes of reunification receded and that policies were adopted which arguably led in a quite different direction did not at first affect the status of the imperative. But gradually – almost insensibly – the emphasis altered: from a concentration on the means of securing reunification as a guiding preoccupation, the parties shifted to preserving it as an ideal or ultimate end, finally incorporating 'Germany' as a symbol, an essential myth of the republic.

The transition from the real to the ideal was not easily accomplished. At successive stages fundamental issues were raised, not just in connection with the prospect of reunification but all related matters: the position of Western Germany in Europe, relations with Eastern Europe and the other German state, the elusive problem of how best to keep alive a German national consciousness. That predicament became serious as the German Democratic Republic gradually asserted its claim to sovereignty and regarded itself as a socialist state rather than as a German one. But the Federal Republic was not immune either: not only has there developed a concept of West German national interests but a feeling for a West German national consciousness as well.

If the symbols are quietly left to moulder, then the legacy itself will disappear in the new identities. But no one can be quite certain how future developments may affect the subjective area of 'consciousness': as long as any prospect of reunification remains unreal, the national issue only acts as a weak constraint on politics. Yet the parties have to maintain the ideal of German unity and have to be constantly aware, too, that in one form or another it could suddenly be given a new life.

Thus if we examine the post-war contribution of the parties in terms of two completed cycles – consensus, polarisation, realignment – we have to leave open the possibility of the commencement of a third cycle as well, even though it may be doubted whether the German Question has any dynamic left. The two cycles which have been completed indicate the strength of the individual parties and the resilience of the party system, for it is remarkable how they have maintained their cohesion, despite the tensions which were set up. Moreover, it is notable that the conflict has been contained within the single dimension of parliamentary government and parliamentary opposition.

The beginning of the first cycle can be located at the foundation of the republic, for its establishment naturally implied a consensus of viewpoint about the situation of Germany at that time. There then followed the long second phase during which the polarisation between the SPD and the CDU became acute, but by 1960 the SPD had come to identify itself with government policies. The second cycle started with the growing flexibility of the CDU in its *Ostpolitik*, and the inter-party agreement reached its peak with the formation of the Grand Coalition and for a year or so afterwards. That mood then soured, and the confrontation became intense once Brandt launched his own policies in 1969, reaching a climax in 1972 with the opposition's all-out attack on the government. Once again, however, the polarisation ebbed, and the CDU ultimately, perhaps unwillingly, accepted the outcome of the *Ostpolitik*. If it is not quite a consensus, the present uneasy peace between the parties shows that neither side is able to initiate a new policy.

First cycle: The Adenauer line

Two factors determined the early cleavage between the SPD and the CDU. One was the fact that the SPD was thrust into opposition, and the nature of that opposition was quickly defined by Schumacher: his idea was that the SPD should offer a 'complete alternative' to the CDU government and he insisted that only the SPD could speak for 'Germany'. The second factor reinforced the first: Adenauer proceeded with his immediate objectives – unreserved alliance with the West, unremitting hostility to the Soviet Union – in a single-minded way which brooked no compromise with the opposition.

Two assumptions dominated Adenauer's thinking. Firstly, he believed that the Soviet Union sought a hegemony in Europe and over the whole of Germany, and if that supposition were true then – unless the Federal Republic was prepared to make a willing capitulation – the Soviet Union had to be resisted at every turn. All her initiatives, her dangling of the prospect of a united Germany, were no more than ploys, delaying tactics to hinder the emergence of a strong West German state, ultimately the sole barrier to Soviet ambitions in Germany. His second assumption followed from the first: only by means of the security of Western alliances and through an unswerving commitment to their cause could the Federal Republic become sufficiently strong to further the chance of reunification – not entirely by her own efforts, but by working from within the network of alliance.

Adenauer's 'policy of strength' was based on the fixed belief that, sooner rather than later, the Soviet Union would be forced to make a settlement in favour of a reunited Germany on terms acceptable to the West. Meanwhile the Federal Republic had to avoid all actions which might help the regime in East Germany to become firmly established; the illegitimate puppet state would soon become a burden to the Soviet Union and would be treated as expendable. In the end, reunification would come about of itself.

If the electorate did not quite follow all of Adenauer's reasoning, the conclusions were at least attractive: the Federal Republic would eventually become the heir to the estate of unified Germany. Natural justice would be done, for she was the only rightful claimant. All of that could be achieved without sacrificing the protection and material benefits afforded by the Western alliances. Why embark on other risky enterprises in the cause of unity? Neither the gamble with neutralism nor reliance on the chance that Soviet initiatives might possibly be genuine were attractive propositions.

The SPD could see the flaws in Adenauer's case. His policy of full-hearted identification with the West might have the objective of reunification, but in the meanwhile the practical effect was that the two parts of Germany were being forced wider apart. Adenauer was also endangering legitimate German interests by accepting the principle of supra-national control (as with the establishment of the International Ruhr Authority) and by the other concessions he was bent on making to France in the cause of *rapprochement*. Above all the SPD saw the dangers that would result if the Federal Republic were drawn into the Western military camp as an active partner, for that step would make it very difficult, if not impossible, to negotiate a settlement with the Soviet Union. The full fury of the SPD's onslaught on Adenauer's government was reserved for that issue, especially in the debates on German membership of the proposed European Defence Community, a way of rearming West Germany without the embarrassment, for the Western allies, of an independent West German army.

The SPD did not wish to be entirely negative. The party was not, after all, opposed in principle to West European co-operation or even completely to economic integration. But such matters had to be seen in the context of this question: would their implementation make reunification more difficult to achieve? The postulates behind Adenauer's severe logic were suspect, and the SPD doubted if Adenauer's headlong rush towards Western Europe would really achieve the proclaimed objectives. Moreover, there were even doubts concerning Adenauer's commitment to the all-German cause: as a Catholic and a Rhinelander, he was incapable of grieving over the fate of Bismarck's Reich for very long. What Adenauer could afford to do, the SPD could not: to identify itself with his policies might – as Schumacher dreaded – result in the old anti-national charge being levelled against the party. The SPD saw that identification with the West almost necessarily meant rearmament in consequence, but that also raised the spectre of German militarism and was alone sufficient grounds for total opposition. Schumacher had once taunted Adenauer with being 'the chancellor of the allies'. That jibe epitomised the degree of polarisation between the two parties.

Yet circumstances gradually changed so as to make the SPD's intransigent position untenable. The party was essentially powerless in opposition and it was overtaken by events. The hardening lines between East and West made it ever more difficult for the SPD to present its policies as a realistic option. There might have been opportunities had the SPD been in power: the Soviet note of March 1952 promised substantial concessions in order to head off West German rearmament, and the possibilities of a reunified if 'neutralised' solution for Germany were confirmed by the case of Austria, which managed to shake off the yoke of occupation by the terms of her State Treaty of 1955. But was that example appropriate to Germany? Her strategic and political position was vastly more important than that of Austria, and no one could be sure just how much the Soviet Union was prepared to give way on Germany. The catch was that once West Germany followed the lines of a Soviet initiative her Western ties would be weakened, perhaps irretrievably so. Whatever positive substance lay in the Soviet willingness to negotiate a peace treaty for a united Germany, whilst Adenauer was in power a brusque rebuttal was inevitable: free elections throughout the whole of Germany had to be the precondition.

Correct as the SPD may have been about the direction of Adenauer's policies, the party was overwhelmed by the defeats in the elections of 1953 and 1957. Belief in a united Germany was as strong as ever, but the electorate was lulled into supposing that unification would occur as a natural dispensation of justice. Moreover, the sharp alternatives once offered by the SPD were becoming increasingly blurred. No longer did the party reject all participation in the affairs of the European Coal and Steel Community or oppose further steps to integration, as those offered by the setting-up of a European Economic Community in 1957. Nor did the SPD continue to fight Germany's entry into the North Atlantic Treaty Organisation. Gradually the SPD had dismantled the various pieces of its opposition, but it did so without any sense of a total strategy to replace its across-the-board negation in the first years of the republic.[1]

One remedy was the Godesberg Programme adopted in 1959, for it set the lines of a new strategy, and the implications for the national question were confirmed in the following year, when Herbert Wehner committed the party to a bilateral foreign policy with the CDU.[2] At the same time the SPD quietly buried its own *Deutschlandplan*, preferring thenceforward to work in tandem with the CDU. It is an ironic commentary on the movement made by the SPD that so soon afterwards the basic premises of Adenauer's doctrine should have been exposed as false. The erection of the Berlin Wall in August 1961 laid bare the essential frailty of the 'policy of strength'. Although the severance between East and West Berlin was a confession of the economic and political near-bankruptcy of the East German regime, the inability of West Germany to capitalise on its crisis was equally apparent. The simple fact was that the Soviet Union had no alternative but to prop up the German Democratic Republic, especially in the face of growing West German power. The Federal Republic was furthermore absolutely dependent on her Western alliance (her strength could only be expressed with and through her allies), but at no point were they prepared to risk a confrontation in the cause of reunifying Germany.

The shortcomings evident in Adenauer's conception did not make the SPD's alternative – which inevitably would have involved some form of non-alignment – suddenly once more relevant. Too much had happened to make reunification on the basis of neutralisation realistic any longer. The SPD had also seen some of its other objections to government policy become inoperative: the opposition had always insisted that the Federal Republic should be treated as an equal by its allies, a demand for *Gleichberechtigung* which in the early years was not realised. But that equality was earned during the 1950s, within the alliances and by means of West Germany's economic progress. The growing stature of the Federal

Republic, on its way to becoming the foremost West European power, made the SPD's former attitudes redundant. The party might still feel that the chances of restoring German unity had been sacrificed, but it had to proceed from current realities. If the SPD were one day to achieve its aim of entering government, then it was inconceivable that it would renege on the Western commitments.

With the emergence of a consensus between the SPD and the CDU around 1960, the first cycle of the national issue was complete. In terms of progress towards the goal of reunification, nothing at all had been achieved. But for the internal development of the republic the conflict had been both inevitable and essential. The polarisation was contained within the limited opposition of the major parliamentary parties, and their antagonism was modified by an underlying consensus, the acceptance of the republic and its institutions. A polarisation not based on that consensus could well have led to progressive instability of the political system: if the SPD had not supplied the limited polarisa-tion, then other political forces would have arisen to do so. Again, without the substantial agreement the parties finally developed, the subsequent changes in popular outlook and in policy could not have come about.

Second cycle: The changing Ostpolitik
No sudden switch in course resulted from the 1961 Berlin crisis, but even before the close of Adenauer's rule in 1963 the *Ostpolitik* changed in character. Its negative features were still prominent: thus the Federal Republic still insisted that she alone had the right of representation for the whole of Germany. This claim, the *Alleinvertretungsanspruch*, was given teeth by the application of the Hallstein Doctrine: the potent threat to sever diplomatic relations with countries recognising the East German regime and the exclusion of those which already maintained them, chiefly the communist states of Eastern Europe.

The sole exception to this rule was the Soviet Union, with which the Federal Republic had maintained relations since 1955. The adoption of an ostrich-like attitude was not feasible in her case, but it could also be argued that the Federal Republic was losing out by using the discriminatory tactic against other East European states: unqualified insistence on the claims of the Federal Republic meant that West Germany had no opportunity to conduct a positive *Ostpolitik*. A new 'policy of movement' (the *Bewegungspolitik*) was initiated, which gave greater flexibility to the Hallstein Doctrine: the East European communist states could be exempted, since through 'an accident of birth' they had had no choice but to recognise the German Democratic Republic. The hope behind the *Bewegungspolitik* was that normal relations with those states (trade agreements and diplomatic recognition) would help 'unfreeze' the East European bloc as far as the Federal Republic was concerned.

But the new policy by no means implied that basic West German goals had changed. There was a continuing insistence that any loss of the eastern territories could only be settled by a general peace treaty; Germans still had a claim on their homelands and a right of return. Furthermore, there was no intention of extending the policy of movement towards East Germany, for that would have implied some form of recognition. Indeed, the shift in policy could be construed as having as its major aim not a reconciliation with Eastern Europe for its own sake but an attempt thereby to weaken the ties of the smaller communist states with the Democratic Republic.

That overly negative aspect was toned down in the course of the Grand Coalition, for an attempt was made by Chancellor Kiesinger to open a dialogue with the East German government; even though there was no question of the GDR being regarded as a 'state', nevertheless he was prepared to admit that an 'artefact' of sorts did exist. That concession justified a fresh appreciation of West Germany's *Deutschlandpolitik*. In particular, since a start had to be made somewhere, proposals were made for discussion and co-operation with the East German authorities on a range of practical and technical matters which concerned both countries. The new approach, dubbed the 'policy of little steps', was a significant change of strategy on the part of the Federal Republic, but it did not mean a change of heart, nor the relinquishment of ultimate objectives: the 'little steps' were directed towards reunification, not recognition.

Both the policy of movement and its later extension in the *Deutschlandpolitik* represented attempts to regain the initiative which had been lost through Adenauer's failed policy of exclusion. Yet both misfired badly. The 'movement' in the *Ostpolitik* ran directly into opposition from the Soviet Union: it was seen as an attempt by West Germany to pursue a divisive strategy in Eastern Europe. The climax came in 1968 with the 'invasion' of Czechoslovakia by the Soviet Union, when that country attempted to go its own way. The Federal Republic was one of the scapegoats, accused of meddling and of encouraging the forces of counter-revolution. The *Ostpolitik* ground to a halt and the *Deutschlandpolitik* fared no better. West German overtures met with a negative response from the GDR: the recognition of the Democratic Republic had to precede reconciliation, a sequence which anyway precluded the hope of reunification.

With their common policies in tatters, the CDU and the SPD in coalition had little prospect of reaching agreement on new ones, and differences between them became apparent, so that the *Ostpolitik* was effectively 'bracketed out' for the remainder of their joint rule. But the impasse of government was accompanied by signs of a revaluation of the Federal Republic's position at other levels. In party politics the change was necessarily slow, since there were strong political taboos against any advocacy of recognition or premature concessions regarding the loss of the eastern territories: the parties naturally were wary of alienating support, especially amongst the 'refugee' sector of the electorate, but more generally there was the risk of being denigrated as a 'party of recognition'. Thus it was at a non-official level that the debate was opened. A memorandum published by the evangelical Churches in 1965 was perhaps the first significant challenge to the orthodox position. The authors questioned the justice of the one-sided insistence on a German *Recht auf Heimat* and a dogmatic claim to the return of territories regardless of the changes that had actually taken place in Europe since 1945.[3] Taking their inspiration from such sources, the Free Democrats – who were out of power – were able to advocate a policy of radical reappraisal, and it was the identity of viewpoint between the new FDP leader, Walter Scheel, and Brandt, with his experience of the problems as foreign minister in the Grand Coalition, which gave the most promising basis for a coalition of the FDP and SPD.

What Brandt had learned from the collapse of the CDU–SPD policy was that a new *Ostpolitik* only had a hope of success if it were instituted with the agreement of the Soviet Union: the road led through Moscow. The new government lost no time in negotiating a major treaty with the Soviet Union as the precursor of all subsequent settlements. A treaty was concluded in 1970 which contained both a renunciation of force as well as a recognition of the territorial *status quo* as far as those two countries were concerned. It was followed by a similar agreement with Poland, following the lead given by the Soviet Union. Those treaties (in a sense substitutes for the German peace treaty which had never materialised) were also an essential preamble for an inner-German settlement, as was the four-power agreement on Berlin which was reached in 1971.

A treaty with the German Democratic Republic was altogether more difficult to negotiate, since it concerned more than a recognition of the *status quo*. Any agreement had to accommodate two vastly different positions: the demand on the side of the GDR for international recognition and the insistence by the Federal Republic that the two states could never be considered 'foreign' to one another. In launching his *Ostpolitik* Brandt had used the formula 'two states of a single German nation', which made it clear that his government would not be content simply with 'normalising' relations. The incompatibilities led to long-drawn-out negotiations before the terms of the proposed Basic Treaty, the *Grundlagenvertrag*, were published in November 1972.

If for no other reason, the West German reluctance to concede full recognition was determined by the necessity of keeping within the requirements of the Basic Law, the overriding injunction to secure German unity. The outcome in the treaty was a number of partial concessions and approximations to full recognition: the inviolability of the frontiers and the territory of the two states, the renunciation of force, the restriction of the jurisdiction of each state to its own territory, separate international representation. Together they were tantamount to full recognition – but not quite. Nowhere in the treaty is the relationship between them described in terms of that which exists between two foreign states, and diplomatic representation is not conducted through ambassadors but through 'permanent missions'. In additon, there were numerous clauses in the Basic Treaty which underlined the special nature of the relationship between the two states – clauses which covered trade, cultural affairs, and especially the provisions for the freer movement of people within Germany – thus denying the absolute nature of the 'frontiers' between the two countries. On the other hand, the West German commitment to eventual re-unification had to be expressed unilaterally by the Federal Republic, not as a part of the treaty.

No doubt the CDU was caught unprepared by the speed at which the new *Ostpolitik* and *Deutschlandpolitik* unfolded and by the consequential way in which the SPD–FDP coalition proceeded once the initial decision to reach a comprehensive settlement had been made. The pique that the opposition felt in being powerless to dictate policy, as it had been accustomed to do for so many years, may in part account for the bitterness of the attack which was launched on the government: the polarisation was reminiscent of the furious polemics of the early 1950s. In itself the government's justification of its policies was entirely reasonable: nothing was really conceded in the treaties, territorially or otherwise, which had not long ago been forfeited. Given the impossibility of securing a peace treaty for Germany, a continued legalistic insistence on her 'rights' was increasingly irrelevant to the situation of contemporary Europe. Even more, it was a major stumbling-block in the way of securing a general European détente. Too much ground had been lost during the years of 'negative exclusion' and, later, half-hearted conciliation. The government's effort to 'catch up with the reality' created in 1945 represented the only chance for the Federal Republic to influence future development positively.

Reasonable as this defence of the *Ostpolitik* was, the counter-arguments put by the opposition had force. True, there was a promise of better relations with the countries of the communist bloc, but the various treaties brought little of tangible benefit to Germany. Since it was abundantly clear that the East European states placed great value on a settlement, and in view of the substantial assurances they received from the Federal Republic, a much stiffer bargain could have been struck. That applied to the Basic Treaty as well. The government argued that its policy of bringing about change through *rapprochement* was the only practicable one, since anyway all the cards held by the Federal Republic – especially the trump one of recognition – were rapidly wasting assets: the German Democratic Republic could not indefinitely be relegated to second-class status merely by the will of the Federal Republic. But the CDU did not regard this as a conclusive argument. What, after all, did the Basic Treaty achieve? The opposition dismissed the provisions aimed at 'humanising' the relations between the two states – chiefly the measures for easing the movement of people – as 'mere bagatelles'. It was a small return for the prize of international recognition and the bestowal of legitimacy which the GDR obtained as a result of the treaty.

In the background lurked a fundamental hostility to the enterprise. No German government should be guilty of writing off German territory; some of the utterances in the debates contained more than a hint of nationalist and even 'anti-Versailles' sentiments. Many opponents within the CDU–CSU harped on all the old antagonisms: once more a Socialist-led government was selling German interests short. The charge, made in relation to the Basic

Treaty, that the government had acted 'in collusion with' the Communists was calculated to reawaken the suspicions that Social Democracy was an 'anti-national' party. These attacks were joined to the assertion that ultimately aspects of the treaties were patently in conflict with the stipulations of the Basic Law.

Yet for all the strength of feeling displayed by the opposition, it could hardly afford to be saddled with the responsibility of outright rejection. The CDU was well aware that public attitudes had changed and that Brandt's *Ostpolitik* had captured popular imagination. Moreover, did the party wish to be seen as an enemy of détente? If the negotiated treaties were not ratified by the Federal Republic, then relations with the communist states would be permanently soured, and a future CDU–CSU government would suffer considerable handicaps in its dealings with them. It would be all too easy to depict the CDU–CSU as the home of all unrepentant revanchists who had learned nothing since 1945. The Christian Democrats had their full share of die-hards, but the moderates in the party were by no means inclined to wreck the treaties; their main complaint was that the opposition had not been sufficiently consulted by the government in an attempt to reach an all-party accord. Yet, judging from the furore the treaties caused, it seems unlikely that any agreement would have been reached.

The CDU was in two minds what to do about the *Ostpolitik*. Root-and-branch opposition could prove a disaster for the party, yet acquiescence would be equally harmful – not just with regard to the substantive issues, but also in relation to the struggle to bring down the government. The slender SPD–FDP majority from 1969 until 1972 was a positive incitement to the opposition to use all means at its disposal, and the *Ostpolitik* had to be one of them.

Nonetheless, the CDU drew back from the brink. The CDU–CSU majority in the Bundesrat was not in the end used to block the ratification of the USSR and Polish treaties in 1972, and the opposition's decision to 'abstain' in the Bundestag vote reflected deep divisions in the CDU–CSU. Instead, the opposition in the Bundestag sought to dismiss Brandt *beforehand;* had that move succeeded, the CDU in government would have been able to play about with 'renegotiation', make some amendments, and lead its own dissenters to accept the outcome with good grace. That more attractive path could not be taken, in view of Brandt's survival, nor was the opposition any better placed when the issue of the Basic Treaty came to the fore later in the year.

To the discomfort of the CDU, the terms of the treaty were published during the election campaign of November 1972. Again the party was in a dilemma, since approval could only present the governing parties with an electoral bonus, but rejection was equally likely to meet with electoral disfavour. During the election campaign the CDU took the latter course, with the result that the victory of the SPD and FDP was interpreted by them as a favourable plebiscite. That left the opposition in a weak position, fully reflected by the internal divisions in the CDU–CSU. These had become apparent in the decision to abstain on the Moscow and Polish treaties in the Bundestag (the 'compromise' between supporters and opponents in the party), and that indecision continued for the Basic Treaty, although the opposition in the Bundestag did vote for rejection. The party's spleen was vented on the CDU leader, Rainer Barzel: he had lost the 1972 election and had also favoured accepting the treaties. The Bavarian CSU government then fought a rearguard action by appealing to the Constitutional Court to have the Basic Treaty declared incompatible with the Basic Law. Its verdict, given in July 1973, although hedged with qualifications, found no conflict. The opposition had by that time run out of ammunition.[4]

Effectively, the year 1973 marked the completion of the second cycle. It would be too much to say that the parties had re-established a consensus, and it took some time for the opposition to 'accept' the *Ostpolitik*. Like the SPD in the 1950s, the CDU could still argue that it had been in the right but that it had to work in the changed circumstances which the party would inherit in power. Brandt's own resignation in 1974 signalled the end of an era, and there was little enthusiasm left to continue the great debate on the national issue.

Material for a third cycle?

The guiding hope of Brandt's *Deutschlandpolitik* was that the Basic Treaty would rescue the idea of the German nation, that the two states, instead of just being alongside one another (*nebeneinander*), would increasingly work together (*miteinander*). The hope was attractive, electorally comforting, and possibly naïve. It rested on the supposition that the East German government thought on similar lines – or at least would not have the strength or temerity to act otherwise.

Yet as far as the GDR was concerned, once the blessing of recognition had been won, the conditions of the Basic Treaty, though irksome in particular respects, placed no real restraint on her sovereignty. There was not the slightest intention of succumbing to West German blandishments or of co-operating to keep the national ideal alive. In earlier years, it is true, the official GDR line had been quite different. The 1949 constitution, unlike the Basic Law, was drawn up as a document which in principle could apply to the whole of Germany. Responsibility for the division of the country rested with the West and with those forces which had helped to set up the Federal Republic. Even the new constitution of 1968 aspired to reunification on the basis of 'democracy and socialism' and described the Democratic Republic as 'a socialist state of the German nation'. Those vague allusions cost nothing as long as vital concessions had to be wrung from the Federal Republic. But the true standpoint was revealed in October 1974, when the constitution was amended to delete all reference to unification and to the German nation.[5]

The official attitude of the GDR can be summed up in its declared policy of *Abgrenzung*, which calls for a strict 'demarcation' between the two states. It means that all contacts should be kept as far as possible to a 'correct', official level and that where there are closer relationships, as in matters of trade, they should not spill over to a more general infiltration. Those reservations also apply to the areas specified in the Basic Treaty relating to cultural matters and other forms of co-operation. In the main they require separate and additional agreements, but apart from a range of technical co-operation little has resulted.[6]

The policy of *Abgrenzung* is directed towards the external relations of the GDR with the Federal Republic, but of equal importance is the attention given by the East German government to internal development: the Democratic Republic is represented as a new type of society; it is a state of the working classes, not one of the German nation. That is not an empty formula, since besides the obvious changes which have been made in society and economy, the regime also emphasises the creation of a new culture, the fundamentally different interpretation placed on German history, even the changing nature of the German language in the socialist society.

Seen against these determined efforts to bury the idea of a German national consciousness, the high hopes behind the Basic Treaty in the Federal Republic seem totally unjustified. The strategy of *Wandel durch Annäherung*, of securing change through *rapprochement*, went awry: the only change which did accelerate pointed in the opposite direction. The attempt to salvage Germany in the form of a *Kulturnation*, an association of peoples with a shared affinity in a common cultural heritage, proved to be equally misplaced.

A less obvious result of the *Deutschlandpolitik* was the effect that it had on Western Germany. The question of recognition cut two ways: the emancipation affected the Federal Republic as well, for it involved a process of self-recognition which had been delayed for as long as the pretence of reunification and the provisional nature of the West German state had been sustained. Thus the Federal Republic in the wake of the Basic Treaty finally emerged as an entity which could develop its own 'national' interests and increasingly rely on the presence of a West German national consciousness.[7] In contrast to the deliberate moulding which has taken place in the GDR, the outcome in the Federal Republic has been a natural consequence of political and social evolution.

These arguments lead to the conclusion that the national issue has reached a point of almost complete attenuation: there is no material left for a further cycle of party dispute and it ceases to act as a constraint on politics. Yet the case can be overstated. It may be premature to bury the *Deutschlandpolitik* or treat it just as part of the portmanteau of foreign relations. There are grounds for arguing that, precisely in the nature of the relationship between the two states, the national issue is preserved in a new form.

The basis of their relationship is an antagonism which reflects the contrasting nature of the two societies, not simply in their juxtaposition – since that would apply equally to any two socialist and capitalist systems – but in the essentially competitive attitude they share in relation to the German inheritance. There has been no sign of an ideological disengagement occurring; indeed, quite the reverse is true: each maintains the other as its negative reference, the *Feindbild*, the necessary enemy. This peculiarly German confrontation supplements and complicates the conflict between two ideologies, one socialist the other capitalist.

Accordingly there is a built-in enmity between the regimes of East and West Germany which differs qualitatively from the kind of antagonism which may obtain between two 'foreign' states. Rather paradoxically, the Basic Treaty has underlined rather than diminished their competitive stance their legal parity providing a common base. Neither is at all indifferent to the internal affairs of the other: the attention paid in the GDR to such matters as the employment of radicals in the public service or economic difficulties in the Federal Republic is countered by the latter in the special interest taken, say, in the treatment meted out to dissidents or the shortcomings of the planned economy.

Adequate fuel for a continuing sense of engagement is always available. Thus the position of West Berlin remains exceptional. Even though its status was partially regularised by the Quadripartite Agreement of 1971, essentially giving West Berlin a permanent form of occupation by the four original occupying powers, their guarantees cannot settle the position for all time. West Berlin is in an anomalous situation, since the four-power agreement did concede that it had special links with the Federal Republic (which can be strengthened), but West Berlin is not an integral part of the republic. At the same time, the presence of this capitalist enclave in the heart of the GDR acts as a constant source of irritation to the socialist state. It is not without significance that the 1968 constitution of the Democratic Republic describes 'Berlin', not just East Berlin, as the capital city.

West Berlin perhaps no longer has the aura of a front-line force for the Western world as it did during the various crises beginning with the Berlin blockade of 1948, but it would be wrong to suppose that the basis for confrontation no longer exists. In addition, it is necessary to bear in mind the problems affecting the economic viability of West Berlin. Not only is it cut off from its natural hinterland and consequently dependent on subventions from the Federal Republic, but West Berlin also has a very unfavourable demographic structure, a high proportion of elderly people, which makes its economic prospects dim in the long term. As a result the Federal Republic is likely to remain especially sensitive to any pressures exerted against West Berlin by the GDR, or for that matter by the Soviet Union as part of its wider European strategy.

The inability of the socialist regime to countenance open dissent from its own intellectuals, writers and party members is evidence of a weakness and insecurity which is seized upon in the Federal Republic to hammer home its own cause. There is also the distinct lack of trust shown by the GDR government towards its own citizens. Attempted flight from the republic is treated as a heinous criminal offence, and the presence of the 'death strips' on the borders with West Germany is a constant aggravation to the sensibilities of public opinion in the Federal Republic. As far as the free movement of people within the whole of Germany is concerned, the Basic Treaty raised false hopes; even allowing for the considerable number of visits to the GDR made possible for

West Germans (including West Berliners, almost eight million 'visits' were made to the GDR in 1978), the resentment they feel towards the restrictions remains. Any sign of widespread discontent within the GDR – noticeably absent since the Berlin 'uprising' of June 1953 – would immediately lead to demands that the Federal Republic should take action, even though legally, under the terms of the Basic Treaty, it would be powerless to do so.

The Democratic Republic finds itself in a cleft stick in its relations with the Federal Republic. On the one hand, its policy of *Abgrenzung* was devised as a means of sealing itself off from the attentions of the Federal Republic, but the economic links are extremely important and valuable to her: West German credits, her technology and the provision of an exceptionally secure market in Western Europe all combine to make the Federal Republic an indispensable trading partner. These links, also given prominence in the Basic Treaty, ensure that the imbalance in favour of the Federal Republic has an underlying political significance as well.

Finally, the ruling given by the Constitutional Court in 1973, by which it reached a favourable verdict on the Basic Treaty, has to be considered as supplying further material for future debate on the national issue. In reaching the conclusion that the treaty was compatible with the Basic Law, the Court had to square legal obligation with political reality, requiring from it a display of constitutional tightrope walking. Besides noting that the treaty nowhere treated the GDR as a foreign state, nor renounced the goal of reunification, the Court added its own provisos. One flowed more or less naturally from the reunification imperative of the Basic Law: all organs of state, therefore, including the political parties, were constitutionally bound to promote reunification. Other riders appended by the Court were that the inhuman conditions on the borders were at odds with the treaty, hence the federal government had a legal obligation to remove those barriers; that West Berlin was a part of the Federal Republic, even though at the time its position was modified by the rights of the three Western powers; that any agreement in the treaty should not prejudice the freedom of communication throughout the whole of Germany; that the 'frontier' between the two states was essentially the same as the borders between any of the West German *Länder*.

Some of these conditions may seem so unrealistic as to verge on a cloud-cuckoo-land of the Court's own making. In its attempt to render the treaty acceptable in strict constitutional terms, the Court may have helped to lay a political minefield. All future treaties, legislation and governmental action can be judged according to the Court's authoritative view. At the least there is a standing invitation to prolong the issues of recognition and reunification indefinitely.

All of those factors which point to potential confrontation have to be set against others which indicate a diminished salience of the national issue for West German politics. The special form of the antagonism between the two German states has to be modified by the recognition of the specifically West German consciousness, but there is no way of telling which might be the predominant expression at any given critical juncture. Meanwhile it would be unwise to assume that the German Question has been totally extinguished: the apparent lack of concern is explicable on the basis that the goals are, in the foreseeable future, quite unattainable.

Undoubtedly the parties would be immediately susceptible to any fresh stirrings of sentiment and resentment. But the issues in a further cyclical process can not be simply manufactured. That was evident in 1976, when the CDU threatened to use its majority in the Bundesrat to block a treaty with Poland which, in dealing with various matters consequent to the 1972 treaty, included a provision for the return of ethnic Germans still in Poland. The CDU insisted that the Polish Government should be obliged to allow free return, not just show a general willingness; the deletion of 'may' and the substitution of 'will' in the treaty was sufficient for the CDU objection to be withdrawn, a compromise which marked the tail-end of the *Ostpolitik*, not the commencement of a new round of polarisation. Helmut Schmidt's chancellorship has coincided with the move away from an active concern with the *Ost-* and *Deutschlandpolitik*, the realisation that the climate of détente did not produce a magic key. The Schmidt era could be symptomatic of a permanent shift of interest in the Federal Republic; in that case, one constraint on politics may have been removed.

Law and Politics

Commentators often remark on the atmosphere of legalism which surrounds political debate in Germany. Arguments need the backing and sanction of law, whilst conflict is resolved not so much by compromise as by correct interpretation. This feature of political style is evident in the unremitting emphasis placed on the Basic Law: political questions become constitutional questions as an almost regular occurrence. The relationship does appear to be important, but why should the law have this paramount status?

German legal traditions

The period after 1945 can be said to have witnessed the 'emancipation' of the *Rechtsstaat* in Germany. Yet it is strange that an idea
which for so long had been central to the German legal tradition
should have been made subordinate to the dictates of arbitrary
authority. An explanation may be found in the special qualities of
the *Rechtsstaat* which make it quite different from a state which is
simply based on the rule of law.

There is a correspondence between the two, but in the juxtaposition of *Recht* and *Staat* the translation 'rule of law' becomes
inadequate. The word *Recht* itself has various shades of meaning
('right', 'justice' and 'law') and these are given a direct expression
in the state. The state is imbued with *Recht* and does not exist
merely as a means of enforcement.

Such a rendering was supplemented in the nineteenth century by
a belief that the state itself had a 'moral capacity', that it could act
as the independent arbiter of the public interest. The panoply of
the state's authority could even be represented as the realisation of
the *Rechtsstaat* – which did not depend necessarily on the existence
of democratic and responsible government. That was only one
view, but we can see that the ordinary citizen could believe
Germany was a *Rechtsstaat*: the administration of justice was
impartial, he lived in the security of the laws and he knew that the
attitudes of all concerned, state officials and judges alike, respected
the codes of behaviour which the *Rechtsstaat* implied.

There was no question of the judiciary attempting to carve out
an independent place for itself or making a challenge to the
authority of the state. It was not that the judges were especially
supine but that they were regarded principally as state servants
who exercised a special competence in interpreting the law. The
legal aura attached to the *Rechtsstaat* imposed a structural unity on
the idea of service to the state. The prestige of the judiciary, as for
other state officials, stemmed from a common status as part of the
Beamtentum, not from a distinctive judicial ethos. The contribution
of the judiciary as an integral element of officialdom was made
with and through the state, not by its acting in defiance.

There were other trends in the nineteenth century which
reinforced the passive outlook of the judiciary. One was the
increasing emphasis upon a *Realpolitik* which made judgement on
policies dependent on their results rather than on reference to
absolute standards. A second and not unrelated 'realistic' development stemmed directly from German jurisprudence in the form of

legal positivism. The positivist doctrine was attractive, in that it provided a 'scientific' and 'objective' basis for non-intervention in the affairs of state on the part of the judiciary. The law was 'positive' in the sense that it was already 'given': it was not open to the judiciary to question its provenance or to apply an alternative standard which might undermine the legal authority of the state. The implications of legal positivism were serious for the *Rechtsstaat*, for its substantial content could be whittled away, whilst judicial interpretation was confined to forms and procedures, not to the content of the law. Positivism led directly to a legal formalism.[8]

The fragile quality of the German *Rechsstaat* became apparent: ultimately its guarantees depended on the self-restraint exercised by the ruling authorities. The full extent of the capitulation can be seen in the pathetic response of the judiciary to the Nazi dictatorship. Legal positivism had no answer to Hitler's use of legalised terror. For the most part, the members of the judiciary saw no conflict in continuing to serve the dictatorship as loyally as they had always served the state. But the 'law' they were then called upon to interpret was the expression of the Führer's arbitrary will.

The need to re-establish the place of law in post-war Germany was agreed, but purely as a spontaneous reaction to the excesses of National Socialism it would have been an insufficient remedy. The defective basis of the *Rechtsstaat* had to be replaced; no longer could it be taken on trust from the state and from the political authorities. To achieve the 'emancipation' of the *Rechtsstaat* it was necessary to place the status of law and its interpretation on a level independent of both forces. That entailed formulating an entirely judicial definition of the *Rechtsstaat*: legal norms subject to the independent interpretation of the judiciary and, equally important, a secure framework for that interpretation.

It is in these respects that the Basic Law made a notable contribution, and we can see that in defining the Federal Republic as a *Rechtsstaat* the constitution emphasises this attribute more than its republican, parliamentary or even democratic qualities. The emphasis was important, for it suited the mood of the time, a general revulsion from Nazi lawlessness, but perhaps even more significant was that it built on the one sure consensus in German society. Respect for the law – its security, certainty and impartiality – was more widely shared than a trust in political forms, democratic or not.

Another connection proved to be of importance as well: a

consensus was established for the elites. The law acts as a unifying influence in Germany because the higher echelons of the state and political establishment share a common world of discourse in the law and its norms. Traditionally a training in law has been a passport for entry into the public service, and the central core of the bureaucracy was – and is – composed of a legally trained elite. More generally, a legal training in the universities is an important avenue for entry to public life. The loose equivalent of the idea of an 'Establishment', the shadowy unity of a social and political elite in Britain, is the *Juristenmonopol* in Germany.[9] That form of elitism, well attuned to the requirements of the *Rechtsstaat*, survived in post-war Germany and became a vital source of support.

The scope of judicial review

The German system of judicial review was to some extent modelled on the American example, and there are several points of similarity between the Federal Constitutional Court and the Supreme Court of the United States. Both courts have a final jurisdiction over the constitution and both operate within a federal structure. With their power of authoritative interpretation they can settle disputes between all the leading organs of the state: the federal government, the president, the legislature, the member states. They both have the basic power to rule on the compatibility of legislation with the provisions of the constitution, and their constitutions include a Bill of Rights for which the courts act as guarantors.

There are also important differences. The Supreme Court normally makes its judgements by acting as a final court of appeal, except in direct conflicts affecting the competence of the leading organs of state. The rulings of the Supreme Court are made through hearing 'a ripe and living lawsuit', at a final stage of the proceedings and quite possibly years after an action was originally initiated. The West German Court can also make this delayed response, although points of constitutional interpretation may be referred to it in the course of deliberations in a lower court. But the Constitutional Court is not necessarily restricted in this way and can apply a direct jurisdiction as well. The immediate application occurs when federal legislation is challenged by one or more of the interested parties: the federal president, the Bundesrat, the individual *Länder*, the Bundestag (or rather, one third of its members, in effect the parliamentary opposition).

Here a distinction should be made between the 'concrete' control of norms exercised by the Court, which it enforces as an integral part of the legal process, and the 'abstract' control of norms, *abstrakte Normenkontrolle*, which is involved in giving an immediate ruling on the constitutionality of legislation (it is 'abstract' only in the sense that the Court's judgement can be made before a law comes into effect, rather like a form of injunction).

The immediacy of the Constitutional Court's involvement, seen in the 'abstract control of norms', has the consequence that the judicial function frequently appears to merge with the legislative one. At times constitutional jurisdiction verges on being a continuation of the political process, with the result that it may be difficult to draw a sharp line between law and politics.

The scope of the Constitutional Court is further widened by its power to hear 'constitutional complaints', *Verfassungsbeschwerde*, brought by aggrieved individuals. Grounds for complaint may arise through the actions of the federal government or in the effect of laws which can conflict with individual or group rights as listed in the first nineteen articles of the Basic Law. In this respect, with its power to make an immediate and final ruling, the Court resembles a more powerful version of the office of the Ombudsman. The latter is chiefly concerned with the investigation of arbitrary executive action, but both have an important popular connection. There is no danger of the Constitutional Court becoming a rather remote body: in purely numerical terms the category of 'constitutional complaints' vastly exceeds all other cases – to the extent that a sifting procedure is used to eliminate spurious or trivial actions.

With this wide spread of functions, the Basic Law clearly intended that the judicial role in the *Rechtsstaat* was not limited to providing a constitutional longstop, to be used only in the last resort to break a political deadlock. The Constitutional Court operates alongside the political institutions as a potent constraint.

Judicial review and the political process
There has been no crisis in Germany on the lines of 'the Court versus the People', nor has one or other of the political parties in recent years felt sufficiently incensed by a decision to threaten an overhaul of the Constitutional Court and its competences. The absence of confrontation is not guaranteed. Unlike the Supreme Court, West German practice does not exclude certain issues on the grounds that they are political questions. Rulings have to be given and the ability of the Constitutional Court to exercise judicial self-restraint is limited by its direct and inclusive jurisdiction.

Extrication is made more difficult by the widely held belief that the law and above all the Basic Law, is able to provide the answers. This outlook is illustrated by the long-running debate on the divergence between constitutional norms and constitutional reality (*Verfassung* and *Verfassungswirklichkeit*). The supposition that there is a gap between the two leads to the argument that the shortfall should be remedied: the Constitutional Court should ensure that the constitutional 'tasks' (*Verfassungsaufträge*) are fulfilled. That view is in contrast with the Anglo-American tradition of 'the living constitution', and in seeking a 'realisation' of the constitution, there is a pressure on the Constitutional Court to make an active intervention.[10]

The political parties are most affected by the overarching power of judicial interpretation, but that does not make them averse to using the Court. On the contrary, there is a well-worn track to Karlsruhe, the seat of the Constitutional Court, which has been trodden by the parties over the years. A party which is in a minority in the Bundestag is by no means compelled to wait until after the following election to reverse government legislation. The SPD blazed the trail in the early 1950s in its attempts to have Adenauer's defence and rearmament policies declared unconstitutional. A reversal of roles was evident in 1973, when the CSU appealed against the Basic Treaty with the GDR. Those efforts were unavailing, but the significant point is that in neither case were the complainants content with a political decision alone. A most notable reverse for the federal government occurred in 1975 on the issue of abortion law reform. Legislation passed by the SPD–FDP coalition was successfully challenged by the CDU–CSU opposition and by several *Länder*, on the grounds that the liberalising measure was in conflict with the guarantee of the right to life as provided in Article 2 of the Basic Law, the Court's verdict holding that the right also applied to the unborn child. The case raised a fundamental moral problem, but the lines of party conflict predominated: the result was trumpeted as a victory for the opposition over the government.

The Court is not able to avoid this kind of embroilment, and it is also drawn into a direct supervision of the parties by the terms of Article 21. Its most spectacular power concerns the banning of parties which it finds to be unconstitutional (the SRP in 1952 and the KPD in 1956). But the Court only reacts to an initiative from the parties in government who are intent on seeking a judicial rather than a political resolution of the issue. A realisation that the latter means is preferable, since the procedure of Article 21 has not been employed subsequently, shows that self-restraint on the political side is also possible.

When the Court does intervene, it may impose its own rather arbitrary conditions. Thus in a ruling on party finance made in 1966, it forbade the blanket subsidisation of the parties by the state and allowed only their reimbursement for election expenses. The law was accordingly amended, but again the Court imposed its own view: after the Bundestag parties had agreed that a minimum of 2.5 per cent of the federal vote should be the requirement for a share of the state subsidy, the Court in 1968 substituted a minimum of 0.5 per cent as more in line with its own idea of equity.

These 'conditional' aspects of the Constitutional Court's judgements undoubtedly affect the political process. Cases have occurred where the judges have insisted that their own 'informed opinion' should take precedence over that of the parties and government, without any obvious grounding in the Basic Law. The Court can add its own riders and stipulations – as was made evident in its verdict on the Basic Treaty in 1973 – which may tie the hands of future governments and affect the content of future legislation. Requirements may take the form of imposing a time limit within which the federal government should re-submit legislation which the Court has found to be unsatisfactory, and the Court may even indicate beforehand just what kind of new provision will be most acceptable. At all times the parties have to keep a weather eye open if they wish to avoid having their legislation mangled at a later date.[11]

Nonetheless, the Constitutional Court has had to develop some skill in balancing the claims of what is constitutionally desirable against what is 'politically feasible'. If all the *social* rights claimed to be inherent in the Basic Law were met, considerable financial and political chaos would result. The demand, for instance, that there should be an unrestricted choice in higher education, according to the provision for the free choice of 'trade, occupation or profession' and the freedom to select the 'place of training' as set out in Article 12 of the Basic Law, had serious implications for government. In fact, the Court had to put the stopper on, ruling that the full implementation of basic rights should be in accord with the availability of financial resources and with regard to established political and social priorities.

The examples of cases where the Constitutional Court may become too involved with the political process should not obscure the effect the judiciary has in maintaining the boundaries between the various political institutions, a demarcation which is especially important for a federal state. The rights of the *Länder* are entrenched in the constitution, but their erosion is always likely if the federal government is not limited by third-party arbitration. In a unitary state such questions of constitutional interpretation are finally settled in favour of the party which is able to control a majority in the elected assembly, but in a federal state that unified conception of political will is inadmissible. The balance in the Federal Republic has been maintained by the Constitutional Court, which usually finds in favour of the *Länder*, but not always. A judgement in 1974 concerning the rights of the *Länder* in the Bundesrat over federal legislation resulted in a sharp limitation of the degree to which the consent of the Bundesrat was necessary in the area of the *zustimmungsbedürftige Gesetze*: consent was mandatory for the specific clauses and not for subsequent amendments. Of course, conflicting party interests were the really operative factor in this case, since the CDU–CSU majority in the Bundesrat was mainly intent on using its power to hamstring the governing coalition. The question can then be asked whether the legal procedure is preferable to settling the matter by compromise or to referring the issue to the electorate for a final verdict.

A political judiciary?

Two views of the relationship between the judiciary and politics are possible, although they are not altogether incompatible. One is that the intimacy leads to a politicisation of the judiciary, a loss in real terms of judicial independence. The second reverses the sequence: it postulates that a judicialisation of politics results, and that the content of political decision making is strongly determined by legal norms and by judicial control.

We have seen how much the Constitutional Court can influence the political process. Is that influence offset by political controls? There are indications that the controls, if loose, are nevertheless fairly effective. There are no signs that a judicial caste has emerged on the one hand, or of an open party politicisation on the other.

Although the Basic Law sets out the principal functions of the Constitutional Court, its detailed structure and procedures are governed by federal law. They can be amended by an ordinary legislative majority, so that conceivably the Court could have its necessary voting majorities altered, requiring, say, a two-thirds majority to find against federal legislation rather than a simple majority as at present. But more relevant is the power of appointment as a means of control. The West German Court is composed of two senates, each consisting of eight members, appointed for a maximum term of twelve years. Some of the appointments are reserved for serving judges from the higher federal courts, but otherwise a qualification in law is sufficient. A university professor is therefore eligible to serve.

In the broadest sense appointments are political since they are made on the nomination of the Bundestag and Bundesrat, each body being responsible for half the appointments, and vacancies are filled by a single, agreed nomination from one house or the other. Some party-political influence is to be expected, although blatant party promotions are prevented by a two-thirds majority requirement either in the Bundesrat or in the relevant committee of the Bundestag. What results is a refined form of horse trading and a degree of party-*Proporz* is ensured. Neither maverick, right-wing backwoodsmen nor fiery, left-wing radicals are at all likely to creep through the net.

Successful candidates will have been considered partly on the strength of their expertise and partly by the drift of their political sympathies. A party connection may be useful, but it could be a barrier as far as the other parties are concerned. If a certain political *Weltanschauung* is a recommendation, then there is no sense in which members of the Constitutional Court subsequently can be subordinated to political pressure. Observers are always intent to gauge the party coloration which may determine the direction of a particular judgement, and in its early years the two senates of the Court were dubbed the 'red' and the 'black' respectively. But, in fact, examples of overt bias are not easy to find. The Constitutional Court maintains its independence in other ways: the removal of a serving member is only allowable on application from the Court itself, a remote eventuality. Since the Court was first established in 1951 it has successfully freed itself from administrative and budgetary controls (which were initially in the hands of the Ministry of Justice) and now stands quite separate from the other parts of the federal judicial structure.

None of these details really settles the question of political controls. There are hints of party patronage, but are they necessarily harmful, and what would be an alternative? A glaring fault of the Weimar Republic was its failure to secure a subordination of the state elites: members of the judiciary were generally no exception in their hostility to the republic, disguising their political partiality in the apparent neutrality of 'service to the state'. Even though radical reforms have not been made in the Federal Republic, the positive influence of the 'party state' should not be underestimated. A sanguine conclusion is that the present balance between party influence and judicial independence is sufficient for the Constitutional Court to have become aware of political realities without being overwhelmed by those pressures.

The more difficult question to answer is whether a political culture which supports a legalistic view of social obligations may also encourage a flight from politics and an escape into law. To that extent political democracy in West Germany may have been made that much less self-reliant. Yet the lack of confidence may also prove to be transient. Changes in popular and party attitudes have taken place. There is increasing confidence in the strength of parliamentary institutions, perhaps also a growing feeling that law is an inadequate substitute for politics.

The Parties and the Economy

A dominant economic philosophy

The terms of the West German economic consensus are set by the philosophy of the social market economy. It is a doctrine which is at once both specific and elusive. As first spelled out by Ludwig Erhard in the Frankfurt Economic Council, it implies a commitment to a capitalist system of enterprise based on the operation of market forces, yet modified by an important if nebulous 'social' qualification. Perhaps it is better described as a socially responsible market system. How, it may reasonably be asked, is social responsibility to be achieved through the operation of market forces? At least part of the answer lies in the role ascribed to state intervention. The system does not imply a neutral, passive, *laissez-faire* state, but one which seeks to influence and guide market forces in accordance with established social priorities. It is a policy of steering rather than planning, of indirect rather than direct control, of working through the market forces rather than attempting to set them aside.

Whatever construction is placed on the validity of the social market approach, it is the foundation of the economic consensus in the Federal Republic. In practical terms, the system has an anti-egalitarian ethos: the market does not easily coexist with the apparatus of a fair-share, planned economy, nor in the Federal Republic were restrictions of this kind imposed. From the outset the inequalities of the market system were deliberately encouraged: they constituted the motor of economic advance. Government taxation and financial policies were aimed at encouraging a high level of production and profitability, but they also ensured a high rate of investment and reinvestment of profits through taxation policies which favoured the retention rather than the distribution of profits.[12]

The outcome, with the contribution of other factors, was the economic 'miracle' of the 1950s and early 1960s. The tangible results could hardly be disputed: a poverty-stricken and devastated country was transformed into a prosperous and self-reliant one. If a contrast were needed, one only had to look across to the limping disaster of 'socialist planning' in the Democratic Republic. That picture has changed in the meanwhile, but for West Germany the proven resilience of the economy has made the tenets of the social market system an article of faith.

That resilience has one vital component: the inequality of the market should not operate at the expense of employed labour. Full employment, taken literally, is something of a statistical chimera, but the economic consensus would not have been formed – nor would it have survived – had the general standard of living not continued to rise. The economy proved equal to this demand, and at the same time secured the economic integration of the huge excess labour supply, the millions of people who came to West Germany after 1945.

In the face of this performance it is understandable that the SPD should have wanted to convince the electorate that it had no wish to throw away all that had been won. The formula of the Godesberg Programme – as much freedom as possible, as much planning as necessary – fell short of a complete affirmation of the social market system, but it differed only in emphasis from the proven policies of the CDU. In renouncing a specific class interest, the SPD undertook a responsibility for the whole of West German society, and that implied the maintenance of the existing social balance and the prerequisites for that balance. The social qualification helped to ease the transition for the SPD. Whilst the policies of the ruling CDU were predominantly oriented towards indirect influence on the part of the state, there was also an important contribution stemming from the application of Catholic social theory: the sense for the well-being of the collective whole. For its part, the SPD added the critical factor of the well-being of the people, in practice a bias towards organised labour.

The difference between the two parties should not be minimised. As the Federal Republic reached maturity, the CDU became rigid in its attachment to the orthodoxy of the market economy. Increasingly the CDU in power was rendered ineffective by the cross-pressures of organised interests, and in the process became identified with the protection of the entrepreneurial class, even to the extent of warding off legislative action against the operation of cartels, an attitude quite contradictory to the CDU's belief in the free operation of market forces. Nor did the SPD completely abandon its preference for direct intervention: only as long as the economy showed no sign of faltering was the party content to stay completely within the market orthodoxy.

The extent of the agreement between the two parties and of their common anxiety at the economic downturn in the mid-1960s was made evident in the course of the Grand Coalition, itself a product of that concern. The passing of the law on stability, the *Stabilitätsgesetz*, can be viewed as a reaction to a particular crisis, but it was also a fundamental affirmation of the norms of the market philosophy in a legal form. The stability law specifies the leading priorities of government economic policy: the maintenance of price stability, full employment, a foreign trade equilibrium and the extent of a 'compatible' degree of economic growth. The point is that these objectives have to be balanced one against the other, and the emphasis is placed on the governmental function of promoting stability – hence precluding any radical change or experimentation.

Since the passing of the stability law, economic circumstances have changed but the underlying commitments of the parties have not. The SPD has been in power continuously, and there have been movements within the party to bring the SPD back on to the path of socialist intervention. But it is significant that the CDU in opposition has had to content itself with levelling charges against the government of mismanaging the economy. It is the management function which they both accept. The changes that have taken place are more general (the preparedness, for example, to accept a moderate rate of inflation if that will secure a lower level of unemployment), but they do not signify a resurrection of socialist economic doctrine.

Corporate traditions
The main conditions of the West German economic consensus rest on agreement between the parties, between the major economic

interests and finally between those interests and the parties. A degree of mutual adjustment is implied: if the organised interests accept the leadership of the parties, it is also true that the parties themselves act within a set of well-defined constraints. The result is a very broad social agreement, something apparently quite new in the German experience. How is it to be explained? The contrast with the Weimar Republic is so striking that we have to look first at recent history. The chaos of the parties, the jungle of interests in the first republic and the harmony and order of the second stand in contrast. The Weimar Republic is separated from the Federal Republic by the intervening Nazi dictatorship, by its 'social revolution'. The imagery of the *Volksgemeinschaft* was reinforced by the practical policies of *Gleichschaltung*, which brought the conflicting forces of the pluralist society firmly to heel. The outcome of Nazi rule was not merely to blur the divisions but to put the whole society into the melting-pot, the precondition for the 'new' society after 1945.

Yet exclusive concentration on this relatively brief period of German history – as if German society was at one stroke bludgeoned into a new shape and outlook – falls short of providing a completely satisfactory explanation. It is, for instance, relevant to ask just why the vision of a *Volksgemeinschaft* should have proved so seductive in the first place, and how it was that the orderly structure of National Socialism should have been so rapidly erected.

Therefore we should also look at certain features of German society which ante-date the modern period, in particular at those 'solidaristic' traits which favour co-operation and participation as opposed to majoritarian and adversary styles of conflict regulation. Revival of interest in the concept of 'corporatism' – freed from its association with Fascist ideology and the 'corporate state' – has a special relevance for Germany. It draws attention to elements of the social structure which are far older than the competitive pressures of pluralism. The corporatist strands cut across and obscure the other divisions of society and preserve social segments reminiscent of the 'corporations', self-regulating entities which also exercise a semi-public regulative function.

It would be fanciful to imagine that any pre-modern influences could overcome the divisions of contemporary industrial society. Yet it is also true that West Germany has been largely exceptional in the harmony displayed by the leading economic groups and evident at all levels. It seems doubtful whether an explanation

related only to the performance of the economy or to the common
standpoint adopted by the parties would be sufficient to account
for the extent of social agreement. That accord can be expressed
on one level by a sense of identity, the old paternalistic responsibility of the employer matched by the loyalty of the workforce.
On another level there is the assumption of a common purpose
which unites the two sides of industry: it is hardly accidental that
they are referred to as the *Sozialpartner*, a description which would
ring strangely if adopted in British or American terminology. On a
third level there is the concept of a shared responsibility which is
partly expressed in the idea of industrial co-determination. Again
we have to be wary of reading too much of a pre-modern continuity
into the implementation and practice of *Mitbestimmung* in German
industry. The extension of co-determination, since it was first
applied to the coal and steel industry in 1951, is an index of growing
trade union power, and the wranglings which accompanied the law
finally passed in 1976 to make the system apply to all medium-
sized and large firms was concerned with the balance of power –
whether the final weight of influence on the supervisory boards of
the firms affected should lie with the trade unions or not.
Mitbestimmung is therefore partly an expression of the modern
power struggle. But the significant point in the present context is
that industrial relations in the Federal Republic should have been
amenable to this type of 'corporate' solution, in contrast to the
great majority of industrialised countries.[13]

Interests and their 'concertation'
The force of the economic consensus depends on the co-operative
role taken by the organised interests, the 'autonomous' groups,
principally the trade unions and the various associations of
commercial and industrial organisations. It may be going too far to
suggest that the economy has become substantially 'depoliticised',
but it is evident that the autonomy of organised interests does
consist in the relative freedom they enjoy from the political sector,
or at least in the lack of a strong attachment to any one part:
the conception of the *Volkspartei* itself precludes an exclusive
association.

The most significant post-war change affected the trade unions.
A radical rationalisation of union structure created a unified
movement: in place of the former division between the 'Free' and
'Christian' trade unions an inclusive *Deutscher Gewerkschafts-
bund* (DGB) was established. The DGB is a federation of sixteen

large 'industrial' unions, that is, an organisation comprising all members on an industry-wide basis, generally with only one union representing members in any one firm. Of itself this simplification must have contributed substantially to the improvement of industrial relations, but an equally important development was the ending of the political divisions. In consequence the DGB has no formal ties with the political parties: that was a precondition of the unification in the first place.

Only certain white-collar and civil service unions are outside the DGB, and the later attempt to re-establish a 'Christian' organisation met with little response. The DGB thus speaks with authority for the great majority of organised labour, although it should be noted that trade union membership is not particularly high: approximately 30 per cent, compared with over 40 per cent in Britain. The DGB has just as little coercive power over its member unions as does the British TUC, but its authority is apparently greater. Within the DGB one union has an overriding numerical superiority, the IG-Metall, with over a third of the DGB's total membership of some seven and a half million workers. Its influence, and that of a handful of others, is decisive in determining the policies of the whole movement. It is notable that the unions show a readiness to take their cues from above, a feature which is evident in particular to the regional and *Länder* hierarchies.

It would be naïve to suppose that the formal political neutrality adopted by the DGB accords with all the facts of political life. Trade union membership is after all one of the best single indicators of support for the SPD, and there are numerous links between leading trade union officials and the party. There is no doubt that union leaders prefer to have the SPD in government, but that desire does not mean that the DGB can – or would wish – to stand unreservedly behind the SPD, nor could it do so without risking an embarrassing fragmentation. The DGB loses in being unable to express an open political commitment, but it gains in flexibility towards governments of all persuasions.

A similar outlook prevails on the other 'side' of industry. But the route to political neutrality has been different. The various business organisations have learned in practice that they can work almost as well through an SPD government as through one run by the CDU. Even though the CDU may be considered the 'natural' partner of business, the fact that the party has been in opposition for a decade has decreased its value. Moreover, if the purity of economic philosophy were the only guide, then the FDP has even more to offer than the CDU. In practice it has been the impressive stability of government policy, reinforced by the high continuity of parties in office, which has made it less desirable for business organisations to become too closely identified with any one party. An additional factor has been the state financing of the political parties. The close association of industrial interests with any kind of 'anti-socialist' party is a matter of record – their beneficent support for the NSDAP in the Weimar Republic illustrated this. But the links, although still of importance, are no longer so critical as far as the parties are concerned. Neither side would wish for a return to a paymaster relationship.

In a similar fashion to the trade union movement, the 'entre-preneurial' groups are dominated by a few, large organisations, and often by certain firms within them. There are two major bodies which together span the same field as the British CBI: the Confederation of German Industry (BDI) and the German Employers' Confederation (BDA). The division is largely a func-tional separation – Hanns-Martin Schleyer, until his murder by political terrorists in 1977, was the president of both organisations: In addition there is the powerful Federation of Chambers of Industry and Trade (DIHT) which effectively puts the views of local areas and smaller firms. The DIHT, the BDI and the BDA are, like the trade unions, organised along federal lines. For both the business interests and the unions this decentralised structure is of importance, since the constituent units have an importance in their own right within the *Länder*, an infrastructure which ensures that the federal leadership, in business and the unions, does not become a remote force: there is a balanced articulation at the various levels of government.

The 'confederal' basis of interest representation in the Federal Republic nonetheless leads to a final concentration of policy at the federal level. The position of a handful of giant corporations on the one hand and a few very large unions on the other inevitably gives the federal organisations a dominant voice. A few leading organisations, the DGB, the BDI and the BDA amongst them, make up the so-called *Spitzenverbände*, and it is with the *Spitzen-verbände* that the federal government has to conduct its dealings. It is their authority over their membership which makes the theory of concerted action at all practicable.

The 1967 law on stability, in enunciating the principle of *Konzertierte Aktion*, gave expression to an accepted pattern of behaviour rather than making a new legal imposition. The idea of concerted action is that the formulation and the execution of economic policy should bring in all those groupings which exercise an economic responsibility: the *Länder* governments as well as the federal authorities, together with the autonomous groups. Concerted action does not mean that all participants have equal rights; it is an acknowledgement of the need to secure wide consent. Its *legal* form makes *Konzertierte Aktion* a commitment binding on the parties and interests alike, not something to be discarded at will. There is an affinity with the concept of tripartism, although the German form expresses more the corporate tradition, whilst the tripartite relationship is more a bargaining model involving government, industry and the trade unions, a modern reaction to economic vicissitudes. The ability of successive West German governments to combat economic difficulties without resort to draconian measures (price controls and mandatory incomes policies) is evidence of the powerful drive to reach an accommodation.

If the competing interests are to be harmonised, the central direction of economic policy must be based on wide consent. The autonomous groups – the major farming interests, the federations of trade and commerce, the DGB, BDI, BDA – are the *Spitzenverbände*, but they are only a part of the whole network of 'authoritative opinion'. The *Länder* also have to be included in the scheme of policy formulation, since the *Länder* governments account for at least half of the total government expenditure, and it is important that they should not pursue budgetary and other policies which are at odds with the federal government. The *Länder*, through the entrenched powers of the Bundesrat, especially in such matters as the apportionment of tax revenue and the approval of the budget, can at no stage be neglected.

Policy has to be rationally based and must build up a mainstream consensus. But it is also important that it appears to be 'objectively' based, not merely the policy of the party controlling the federal government. The Council of Economic Experts – in popular parlance 'The Five Wise Men' – is one source of impartial opinion. The Council in its annual report on the direction to be taken in macro-economic strategy (thus supplying a 'supra-party' sanction) sets the guidelines for subsequent concerted action. A similar impartial constraint on the federal government comes from an equally authoritative source: the Federal Bank. The *Deutsche Bundesbank*, unlike the central banks of most countries, is relatively free from government control. It is able to operate monetary policies which elsewhere could only be directly sanctioned by the government. It is not that the *Bundesbank* works against govern-ment policy, but that it is assumed to have the same objectives – as the law on stability specifies. The Federal Bank is not at all reluctant to air its own views on public economic policy nor to indicate to the autonomous groups how they should behave in relation to wage negotiation and pricing policies.

The structures related to concerted action are extremely stable, and the underlying economic consensus has hardly shifted since the early 1950s. The parties are secure in the knowledge that the organised interests have no inclination to challenge or undermine their authority. But the parties are also circumscribed by the constraints of the system, and neither the CDU nor the SPD could initiate radical changes on its own volition.

That does not mean that change is impossible. The doctrine of the social market philosophy can wear thin if its central tenet, the market, is destroyed by the growing concentration of power in the hands of a few firms. The SPD itself, in *Orientierungsrahmen '85*, has shown that the party still hankers after increased powers of direct intervention by the state. A similar restiveness is evident in the trade unions: younger officials, especially those at branch and factory level, do not altogether share the acquiescent approach of the trade union leaders of the post-war generation. *Konzertierte Aktion* has also lost much of its earlier gloss.[14] Whether any of these changes is sufficient in itself to restore politics to the economy remains to be seen.

The Question of Toleration

A German problem. Few issues have caused such acrimonious debate in the Federal Republic as that of political toleration: the question goes to the heart of 'liberal democracy'. In Western Germany there are special overtones; the debate is coloured by the history of intolerance from the anti-socialist laws of Bismarck to the experience of National Socialism. Added point is given by the presence of the German Democratic Republic: the Federal Republic cannot afford to be labelled crudely as the 'anti-communist' state.

There are really two interrelated issues. One is the broad sense in which the term 'political toleration' is used: in this context it refers to the tolerance of political ideas and movements which are hostile to the established order. The other concerns the specific problem of the employment of 'radicals' in the public service. The wider question is faced in the Basic Law. The constitution establishes several rights which guarantee the free expression of ideas and the formation of associations and political parties, whatever their political persuasion. These rights, however, are restricted and the 'privileges' can be withdrawn, as Article 21 of the Basic Law makes plain, in the case of parties threatening the 'free democratic basic order' or endangering the existence of the Federal Republic. But unless or until the Constitutional Court finds them to be unconstitutional, 'party privilege' is guaranteed.

Every 'liberal democracy' has to find its own way round this problem. In West Germany the memory of the dictatorship makes it impossible to take a relaxed attitude towards right-wing extremism, and the proximity of the GDR makes it equally hard not to be wary of the potential danger of disruptive infiltration, of the setting up of democratic 'front' organisations, the major function of which may be to weaken the West German state or political system. Given the German predeliction for legal forms and norms, the apparatus of the Constitutional Court is the obvious way to deal with 'hostile' movements.

That course finds its justification in the conception of the Federal Republic as a 'militant democracy', a *wehrhafte Demokratie*.[15] The awkward question is how far a 'liberal democracy' can proceed with its militancy before it merely becomes an intolerant one. The general debate came to a head once in the 1950s, on the occasion of the banning of the SRP and the KPD, and signs of a more relaxed approach became evident when the successor parties, the NPD and the DKP, were left alone and allowed to die a natural death at the polls. But a new pitch was reached in the late 1960s with the student protest movement, the extra-parliamentary opposition, and the adoption of violence both as a political means and as an end in itself. Unlike conventional political parties, the new movement was not easily rendered harmless: to the authorities it appeared hydra-headed, for splinter groups could detach and re-form with bewildering rapidity.

On one level the confrontation was straightforward: the revolutionary theories of the extreme left (for that is what the extra-parliamentary opposition soon became) demanded the destruction of the existing repressive state. As long as the theory was mainly rhetoric and the violence sporadic, the resources of the liberal state were adequate. But the confrontation took a novel form in the practice of realising revolutionary aims by taking 'the long march through the institutions'. One of those institutions was the state, and many of those students who, naturally enough, took part in the great intellectual debate also cherished the idea of following their careers in the state service. Could the political authorities face that prospect with equanimity?

The solution of the Radikalenerlass

There are two 'structural' peculiarities attached to the concept of state service in the Federal Republic, and they may go some way in explaining why the issue of the employment of radicals has become both long-lasting and complex. One special feature of the German system is the very extensive interpretation given to state service. In most West European countries the term applies principally to civil servants, that is, to officials of central government departments, the administrative bureaucracy. In Britain it would be reasonable to include those people who are covered by the restrictions of the Official Secrets Act. But the West German definition of a public official is exceptionally broad. Part of the reason is the federal nature of the state and, in consequence, the decentralised character of the administrative system (the great majority of civil servants are employed in the *Länder*), yet at the same time the conditions of service are laid down by federal law, so that a uniformity is required between the *Länder*. Once the *Länder* are included as well as the federal government departments, the scope for widening the definition of state service is enormous: it covers not only the *Länder* departments but also local government, the schools and the universities. Furthermore, other areas of public service, notably the federal postal system and the federal railways, also fall within the category of state service. In principle the same tests of loyalty may be applied to relatively menial local government employees as to high officials in federal ministries, and a university professor of philosophy may find himself in the same boat as an engine driver on the *Bundesbahn*.

A second complicating factor is the division of responsibility between the federal government and the *Länder*, since neither can have an overriding competence in deciding what standards of loyalty are to be set. Thus unless a wide measure of agreement is forthcoming, all the *Länder* are virtually free to establish their own criteria, even their own standards. The federal government is simply not able to make an authoritative intervention.

These difficulties have to be conceded. For one thing, it is just not practical politics to impose a wholesale change in the status of public officials. The immediate effect of attempting to make a distinction between 'sensitive' and less-responsible appointments would be to threaten a large number of vested interests amongst the various categories of public officials themselves, and it is fairly certain that the CDU–CSU majority in the Bundesrat would have no truck with any substantial 'liberalising' reform.

The most notable attempt to reach at least a common basis of agreement was the *Radikalenerlass* of January 1972. This document has since achieved a degree of notoriety, but in fact it was not a decree but a statement of policy. It did not establish any new principles and, ironically, those who had initiated the discussions leading to the agreement had done so to improve the situation, not to make it worse.

As early as 1950 a directive had been issued listing a number of organisations considered to be opposed to the Federal Republic and making dismissal from public service the penalty of membership. The wording of the *Radikalenerlass* also came close to the relevant provisions of the 1957 civil service law. What was different was that certain SPD-governed *Länder* were concerned at the arbitrary differences in treatment from one *Land* to another and hoped to evolve a system for testing loyalty based on the consideration of individual cases rather than apply a blanket policy of exclusion based solely on the criterion of membership of a 'hostile' organisation. The *Radikalenerlass* of 1972 represented, therefore, a statement of policy agreed by the minister-presidents of the *Länder* together with a separate agreement between the *Länder* and the federal government. The text of the former document, the *Radikalenerlass*, reads as follows:

> According to the Civil Service Law of the Federation and the *Länder*, a person may only be admitted to the civil service (*darf in das Beamtenverhältnis nur berufen werden*) who pledges at all times to uphold the free democratic basic order as understood in the Basic Law.
>
> Civil Servants (*Beamte*) are duty bound, within and without their course of duty, actively to support the preservation of this basic order. These requirements are mandatory.
>
> Every individual case must be investigated and decided separately.
>
> The following principles are to be applied:
>
> *Candidates:* A candidate who becomes involved in activities hostile to the Basic Law will not be employed in the public service. If a candidate belongs to an organisation which has aims hostile to the Basic Law, it is to be assumed that this

membership gives reason to doubt whether he will at all times uphold the free democratic basic order. This doubt will normally justify the rejection of a candidate.

Civil Servants: If an official by his actions or through his membership of an organisation with aims hostile to the Basic Law fails to satisfy the requirements of Paragraph 35 of the Civil Service Framework-Law*, his employer has to reach a conclusion as indicated by the relevant evidence, and in particular to determine whether the dismissal of the official is desirable. For workers and employees in the public service the same principles are to be applied in accordance with the contracts regulating each case.

The terms of the *Radikalenerlass* are sufficiently clear not to need much comment. As the reformers wished, cases were to be judged on their individual merits. Account could be taken of 'mitigating' circumstances: degree of .involvement, length of membership, whether it was still in force or belonged to the past. But what was insufficiently appreciated was the implication of making a detailed study of an individual's background. The system of evaluation encouraged a massive bureaucratic intervention, which involved investigatory techniques, the compilation of bulky dossiers with relevant and irrelevant information, interrogations of candidates in the provision for 'hearings' and a regular channel of appeal against decisions to be dealt with by the administrative courts.

It is a quite inadequate response to claim that not more than a thousand or so people have been directly affected by the *Radikalenerlass*, either by dismissal or through having their applications rejected. The screening process has involved perhaps a million people all told, since the net is cast wide. In addition, concern is felt about the enormous data-gathering capacity which has been established, both at *Land* and at federal levels. The Federal Office for the Protection of the Constitution, the *Verfassungsschutz*, and the Information Service, the *Nachrichtendienst*, are in a position to supply information about suspect organisations (their listing by the *Verfassungsschutz* is a definitive ruling as to their 'hostility') as well as information necessary to

---

* 'On the basis of which he is obliged to commit himself to the free democratic basic order in the sense of the Basic Law and to work for its preservation by his whole conduct.' (The 'framework' law in question has its basic principles established by the federation, with the *Länder* legislating for its detailed application.)

reach decisions in individual cases. The *Länder* governments also maintain their own '*Verfassungsschutz*' departments, responsible to their interior ministries and independent of the federal office, although there is co-operation between them.

Because the *Radikalenerlass* only made matters worse, the federal government sought a remedy in legislation, with the objectives, firstly, of securing uniformity and, secondly, of weakening the whole atmosphere of political scrutiny by making the test of loyalty only the final, deciding factor rather than the central issue in the consideration of a candidate's suitability. But the SPD–FDP legislation foundered on the opposition of the CDU–CSU in the Bundesrat, since any bills in this field require the consent of the Bundesrat. The failure to obtain an inter-party agreement in 1976 meant that nothing at all had been achieved: the CDU – and particularly the CSU – took a hard line, whilst the SPD opted for a more flexible approach. In fact, the operation of the *Radikalenerlass* has worked overwhelmingly against left-wing radicals. There were more of them perhaps, and certainly they were more 'visible', but the saga has given credence to the view that intolerance is directed mainly towards the extreme left, not the extreme right.[16]

An answer in the Basic Law?

Since in the final analysis the constitution has to sanction public policy, the Basic Law must speak with more authority than any legislation or ministerial decree. We should therefore look to the Constitutional Court for an authoritative view of how loyalty is to be judged. Yet absolute clarity does not follow.

A straight reading of the Basic Law seems to give an unequivocal answer. Article 33 states in part: 'Every German shall be equally eligible for public office . . . No one may suffer any disadvantage by reason of his adherence or non-adherence to a denomination or ideology.' Article 3 holds: 'No one may be prejudiced or favoured because of . . . his political opinions', and Article 12 gives the right to free choice of 'trade, occupation, or profession'. These provisions also have to be read in conjunction with the concept of party privilege as set out in Article 21. The implication of the privilege is that there should be no discrimination against the members of a party who seek to implement its policies or propagate possibly unpopular views as long as the party itself is fully constitutional. Taken together, these elements of the Basic Law would seem to make the toleration of dissident political views an obligation.

The ruling by the Constitutional Court of May 1975, however, paints a quite different picture, at least as far as the public service is concerned. The basis of the Court's judgement rested on another clause of Article 33: 'The law of the public service shall be regulated according to the traditional principles of the professional civil service.' Now these traditional principles, the Court held, include a special duty of political loyalty (a *Treuepflicht*) towards the state on the part of public officials, a positive commitment to the constitutional order, not just a formal acceptance. Following this line of argument, the Court maintained that there was no conflict between the loyalty requirements of public service law and the guarantees in the Basic Law.

In the course of its 1975 judgement, the Court also redefined the idea of party privilege. To the objection that a person should not suffer discrimination through belonging to a party which had not been found to be unconstitutional, the Court formulated its own new classification, distinguishing between those parties which were *verfassungswidrig* (found to be unconstitutional) and those which were on the lesser plane of being *verfassungsfeindlich* (deemed to be hostile to the constitutional order although perfectly legal). Membership of this latter category of organisation could be sufficient ground for exclusion from the public service, even though the party or association could participate fully in political life.

By these means the Constitutional Court was able to justify an apparent contradiction between public service requirements and the Basic Law. The concept of *Verfassungsfeindlichkeit*, however, is nowhere to be found in the Basic Law. The new category also raises the question of how hostility is to be determined. In fact, the matter is left to executive discretion, to the office of the *Verfassungsschutz*.

Perhaps the Constitutional Court chose the course of the lesser evil in devising a way of underwriting established practice. Without the half-way category of *verfassungsfeindlich*, the federal government would have been encouraged to initiate proceedings against extremist associations (Article 9) or against political parties (Article 21) which could have led to the wholesale banning of a host of splinter organisations just to protect the public service.

Yet the continuing operation of the *Radikalenerlass* and the Court's ruling have done nothing to dispel a widespread belief that the West German system is intolerant, not just militant. The ripples extend beyond employment in the public service. Since its domain is so extensive, critics have claimed that exclusion amounts to a *Berufsverbot*, a ban on following a particular occupation. Doubtless this is an exaggeration, but the claim has some validity in relation to the field of education, which is almost entirely within the public sector, and for a part of the legal profession (or rather, those who have a university training in law), since large numbers are engaged in public administration.

Nor can the issue of toleration be limited to those who, possibly with justification, are directly affected. There is, for instance, a widespread feeling in universities that to be associated in any way with radical activity – or even to engage in any kind of legitimate protest – could invite the attention of the authorities and thus endanger a student's future career. That atmosphere may lead either to an undesirable conformity or, for a small minority, to an implacable hostility towards the state. Either way, the spirit of liberal democracy suffers.

A conclusion may be that, after all, the democratic system is not firmly anchored in the Federal Republic and that authoritarian traditions have been maintained. But the fault may lie elsewhere: in the desire to look too readily for solutions in the certainty of the law, with all the rigidities that the reliance can entail. The question in the end comes down to the problem of striking a reasonable balance between the exclusion of a possible risk and the preservation of a desirable degree of non-conformity in a society. A relaxed attitude towards dissent would require using the flexible doctrine of 'a clear and present danger' towards the state. But the German tradition requires all things to be made quite explicit; it hankers after definitional exactitude. In the West German case, this constraint on politics is still in evidence.

Ideology: The West German Consensus

Nature of the consensus
We have examined some of the constraints affecting politics in the Federal Republic, and each can be seen to impose its own special requirements on the political system. But they are also related to one another and form part of a pattern. Thus the three basic elements – the national issue, the pervasive *Rechtsstaat*, the dominant economic philosophy – can be brought together in the totality of opposition towards the German Democratic Republic. Their conjunction can also be expressed in practice as a militant

form of anti-communism, and that trait highlights the particular constraint of the toleration issue.

Emphasis on the repressive nature of these constraints can be misleading: seen from another point of view, they are also the foundations of the political consensus of the Federal Republic. So widely shared are the prevailing norms that it often appears as if ideology itself has waned, but in reality the overwhelming consensus merely obscures its presence. The initial impression of West German society may be that it is motivated by an everyday pragmatism, but that impression is contradicted by an evident inability to show a relaxed attitude towards a questioning of any aspect of the prevailing consensus. On the contrary, the pressures towards political conformity are considerable. That leads to the formulation of the West German paradox: the liberal state lacking in the liberal spirit.

The paradox should not be exaggerated. We can point to deficiencies in the working of 'liberal democracy', but should not their incidence be weighted against all previous German experience? Is it not also important to retain a sense of proportion and view the Federal Republic in a comparative light? Answers to these questions probably lead to a more favourable judgement: not only is the present order far superior to anything Germany has hitherto produced, but its aberrations pale into insignificance when contrasted with the totalitarian indignities of the East German state.

Yet the system also has to be judged against the level of its own pretensions; gaps between norm and reality have to be explained, and it is also relevant to try to isolate the special character of West German democracy. One approach is to examine the traumas of German politics, for they have had the effect of exerting a peculiarly centralising pressure and go some way to explaining the qualified nature of West German pluralism.

Der Feind steht rechts!

In the turbulent early years of the Weimar Republic, it could have been anyone's guess where the major threat to the republic was to be found. The warning given by Chancellor Wirth – 'The enemy is on the Right!' – proved later to be correct. It is a warning which has been frequently voiced in succeeding years: there is a prevailing suspicion that, given the suitable occasion, right-wing forces would be eager to supplant the republican system by an authoritarian regime or, failing that, to distort the democratic system by introducing measures (such as the *Radikalenerlass*) so that the liberal order would be eroded from within.

That suspicion is endemic, but it does not amount to a trauma. The experience of National Socialism was the fundamental catastrophe. If it were at all possible to believe that the dictatorship somehow 'just happened', then its memory would by now have receded. But too many people were actively involved and the movement drew on too many German political and social traditions for it to be explained as the product of a wayward evil genius. So far it has proved impossible to rehabilitate any aspect of the Third Reich. Its consequences extend beyond the simple discrediting of one political expression: any right-wing movement now bears a taint of association, often justifiably so, and the spectrum of the right is broad.

One casualty is conservatism. Conservative values are, of course, not directly associated with National Socialism but with a more general form of reaction. Historically they were anti-republican and unrepentantly nationalist. In the Weimar Republic those values were reinforced by a crusading anti-communism and by leanings towards an authoritarian state. Whatever the merits of a traditional conservative outlook may have been, in the Nazi creed most aspects of such conservative values reappeared in an intensely magnified form.

The failure of any party to the right of the CDU to survive illustrates the difficulty of re-establishing an 'orthodox' conservative movement. One consequence is that Christian Democracy has to express a variety of political inclinations. A measure of its success is that the party has never been pulled too far from its predominantly moderate course, whilst it has also managed to retain the support of its right-wing adherents. A second consequence is that more extremist values themselves circulate more diffusely, permeating a part of the political system without taking a definite party expression.[17]

In formulating this interpretation, we can visualise the existence of an ideological continuum which, instead of tapering off towards the extreme Right, shows a sharp rupture at a much earlier point: there is a gap separating Christian Democracy from anything else. The CSU represents one way of making an extension but, significantly, as yet only by keeping its attachment to the CDU.

Der Feind steht links!

A similar break in the ideological continuum affects the German

Left, but if anything it is even sharper. Whilst the German Right has to contend with one major historical disability, the Left has two kinds of handicap. The first is the almost permanent 'anti-national' charge which, despite changes of form and context, has been preserved since the nineteenth century. The second is super-imposed on the first: the fragmentation of the Reich was a national disaster, and the creation of the communist state was the prime reason. Moreover, the continued existence of that state serves as a constant reminder.

We have seen how the SPD made a determined effort to rid itself of these negative associations. Under Schumacher the SPD became a 'national' party and dissociated itself entirely from the KPD. By degrees the party also came to subscribe to all the leading values of the Federal Republic. From this perspective, the emergence of the SPD as a 'new-type' party was integral to the process of extrication. The vulnerability of Social Democracy has not been entirely overcome. At all times the SPD has to demonstrate that there is a gulf separating it from any movement further to the left. The demarcation must be kept visible and complete.

The position on the German Left is complicated by the two handicaps it faces. There is a general suspicion of left-wing motives. The 'anti-national' suspicion finds sustenance in a roundabout way: to seek to erode the existing social order is to be hostile to the 'free democratic basic order' on which the Federal Republic is based and therefore to be a threat to its existence. To that extent it makes no difference whether a group, in propagating its aims, is favourably disposed towards the German Democratic Republic or not. Those who specifically reject the East German model may even be treated with greater mistrust, for their often unconventional strategies present a more insidious challenge to the existing system than the traditional forms of party politics.

In contrast, the DKP, which takes the German communist state as its exemplary reference, may even appear relatively innocuous. It is a convenient whipping-boy for the sins of the GDR, but scarcely a real threat. The party is painfully orthodox and with a miniscule following, a sorry successor to what was once – in the KPD before 1933 – the strongest of West European communist parties. But the weakness of the DKP is not an exculpation, nor can the threat implied by the GDR be treated as one coming from a 'foreign' state. The regular spy scandals which disturb the Federal Republic, usually taking the form of the discovery of East German agents operating in high places, have to be appreciated as having a significance at two distinct levels: the 'normal' one of inter-state relations and the special one on which the German fear of 'the enemy within' operates. Frequently it is difficult to disentangle the various threads of argument presented by the left-wing groupings, nor from the point of view of the established order is it really necessary to do so: the SPD is the point at which serious debate should stop.

Political centrality as the key

If we briefly return to the concept of the *Volkspartei* and to the logic of the catch-all party system, a convincing picture of the functioning of a political system can be drawn. Its main features are illustrated by the *Volksparteien:* they can be said to stand in a centripetal relationship to one another. The centripetal drive – 'flying towards the centre' – arises from the strong attractive power exercised by the *Volksparteien* over the electorate and through the necessarily intense competition between the parties, for they are competing for substantially the same support.

That this representation applies to the Federal Republic seems to be scarcely a matter of dispute. The situation has only to be contrasted with the alternative of centrifugal politics – the fragmentation and extreme polarisation of the Weimar Republic. Yet this simple dichotomy may be insufficient to give an accurate impression of how the West German system operates.

It is here that the idea of 'centrality' can be introduced. Whilst an unadulterated centripetal system exerts a powerful appeal, the effect of centrality can be regarded as a strong negative pressure. These two forces are absolutely different in nature, but they can reinforce one another as well: in both cases the ideological continuum is abbreviated, attenuated in the one, truncated in the other.

If that combination is indeed true for the Federal Republic, then it helps to explain some of the more puzzling features of the political system. It helps to account for the massive stability of the system at the same time as that stability is constantly under question. It makes it easier to understand why the unforced consensus of an open democracy is joined with some features of a less tolerant one. We can also appreciate how, in accord with the centripetal model, ideology has lost its strength and yet at the same time the *Rechtsstaat*, the militant defence of the 'free democratic order', becomes a substitute for the missing ideological engagement. Finally, the contribution of centrality to an analysis of the West German party system makes it easier to comprehend the rapidity with which the post-war transformation took place and, probably, why it has remained so complete.

The West German consensus is composed of positive and negative elements. It is possible to argue that the domestic consensus is only so pronounced because the external polarity – that with the German Democratic Republic – is so profound. But that formulation provides only one factor in the equation: the nature of West German society itself acts as a powerful reinforcement to the purely political tendencies.

German pluralism
One of the most controversial descriptions of West German society was that offered by Ludwig Erhard in the 1960s, when he applied the term *formierte Gesellschaft* to the Federal Republic, postulating that it was not a uniform society, but not a completely pluralist one either. Erhard was howled down, yet so many writers have played on the theme that it is reasonable to ask in what ways Germany differs from other countries which in most respects appear similar.

We are certainly presented with a variety of descriptive possibilities. Thus, given the ramifications of the 'party state', the label of 'party pluralism' can be applied – although, since the parties themselves are subject to numerous constraints, it would be misleading to give the impression of unrestricted party power. Other terms have been frequently employed to describe West German society: 'limited pluralism', 'official pluralism', 'corporate pluralism', 'liberal corporatism'. In their different ways they all capture something of the contradictory quality of society in Germany and, for that matter, of her liberal democracy.[18] Too easily, however, the qualifications are interpreted as carrying the seeds of an authoritarian reversion, of a simple desire to be rid of 'democratic' restrictions. Yet are we entitled to impose a normative model of a 'rational' – if not unrestricted – pluralism to all societies, regardless of the terms on which their development has taken place?

In many ways the Federal Republic does represent the archetype of a 'modernised' society, and no one doubts that some kind of metamorphosis did occur in the wake of the Nazi dictatorship. But in a sense it can be argued, too, that Germany became 'over-modernised' in the process: factors were at work which accentuated, even exaggerated, the underlying trends. There is a paradox here, for possibly those other factors were not modern at all, but ones which, in happening to complement post-war developments, were effectively disguised in the rush towards a 'modernised' society. On one level, that is to say no more than that older components of the political culture survived and were incorporated into the new political system. But it is also apparent that we are concerned with more than sets of political attitudes. The connections can be traced in several ways: the values attached to the state – which pre-date the pluralist conception and which enforce a responsibility on the parties to be *staatserhaltend* – are the most obvious on a political plane. They are joined by others from wider social spheres, especially those relating to the law and to economic relationships, which altogether amount to a considerable amendment of the pure pluralist model.

The idea of 'over-modernisation' is naturally one to be treated with some caution. In the present context it is merely used to express a complementarity. We can at least appreciate the kind of relationship involved in the juxtaposition of the two forces affecting the political system, the centripetal one of 'modern' society finding a similar expression in the force of centrality. Likewise, the idea of 'concertation' calls on elements of a pre-modern ethos which nevertheless harmonise with the need for a framework to be provided for the reconciliation of conflicting interests in society.

The grafting process which appears to have taken place makes it imperative to avoid hasty judgements about the present nature of the political system. Even more care has to be taken over any prediction about the future. It may well be that the weight of the past inheritance will gradually be lifted. If so, the incidence of a greater 'democratic polarisation' need not be taken as a definitely negative sign, but simply as a decline in the restrictive effects of centrality. What Western Germany has fortuitously been spared in the post-war era has been a fundamental *choix de société*, and that has given the Federal Republic the benefit of a smooth evolution. It would be unwise to assume, however, that nothing at all was lost by that conflict-free process: the future of the political system is likely to be dictated by the peculiarity of its development since 1945.

Notes and References

1. Especially enlightening on the problems and change of outlook of the SPD up to the beginning of the 1960s is W. E. Paterson, *The SPD and European Integration*, Saxon House, 1974.
2. Wehner made a decisive contribution to aligning the SPD with the CDU in a Bundestag debate of 30 June 1960, a commitment which went too far for

many SPD members, but which in fact became irreversible. For a rather impressionistic account of Wehner's career, see A. Freudenhammer and K. Vater, *Herbert Wehner: Ein Leben mit der Deutschen Frage*, Munich: Bertelsmann, 1978.

3. One of the earliest signs of change in the *Deutschland-* and *Ostpolitik* was a speech made by Egon Bahr, SPD, later an architect of Brandt's policies, in July 1963 when he first spoke of the possibility of '*Wandel durch Annäherung*'. The memorandum of the Evangelical Churches was entitled '*Die Lage der Vertriebenen und das Verhältnis des deutschen Volkes zu seinen östlichen Nachbarn*', Hanover: Evangelische Kirche in Deutschland, 1965.

4. See C. Hacke, *Die Ost- und Deutschlandpolitik der CDU–CSU: Wege und Irrwege der Opposition seit 1969*, Cologne: Verlag Wissenschaft und Politik, 1975.

5. On the 1974 GDR constitutional changes, with texts, see D. Müller-Römer, *Die neue Verfassung der DDR*, Cologne: Verlag Wissenschaft und Politik, 1974.

6. For a political assessment of the benefits, see C. Arndt, 'The Effects of Détente on the Two German States', *West European Politics*, May 1979. Arndt has to concede, however, that the 'technical' co-operation is the only one that can be added to the movement of people (i.e. visits of West Germans to the GDR). Substantial progress has been made in improving telephonic and transport communication.

7. See G. Schweigler, *National Consciousness in Divided Germany*, Saxon House, 1975. His arguments for a specifically West German national consciousness are based chiefly on public opinion polling and hence the conclusions could just as well be invalidated if public opinion were to swing in another direction or were to take other expressions of what was essentially 'German'. See also, D. Conradt op. cit, pp. 211–2.

8. See N. Johnson, *Government in Germany*, op. cit., for a clear discussion in the first chapter of the relationships involved in German thinking on the idea of the *Rechtsstaat*.

9. On the *Juristenmonopol*, see R. Dahrendorf, *Society and Democracy in Germany*, op. cit.

10. See W. Hennis, *Verfassung und Verfassungswirklichkeit – ein deutsches Problem*, in *Die missverstandene Demokratie*, op. cit., also P. Blair, 'Law and Politics in Germany', *Political Studies*, September 1978, and R. Leicht, *Grundgesetz und politische Praxis*, op. cit.

11. The Court's potential was shown in 1979 in upholding the 1976 Co-Determination Law against the objections of employers' associations. Since shareholders have a parity on the supervisory boards with employees and also effectively have the chairman's tie-breaking vote, the Court ruled that 'property rights' under the Basic Law were still protected. But in finding the present 'balance' valid, there is an implication in favour of the *status quo*, a factor which could affect the fate of future legislation.

12. Erhard's own writings on the policy of *soziale Marktwirtschaft* are a fair guide to its philosophy and practice in the Federal Republic: *Prosperity through Competition* (1959) and *The Economics of Success* (1963).

13. A straightforward account of the current meanings and implications to be attached to the idea of corporatism is given by A. Cawson, 'Pluralism, Corporatism and the Role of the State', *Government and Opposition*, Summer 1978.

14. A specific reason for the sudden decline in trade union co-operation in the *Konzertierte Aktion* was resentment that the employers' organisations had challenged the new co-determination laws in the Constitutional Court. Since the Court's decision was favourable to the law as it stood, the trade unions are likely to resume co-operation (see note 11 above).

15. The concept of a 'militant democracy' is expressed in Article 20 of the Basic Law which gives all Germans 'the right to resist' subversions of the constitutional order if no other remedy is available.
16. However, one has to be on guard against too gullibly accepting all the strictures of those critical of government policies. Thus S. Cobler in *Law, Order and Politics in West Germany*, Penguin Books, 1978, presents a distorted picture, and whilst denying that the Federal Republic is a 'fascist' state, proceeds then to show that it has most of the ingredients. The specific causes of government intervention (e.g. the activities of the *Rote Armee Fraktion*) are merely treated as a 'given' factor. Cobler's book shows the difficulty of reaching a balanced perspective for German observers.
17. There are various conservative *tendencies* which do not find an overt outlet at the level of the parties. See M. Greiffenhagen, H. Grebing (and others), *Konservatismus – eine deutsche Bilanz*, Munich: Piper, 1971. Also, M. Greiffenhagen, *Das Dilemma des Konservatismus in Deutschland*, Munich: Piper, 1971. More *extremist* expressions are manifold, see G. Bartsch, *Revolution von rechts? – Ideologie und Organisation der neuen Rechten*, Freiburg: Herder, 1975.
18. See K. von Beyme, 'The Politics of Limited Pluralism? The Case of West Germany', *Government and Opposition*, Summer 1978.

Further Reading

A. Baring, *Aussenpolitik in Adenauer's Kanzlerdemokratie*, Munich: Oldenbourg, 1964.
W. Hahn, *Between Westpolitik and Ostpolitik: Changing West German Security Views*, Sage, 1975.
W. F. Hanrieder, *The Stable Crisis: Two Decades of German Foreign Policy*, New York: Collier, 1970.
P. C. Ludz, *Deutschlands doppelte Zukunft*, Munich: Hanser, 1974.
P. Merkl, *German Foreign Policy: West and East*, Oxford: ABC/CLIO, 1974.
H. P. Schwarz (ed.), *Handbuch der deutschen Aussenpolitik*, Munich: Piper, 1976. (Bibliography.)
G. Schweigler, *National Consciousness in Divided Germany*, Saxon House, 1975.
J. Sowden, *The German Question, 1945–1973*, Bradford University Press, 1975.
R. Tilford (ed.), *The Ostpolitik and Political Change in Germany*, Saxon House, 1975.
F. R. Willis, *France, Germany and the New Europe, 1945–1967*, Oxford University Press, 1968.
Bundesministerium für innerdeutsche Beziehungen: Texte zur Deutschlandpolitik, Bonn, annually from 1967.

M. Fronz, 'Das Bundesverfassungsgericht im politischen System der BRD', in R. Wildenmann (ed.), *Sozialwissenschaftliches Jahrbuch für Politik*, Munich: Günter Olzog, 1971.
W. Hennis, 'Verfassung und Verfassungswirklichkeit', in *Die missverstandene Demokratie*, Freiburg: Herder, 1973.
N. Johnson, 'Law as the Articulation of the State in Western Germany', *West European Politics*, May 1978.
D. P. Kommers, *Judicial Politics in West Germany*, Sage Publications, 1976.
H. Säcker, *Das Bundesverfassungsgericht*, Munich: Landeszentrale für politische Bildung, 1977.
T. Schieder, 'Vom Reichskammergericht zum Bundesverfassungsgericht' in *25 Jahre Bundesverfassungsgericht, 1951–1976*, Heidelberg: C. F. Müller, 1976.

K. von Beyme, 'The Changing Relations between Trade Unions and the Social Democratic Party in West Germany', *Government and Opposition*, Autumn 1978.

G. Braunthal, *The Federation of German Industry in Politics*, Cornell University Press, 1965.

D. Claessens (and others), *Sozialkunde der BRD*, Düsseldorf: Diederichs, 1973.

G. Hallett, *The Social Economy of West Germany*, Macmillan, 1973.

U. Jaeggi, *Kapital und Arbeit in der Bundesrepublik*, Frankfurt: Fischer, 1973.

G. Lehmbruch, 'Liberal Corporatism and Party Government', *Comparative Political Studies*, April 1977.

A. Shonfield, *Modern Capitalism*, Oxford University Press, 1965.

J. Weber, *Die Interessengruppen im politischen System der Bundesrepublik Deutschland*, Stuttgart: Kohlhammer, 1977.

———

E. Benda, *Der Rechtsstaat in der Krise*, Stuttgart: Kohlhammer, 1972.

F. Croner, *Die deutsche Tradition*, Opladen: Westdeutscher Verlag, 1975.

R. Dahrendorf, *Gesellschaft und Freiheit*, Munich: Piper, 1971.

K. Dyson, 'Left-Wing Political Extremism and the Problem of Tolerance in Western Germany', *Government and Opposition*, Summer 1975.

M. Funke (ed.), *Extremismus im demokratischen Rechtsstaat*, Bonn: Bundeszentrale für politische Bildung, 1978.

M. Kriele, *Legitimitätsprobleme der Bundesrepublik*, op. cit.

G. Smith, 'West Germany and the Politics of Centrality', op. cit.

K. Sontheimer, *Die verunsicherte Republik*, op. cit.

Index

For glossary of party abbreviations, see pp. ix–x.